Advertising Campaign Planning:

Developing an Advertising-Based Marketing Plan.

© 2000 Jim Avery

Published by The Copy Workshop.
2144 N. Hudson • Chicago, IL 60614
773-871-1179 • FX 773-281-4643
copywork@aol.com

Advertising Campaign Planning:

Copyright © 2000 by Jim Avery

Publishing Information:

ISBN: 1-887229-06-X

All rights reserved. Printed in the USA
For further information contact:

The Copy Workshop
2144 N. Hudson • Chicago, IL 60614
773-871-1179 • FX: 773-281-4643
copywork@aol.com

Editor: Bruce Bendinger

Cover Design: Greg Paus

Photography: Clark James Mishler

Publishing History:
First Edition • August 1993
Second Edition • January 1997
Third Edition • January 2000   0 9 8 7

Published by The Copy Workshop.

A Division of Bruce Bendinger Creative Communications, Inc.

To George Barrus—

For teaching me to believe in advertising.

Table of Contents:

Chapter Seven. Advertising Creative   168
  A. Target Audience
  B. Objective
  C. Strategy
      1. To Convince...
      2. To Use...
      3. Instead of...
      4. Because...
  D. Support
  E. Consideration
  F. Tone
  G. Rationale
  H. Tactics

Note A. Creative Platform   181

Note B. Ideas & Ideation   184

Chapter Eight. Advertising Media   190
  A. Objectives
      1. Target Audience
      2. Geography
      3. Seasonality
      4. Continuity, Flighting, etc.
      5. Creative Constraints
      6. Reach vs. Frequency
  B. Strategies
      1. Media Mix and Types
      2. Media Format or Classes
      3. Geographic Use
      4. Seasonal Use
      5. Flighting vs. Continuity
  C. Rationale
      1. Support of Strategy
      2. Support of Delivery and Efficiency
  D. Tactics
      1. Media Vehicles
      2. Reach/Frequency/GRP Summary
      3. Cost Summary
      4. Flow Chart
      5. Sales to Advertising Comparison
          a. History
          b. DMA by BDI
      6. Competitive Media & Sales Review

The Presentation:

Bozell Group

Eugene F. Bartley, Jr.
Chairman and
Chief Executive Officer

Dear Reader:

The world of advertising is evolving at break-neck speed; I'm constantly asked to read marketing books for my comments, and often, I find that by the time books make it to market, they're out of date. Or worse, they try to capitalize on some hot new trend, and fail utterly at offering a practical, all-around guide for use in the real world.

I'm pleased to report that Jim Avery has given us the best of both worlds. A book that is totally relevant to today's tough marketing world, and one that provides thorough insight into the nuts and bolts aspects of advertising-based marketing. In short, Jim's book is a comprehensive guide that both the student and the business entrepreneur can refer to repeatedly in order to open doors and succeed in a competitive marketplace.

Avery covers all the elements of a marketing plan with acuity and insight; above all, his recommendations have real-world application. He understands the importance of honing in on consumers' perspective as it relates to the brand, that all the elements of a plan – strategy, creative execution, media buying, etc. emanate from this perspective.

I wish I had a book like this one when I was starting out years ago. They say there's no substitute for experience, and there isn't. But this book certainly comes close!

At Bozell, we've worked hard to cultivate that all-important competitive edge; after all, our clients demand nothing less of us. Nevertheless, I maintain that Jim's book could easily serve as a manual for my employees. It's that valuable. Read it well and you'll be poised for success in the world of advertising-based marketing communications.

Eugene F. Bartley, Jr.

10

Author's Notes:

Prof. Jim Avery • University of Oklahoma.

This is the Third Edition of a book intended for anyone who wants to know how to write a marketing plan.

The First and Second Editions did a good job.

This Third Edition will do it a little better— providing more information on account planning, sales promotion, "IMC," and "idea-driven integration."

But we will try not to let that get in the way of the advertising. It's not intended to define terms or explain why something works the way it does—I assume you are beyond that.

For Professionals, Entrepeneurs, and Students.

If you're a working professional or entrepreneur, you have already been through that period. If you're a student, you've already taken courses like Principles of Advertising, Advertising Management, Media Planning, Advertising Creativity, and possibly even Advertising Research.

There are a lot of other books that provide definitions and reasons why something works the way it does. Some are listed at the end of the chapters. This is not one of those books.

A Detailed Action Plan...

This book gives a detailed action plan for writing a marketing plan. Recognize that the method presented here is just one way to do it.

There are as many different methods for writing a marketing planning document as there are companies that write them. This method is a good one and is easily adaptable to other formats.

...in Three Parts.

This book is divided into three major parts.

The first part, called Planning Points, helps a student agency get organized and lists other information you need to get started.

The middle section—the main part—is the marketing planning document itself.

The third part contains some practical advice on the thing that can make or break a student marketing plan—presentation.

The Book That Feels Like a Marketing Plan...

One of the challenges you'll have is working with creative people— art directors and copywriters who will look for creative ways to address marketing issues. That's the way this book evolved.

Overall, we tried to make this book feel like a marketing plan—it's intended to look like a planning document.

...except for the Subheads.

Except that my editor, Bruce Bendinger, insisted we have sub-heads to help organize the material.

I fought him on this at first, but he's right. The book is better for having the subheads. But in a way, they are interrupters.

Realize that they'll help you learn the subject, but recognize that they would not be in a marketing planning document.

In the majority of cases, your planning document will not have introductions and subheads. But with these exceptions, it will be constructed very much like the middle portion of this book.

Some Words of Thanks.

There are a lot of people to thank:

> People like Bill Impey and Larry Carroll—for insisting on excellence in the marketing planning I provided to them when they were my clients.

> People like Jim Johnson and Peter Parsons—for teaching me, and Larry Singer—for trusting me.

> All the students who survived this book in lecture form before it was written—and helped me refine it.

> People like Tim Bengtson and Mike Kautsch—for encouraging me to begin my writing. And Ann Maxwell and Jim Marra—for their positive reinforcement.

> To my father—for teaching me the value of work, which is what this book is all about.

> And to my mother—for at least thirty years of correcting my grammar and always encouraging me.

To Bruce Bendinger of The Copy Workshop—for hounding me for no less than three years to write this book.

But mostly I have to thank my wife Janet—my love, my first editor, and my partner forever.

Thanks also to:

• Wells Rich Greene—for developing some of these systems before I ever went to work there. It's an agency we all miss.

• The American Advertising Federation (AAF)—for their great student contest, an exceptional learning opportunity.

• The Association for Education in Journalism and Mass Communications (AEJMC)—for teaching me how to make the transition from professional to professor.

Thanks to you all for your help and the lessons learned. I do not construe the writing of this book as sufficient payment.

Jim Avery

About The Author.

Jim Avery • University of Oklahoma.

Jim Avery began an academic career after seventeen years with ad agencies in New York and Chicago. He was Senior Vice-President Management Supervisor on Midas International at Wells Rich Greene. He has won both creative and marketing awards.

He has been at University of Oregon, University of Kansas, Penn State, and the University of Alaska/Anchorage. He is now a Professor at the University of Oklahoma.

Avery-coached student advertising teams have taken first and second nationally in the American Advertising Federation's National Student Advertising Competition (AAF/NSAC).

Avery served on the *Executive Committee for the Advertising Division of AEJMC,* and is a member of the *American Academy of Advertising.* He is an active marketing and advertising consultant, and writes a syndicated newspaper column, *"The Advertising Workshop."*

In 1996, he was appointed to the *National Advertising Review Board (NARB),* an industry group founded by the *American Advertising Federation, American Association of Advertising Agencies, Association of National Advertisers,* and the *Council of Better Business Bureaus.*

Planning Points:

Before you begin writing your marketing planning document, there are a number of areas we should cover:

1. Target Audience:

It is important to realize that the single most important information you will ever gather relates to the understanding of who will buy or use your Brand. This is the essence of account planning.

The more you understand about the people you are intending to reach with the advertising, the better that advertising will be.

For this reason, marketing should be done with a point of view that places the consumer, or the target group, first and foremost.

This book was written with that point of view.

Therefore, this section had to appear first.

2. Working Procedures:

This next planning point will provide direction on how to help your student group run more smoothly.

It covers organization of an advertising agency team—so you can create a similar pattern for yourselves.

It includes reporting procedures and formats—plus a few housekeeping hints for your agency.

3. Writing Style:

Business writing is quite different from the writing style that may have served you well in Creative Writing courses.

This planning point will cover some quick tips that can help move your writing in the right direction.

4. Computer Considerations:

The computer will be a critical resource for your ad agency team.

A. Most of your agency documents will be done on some sort of word-processing program—perhaps with your agency logo on the letterhead.

B. Your Plans Book, a critical document which presents your Marketing Plan, will be prepared using some sort of desktop publishing program, integrating text, graphics, and charts.

C. Your Presentation will probably be prepared on PowerPoint, or some other presentation software, and demand a good level of skill with this type of program.

D. You may use other computer-based resources as well if you produce print ads or videos, prepare a media plan, or develop a direct-mail program.

As you develop your marketing plan, some of you may find yourselves developing new skills on the computer. If you already have these skills, you will find yourself a valuable member of the team as you put those skills to good use.

5. The Outline:

This is the framework for your Marketing Planning Document.

Try to keep this overall organizational structure and discipline in mind as you move from chapter to chapter.

It will help you maintain focus as you concentrate on the details in each section. You may find it helpful to refer back to it from time to time and use it for a guide as you plan and develop your own campaign.

A Starting Point.

The outline listed in this book should be considered as a starting point. You'll be starting with a proven framework.

Remember, you can change anything you want and it will be just fine—if there's a good reason.

But to change anything you'll need to defend your reasons for the alterations. When you're done, you may find yourselves thinking a whole new way—like marketers.

Target Audience of this Book

"I keep six honest serving men (They taught me all I knew).
Their names are What and Why and When and How and Where and Who."

—Rudyard Kipling

Introduction.

In *Advertising Media Planning,* Jack Sissors and Linc Bumba define Target Audience as *"the desired or intended audience for advertising as described or determined by the advertiser."*

I think there are two major groups of people that will be interested in this book—entrepreneurs and students.

They are the Target Audience of this book.

The reason for telling you the target audience of this book is a little like giving you the objective for the book. Once you know for whom the book is intended, you understand why it was written.

The target audience for your ad campaigns will be the people who buy, use, or influence the buying or using of whatever you intend to sell.

A. Entrepreneurs:

People who invent businesses and then try to make them grow usually need a little help with their advertising. If you are one of these people, there is a strong probability that you do not always trust the people from whom you get advice.

This book will tell you how to write a Marketing Plan by yourself so your bank will give you a loan, or so that you can actually use the information to market what you sell.

If you are a very small entrepreneur, then you will likely do the work yourself, or you will convince your brother-in-law, who has been sponging off you for the past six months, to do some work.

This book will show you how to write a Marketing Plan on a step-by-step basis.

From National to Local.

You might have to do a little interpretation because this book will mostly be written with a national skew. That is, most examples will be for advertisers who advertise on a national basis.

Even knowing that, this book will likely be quite a bit clearer than others you may find. Just remember that you will have to translate some of the nationally oriented information to your local or regional marketing area.

If you're a larger entrepreneur, this book will provide you with an understanding of what your marketing and advertising people are doing. If you use an advertising agency, it will give you a chance to see what they do to earn their keep.

There is also some chance that the book will aid you to understand that the schmucks who say they are working on your advertising are incompetent fools who need to be fired. On that basis, the price of this book was the best investment you've ever made.

B. Students:

Three Target Groups.

There are potentially three different groups of students that may be interested in this book:

1. Students in an Advertising Campaigns class

2. Students competing in the AAF (American Advertising Federation) National Student Advertising Contest or "World Series of Advertising"

3. Students who work at student-run advertising agencies

In general, all advertising students will find this book useful. This book is written for an advertising student in an Advertising Campaigns class that has been designed to be a "capstone" class after the student has taken Principles of Advertising, Advertising Copywriting, Advertising Media Planning, Advertising Management, Advertising Research, etc.

This book will not attempt to explain every detail of every element in the campaign planning process. (As slowly as I write, that book would never be published.) This book is intended to explain how to do it once you've learned the theory in another class or contest.

It's written with the Advertising Campaigns class in mind, but this is virtually the same as preparing for the American Advertising Federation's national contest.

If you're in a student-run advertising agency, you'll find the book requires you to make an interpretation from time to time. I still think it will be the most useful guide you will find.

For more information, please also read:

At the end of each chapter will be a list of other books you may read to get more information on the subject.

Here is a list of some of the books we will be referring to:

1. **Strategic Advertising Campaigns**
    Schultz, Don E. and Barnes, Beth E.
    NTC Business Books, Chicago, 1994. Fourth Edition.

    This book is quite comprehensive and will be referred to throughout as a primary resource. You should try to have at least one copy available for your team.

2. **Hitting the Sweet Spot**
    Fortini-Campbell, Lisa
    The Copy Workshop, Chicago, 1991.

    This book will be particularly useful in areas related to your Target Audience and the Account Planning function.

3. **Positioning: The Battle for Your Mind**
    Ries, Al and Trout, Jack
    McGraw-Hill, New York, 1986.

    This classic book is available as an inexpensive paperback. You should get it and read it.

4. **Management Decisions by Objectives**
    Odiorne, George S.
    Prentice-Hall, Englewood Cliffs, NJ, 1969.

Working Procedures

"So much of what we call management consists of making it difficult for people to work."

—Peter Drucker

Introduction.

Welcome to Advertising Campaigns.

This will be the most difficult, painful, time-consuming, and frustrating class of your university career.

It will also be the most fun, the most rewarding, and likely the one from which you will learn the most.

You have already taken several other classes in advertising and understand the axioms of basic advertising, copywriting, media planning, etc.

This book will not seek to educate you in any of those disciplines—after all, you have already survived those classes.

However, it may give you a little different perspective on these disciplines as you see how they all work together.

This book will help you to know what to do when you write a marketing plan or document and give a presentation.

In fact, that is the reason for this book's being.

Housekeeping Issues.

But before we get into how to write a marketing document, there are some housekeeping issues that need to be addressed.

We will assume that you are working in a group of four to six people (this varies from program to program). You will be judged by what you do as a group, and the work should be considered a joint project.

As such, you are all responsible for one another's grade, but more important, you are all responsible for one another's work.

The quality of the final work and the learning that goes with it are much more important than a mere grade.

As you begin, consider these aspects:

A. Agency Organization:

Most advertising agencies are organized into the functions of account management, creative, media, research, and account planning. Each has their own resources and computer expertise.

If you organize your student group to match that of a typical advertising agency, you will increase your translatable learning. You'll undoubtedly know the job descriptions of the people who fulfill the various functions at the advertising agencies, so I've recorded a quick outline here as a reference for the other members of your group.

1. Account Manager:

We used to call these people account executives, but to avoid confusion with sales people in real estate, insurance, and brokerage houses who are also called account executives, we have changed the name to account managers.

It's their responsibility to manage their clients and the account at the agency. In most cases they're actually running a small business—such as the Cover Girl business at Grey.

They're also responsible for the major marketing on the Brand. Their job is identical to that of a Brand manager at the client, except the product they produce shows up in the media, not on the grocer's shelf.

In your student group, the account manager will take control of meetings, issue conference and status reports, and probably be responsible for the marketing objectives and marketing stragety.

The account manager will also have major input into the remainder of the document, including creative strategy, media strategy, sales promotion strategy, etc.

2. Creative:

In most advertising agencies, creative people are divided into copywriters, art directors, and producers.

They may have input into the creative platform, blueprint, or brief, but their major responsibility is to create brilliant advertising.

The creative people in your student group have the same charge.

3. Media:

Advertising agency media departments are sometimes independent entities, and are sometimes married with marketing services.

For the purposes of this book, we will assume they are independent, with account management handling the marketing services. These departments estimate costs, plan media, and buy media.

In your student group, the person you choose should have an affinity for numbers. They will have to be able to determine not just what medium to use, but also where and when to advertise.

4. Research:

The gathering of information is the responsibility of the advertising agency research department and your student group researcher.

5. Account Planning:

This is a new function in recent years and has aided advertising agencies to do a much better job of targeting the advertising for their client.

The account planner is the consumers' advocate at the agency. The account planner's major contribution is the creative strategy or blueprint. It is the result of intense interaction with the consumer, as well as other members of the agency team. At your student agency, you will also want to choose an account planner.

6. Presentations, IT, Computer Skills:

Call it what you will, your team will need good computer skills to put together a winning presentation. "IT," or information technology, is one aspect, and knowing what to do when the hard drive crashes is another.

Within your team, you will have a varying degree of computer skills. This is one more area in which you will be judged as a group, so you should discover your strengths.

And, even though it is not a traditional agency job, many teams appoint someone as the Chief Computer Guru—you can make up your own title. This job may be in addition to one of the jobs discussed previously. For example, your Media Director may also be the resident expert in PowerPoint.

B. Record Keeping:

This class is a very much like a business. The better records you keep, the better will be the quality of your work.

There are two kinds of records you need—a library and reports. But first you need—The Box.

1. *The Box:*

The very first thing you need to do when you start this campaign is to get a box. It should be wide and tall enough to hold a file folder. It can be a file drawer, a fruit box, or a cardboard box designed to hold files.

Appoint a Librarian.

Write "Library" on the outside of The Box, then appoint someone to be Librarian. Anytime a group member finds an article in *Time* or in a newspaper or anywhere else that has anything to do with the campaign, it should be filed in The Box.

There are at least three reasons for this:

a. **The quality of your work will be evaluated by judges.**
If you are an American Advertising Federation student contest group, then you will be evaluated by three to five professionals. They will ask questions after your presentation.

If this is for an Advertising Campaigns class, then your client will most likely attend your presentation and there will be time for that client to ask you questions at the end of your presentation.

Finally, this could be for a student advertising agency. In this case, every time you make a presentation to your client, they will ask questions. You need a resource to keep the answers to these questions.

When they are going to ask questions, have The Box nearby, because it will impress them, and second, because it will aid you to find the answer if you cannot remember.

The latter is not usually reality however, because if you're not bright enough to remember the answer, you're probably not bright enough to remember where you filed the information.

The first reason for The Box is showmanship.

b. **Since there are several of you working on this campaign, each of you will want to keep information in a different place.**

The copywriter will want all the information on how people make purchase decisions at his or her apartment. The media planner will also want to have all the information on rates and costs within easy access.

The Box is the answer.

Everything goes in The Box, and if anyone wants to use it overnight or over the weekend they can just sign it out. If they lose it, they will lose face with the remainder of the group, because everyone will know that they lost it.

So the second reason for The Box is it's a place to store information and reduce arguments.

c. **The Box will become a symbol that the group is now working—kind of like the legislature is in session.**

The Box will make meetings official. That is the third reason.

Learn to use The Box, because if it does not have everything that needs to be in it, it will not serve its function.

2. Reports:

Next, you need to start writing Conference and Status reports. These reports will record your progress.

A copy of these reports should be provided for each member of your group and for your class instructor. This will allow a group member who missed a meeting to know what happened and what they need to do to catch up.

Conference Reports also provide a method to keep your instructor posted on your progress.

a. **Conference Reports:**

These will provide a review of what happened at each meeting (or conference). You should report who was there, what was discussed, what agreements were reached, and what needs to be accomplished before the next meeting.

Each of these is important, especially in a student group for an Advertising Campaigns class.

Consider the flake who has been assigned to your group—

who will not do anything that is required. You have already decided that you cannot let him (or her) have a significant assignment because you know he or she won't do it.

If you include in the Conference Report the fact that this flake didn't even bother to show up, then you know that the instructor also knows—and you didn't need to tattle.

All you had to do was write the weekly Conference Report.

The Conference Report will also serve as a record of who, when, why, and what was discussed.

If you need to know when a specific strategy was agreed to, just check the past conference reports.

An example of a student Conference Report can be found on page 28.

b. Status Report:

This is a record that allows you to see what has been done and what needs to be finished. It records who is responsible and when it is due. An example of a Status Report is on page 29.

Notice that the left-hand column (project) identifies the category of what needs to be done.

As the semester, or year, progresses this column will contain more and more information.

When you're working on the media segment of the planning document, it is likely that there will be an overall heading for "Media Plan" followed by a subhead of "strategies."

Then there will be a notation that you are working on the seasonality strategy. As you look across the page you will find the status—that it's due next week. Everyone will know.

The Status Report should be distributed to every member of the group—and to the class instructor.

This report will also allow you to rip the person who chooses to skate by with as little work as possible because you will simply not change the due date when someone doesn't complete a project on time.

This will help the instructor notice that the flake did not hand in the research interviews when everyone else had completed their work ten days earlier.

C. Financial Considerations:

A Good Presentation Costs Money.

The development of this campaign, including the planning document and the presentation, will cost quite a bit of money. But the money will not be needed until the end of the term when everything starts to come together.

Check with someone who took the class last term, but as of the writing of this book the average group spends about $200 to complete the class.

Virtually all of this cost will be for photocopying. You will need to make copies of weekly reports, status reports, conference reports, and you will need to duplicate your research questionnaires.

The cost of your presentation can be expensive if you produce slides. But most universities and businesses now have computers with programs like PowerPoint, so this work can be done for little or no cost.

Appoint A Treasurer.

If you are like most groups, $200 does not just appear. Therefore, I recommend that you tax yourselves each week or month.

Appoint a Treasurer and make him or her responsible for collecting taxes. Make projections and find ways to earn money.

If you're an AAF group getting ready to compete in the regional contest, you might want to raise some money by getting donations. These donations may require you to provide some work in exchange for funding. Travel costs vary, but unless the contest is in your home town, meals and hotel should be in your budget.

If you're an AAF Finalist, and go to the nationals, congratulations. Now you will also have more money to raise. You can double the costs above, and add money for more travel, hotel, and meals.

Use Your Skills to Make Money.

Another way to pay for this advertising campaign is to earn the money using your advertising knowledge. Here are a few ways:

Campus Coupon Book.

Students at the University of Alaska created a coupon book to be distributed to students. Group members then sold coupons in the book to retail establishments.

Radio Station Raffle.

Another group of students asked radio stations for contributions of time. They traded the time to an auto dealer for a car, then they raffled the car.

Sell Advertising Textbooks.

The company that publishes this book (The Copy Workshop) allows their advertising textbooks to be sold through your student ad club. The ad club then keeps the 20% that normally goes to the campus bookstore. Other companies may have similar offers.

These are just three ideas. You may have more. In fact, you should. Use what you have learned about advertising and marketing.

There's a way to make money to pay for your advertising campaign.

D. Responsibilities:

Be Specific.

Every member of the group will have a specific area of responsibility.

This should be assigned by the group.

It is likely that your class instructor asked you to be in a specific group because your skills complement the skills of others in the group.

Desire Is Good. Capability Is Better.

You probably have someone who wants to work in media, someone who wants to be a copywriter, and someone who wants to be an account manager. That is good, and a great way to start.

But you need to remember that just because someone *wants* to be a copywriter doesn't make them a copywriter. Desire is good, but capability is better. Being able to write copy makes someone a copywriter.

Sometimes you'll have someone who wants to write copy and you'll want them to write for another group because if they work for someone else you will have a better chance of winning.

Welcome to the real world. You will always find people who are incompetent working in good jobs. Sometimes you'll be able to get rid of them, but sometimes you'll just have to put up with them.

If you have one of these people in your group, find a way that they can feel responsible and contribute without destroying your work.

The best way to deal with these people, however, is to not have them in your group to begin with.

Good Advice for Bad Students.

If you are a person who doesn't want to work or if you aren't very capable, your goal in the first week of class is to find a very good group, and then find a way to weasel your way into it.

After all, if you get in the group and do enough to get by you can have a pretty easy semester—if everyone else in your group is working.

This wouldn't work if I were the class instructor—for two reasons.

First, I pick the groups—so there is no way for you to do your weaseling. Second, I allow groups to fire people.

So if you get fired by your group, you have to do the entire project on your own, find another group to hire you, or drop the class. (Hint: there's a zero percent probability that if one group fires you another group will offer you a job.) But on a more positive note, if you are a doer, you will not have to worry about this.

Good Advice For Good Groups.

You should not actually assign individual responsibilities until you are almost finished with the Situation Analysis.

This gives you a little time to work out how you will work with one another and to establish a kind of pecking order. You need to discover who will work and who is reliable, and who will be the object of your active hostility.

Finally, put someone in charge of every section and every element of the project. You may decide that everyone is going to work on the Situation Analysis and as a result, you really don't need someone to be in charge. Wrong.

If everyone is responsible, then no one is responsible.

So put someone in charge and let them do it. Hold their feet to the fire if they don't, and congratulate them when they do a good job.

Hint: If you're an American Advertising Federation group, don't select your presenters until the very last possible moment. As soon as you decide on those five people, everyone else will quit working.

Example: Conference Report

Conference Report

Present for agency: Bill Smith
Present for client: Jim Avery
Meeting place: Room K-136
Date of meeting: August 13, 1999
Date of report: September 1, 1999
Written by: Bill Smith

The purpose of this meeting was to establish the ground rules for the *Advertising Campaigns* class.

Discussion:
Client outlined parameters for Journalism & Public Communications 328, *Advertising Campaigns,* including reading, assignments, philosophy, and grading procedure.

Client provided background as evidence of ability to guide the discussion.

Agreements:
It was agreed that the class would address advertising and the development of a campaign from an advertising agency viewpoint.

It was also agreed that the Agency may write a recommendation to change any aspect of *Advertising Campaigns.*

Agency further agreed to participate in each class period.

Action:
1. Agency to continue to read *AdWeek* and other trade publications.

2. Agency to submit capabilities for campaign teams by September.

3. Agency to read case study as soon as it is available.

BS
9/1/99

Project Status Report
Advertising Campaigns Class

Project	Status	Next Steps	Due Date	Who
Groups	In process	1. Prepare memorandum designating one team member responsible for group assignments	9/01	Student
		2. Make group assignments	9/09	Instructor
AdWeek	Subscribe to	Be prepared to discuss in detail in class	9/02	Student
Conference Report	In process	One due each week from each group	9/16	Group
Case Book	In process	1. Write and publish	TBD	Instructor
		2. Study and prepare for quiz	TBD	Student
Research	In process	Prepare questions for client meeting	TBD	Student
Presentation	In process	1. Review procedure with photo lab	TBD	Student
		2. Rehearsal for final presentation	TBD	Group
		3. Final presentation	TBD	Group

WS
8/31/99

Planning Point Three

Writing Style

"Make clear and simple rules..."
—Louis Boccardi, President, Associated Press

Introduction.

Rules Happen.

Writing style is dictated more by corporate philosophy than by what is right and what is wrong.

The Associated Press maintains an entire book so the writers who work for A.P. will know what style to use.

As time goes on, the rules become more and more numerous.

There wasn't even a standard for spelling until the latter part of the nineteenth century when Noah Webster decided we needed a dictionary. (Quite often I'll tell an associate that my spelling is pre-Websterian.) Personally, I think A.P.'s book is too much in its entirety, but here are a few things to keep in mind when you write.

Fifteen Good Guidelines.

The following is a short list of rules that students should follow:

1. **Use the shortest possible set of words.**
   Flowery adjectives and adverbs are out of place in business writing. Always use the shortest possible set of words to communicate the point.

2. **Use the shortest word when you have a choice.**
   Use "use" instead of "utilize" whenever you can. How often do you utilize the bathroom? Always use the shortest word when you have a choice.

3. **Always spell words correctly.**
   Use spell check and use your dictionary. Proofread your work for incorrectly used words that are spelled correctly.

   You will be fired if you misspell the brand name or the name of your client.

4. **Use good grammar.**
   Remember: if you make mistakes in spelling or grammar the reader will assume that you are uneducated and that there will be no reason to believe your point of view.

   The only other interpretation the reader may assume is that you do not care enough about this communication to check it.

5. **Tell the most important thing first.**
   Don't make the reader wade through a lot of minutiae to find the good stuff. Put it up front.

6. **Use topic sentences.**
   Always make the first sentence of a paragraph the topic sentence. In English Composition class you may have learned that you should vary the topic sentence to add interest to your writing. This thinking does not apply in business writing.

7. **Never start a paragraph with a dependent clause.**
   The reader will get your point faster if you put that phrase later in the paragraph.

8. **Do not start sentences with prepositional phrases.**
   Again, the reader will get your point faster. However this is a harder rule to follow.

   In less formal writing, prepositional phrases at the beginning of a sentence seem to make the sentence friendlier. Still, in business writing, and especially in formal planning documents, do not start sentences with prepositional phrases.

9. **"The purpose is…"**
   When you start a memorandum or letter, you should tell the purpose for that written communication in the first sentence. It is common to write *"The purpose for this letter is …"*.
   I quite often have students start all written communication with the word *"this"*:
   > *"This provides …,"*
   > *"This responds to your request for…,"* or
   > *"This requests …"* are all examples of this usage.

   "This" forces you to write the purpose of the memorandum or letter in that first sentence.

When you are about to graduate, you will write letters to potential employers. Those letters should start, "This requests an interview leading to the position of assistant media planner."

Your potential new employer now knows exactly what you want with the letter. If you want to be clever, that's good. But don't waste people's time with your writing. Get to it.

10. **Never end a sentence with a preposition.**
Winston Churchill once said, *"This is something up with which I shall not put."* There is no preposition at the end of that sentence.

11. **Use the tabs on your typewriter or computer.**
   a. **Make decimals line up under one another.**
   Most computers have a decimal tab. Learn to use it.

   b. **Make numbers or bullet points stand out.**
   Look at this section. The "U" in "Use" lines up over the "a." The "M's" in "Make" and "Most" line up.

   Using tabs makes it easier for the reader to see when there is another point to be communicated. It helps keep the reader organized, and it helps keep you organized.

12. **Never start a sentence with an Arabic number.**
Write it out.

13. **Be specific.**
If you want the reader to believe what you are writing, do not simply write *"Research indicates that ..."*

This kind of statement often creates more questions than it answers. What research? When was it conducted? Under what circumstances?

14. **Write as short as you can to communicate the point.**
We all have more to read than we have time to read. Give your reader a break.

15. **Avoid superlatives.**
In business documents, overstatement and "hype" are treated with suspicion. What may be appropriate for the advertising may not be appropriate for the advertising plan.

Writing As a Group.

There is a good business writing style, and you should stick to it. But you can all make minor decisions within your group as you work to develop a consistent style.

The finished document should look as if one person wrote it.

Most important, it should look as if your entire future career depends on how good your document looks. After all, it does.

Good Writing and Good Design.

Good writing looks good.

Today, you have great control over the look of your writing with computer-based word processing and desktop publishing programs.

Unfortunately, these programs won't usually tell you the difference between good typography and bad typography, they merely do what you tell them to do.

So, it seems worth mentioning that you should either know what you're doing or copy someone who knows what they're doing. This is not as strange as it sounds. If you find some graphic formats that really work—that are easy to read and have an appealing design—well, you should certainly try to do better, but don't feel like you've failed if you follow a format developed by a top professional.

Here's what the legendary art director Helmut Krone had to say, *"I'd like to propose a new idea for our age: Until you've got a better answer, you copy. I copied Bob Gage for five years. I even copied the leading between his lines of type. And Bob originally copied Paul Rand, and Rand first copied a German typographer named Tschichold."*

These are some of the finest art directors and designers in the history of advertising. And they followed formats developed by others. So don't feel you have to invent a whole new graphic format. You've got enough to deal with. Or should that be you've got enough with which to deal.

33

Computer Considerations

"What's the difference between Apple Computer and the Boy Scouts?
Answer: The Boy Scouts have adult supervision."

—early Silicon Valley joke

A. Hardware & Compatibility:

In many ways, we're only as good as our tools—mental and physical. For your ad agency team, this means your computers.

You should make an assessment of who has what.

You should know what is available at your university's computer lab.

You should have compatible programs and either be able to swap disks or send files to each other as e-mail attachments.

The Need for Backup.

There is an unconfirmed rumor that your computer knows when the deadline is approaching. This rumor gets confirmed every semester—right around deadline time.

Back up on a regular basis and have a backup plan in place for when (not if) some key piece of equipment decides to test your stress tolerance.

B. Software and Ability:

As we've mentioned, desire doesn't make a good copywriter, ability makes a good copywriter. The same goes for computer skills.

What can take one person the better part of an evening, another can do in less than half an hour. Who do you want working on your charts?

Put your ego on hold and evaluate who is best at doing what. If you find that you have some weaknesses—maybe more than one—figure out what you have to learn. Or, figure out who you have to recruit.

Commonly Used Software.

These are some of the programs and their uses:

Word Processing and e-mail Software:

Every member of your team should be proficient. This is how you and your team will communicate. Almost everyone uses Word, but this was written in Claris.

Desktop Publishing and Graphic Software:

You will need to use this software for your Plans Book and for preparation of print materials. Quark is the current favorite, though many use PageMaker. Someone will have to know how to scan and use an image manipulation program, such as Photoshop.

You will need a good selection of fonts and access to printing in black and white and color. Some pieces may need to be printed in larger sizes.

Spreadsheet and Database Software:

Your Media Director will need to be able to use this type of software, for preparing your media plan and budgets. You may also need to access some specialized media planning software.

Some of the information you will need will be available over the Web, so good searching capabilities on the Internet will also be useful.

Presentation Software and Hardware:

In a word, PowerPoint. This is the current software of choice. It has interesting capabilities in both audio and video—learn to use them.

Projection capabilities are also critical with this type of software, and you should find out as early as possible what equipment you will be able to use for your presentation.

And more...

Your plan may call for a Web site. You may create an audio logo. You may produce and edit a TV commercial.

Each of these tasks has their own specialized software. As you identify your needs, try to identify who, what, and how you will meet them.

There's only one type of software to avoid—games. You've got a lot to do, try to keep those time-wasters far away from your computer.

The Outline

"Make no little plans; they have no magic to stir men's blood."

—Daniel Hudson Burnham

Introduction.

This section will provide an outline for your planning document.

It is reasonable to assume that if you know what you are going to write and know where it is going, it will be easier for you to write it.

Many good outlines exist. The outline found here is one example.

The First Part.

The first part of the marketing planning document has three sections.

Section I (Situation Analysis) and Section II (Research) contain a review of what you have learned. This material will help give you the expertise to write the marketing document.

Section III (Problems and Opportunities) summarizes what you have learned that may be actionable in the coming year.

The Second Part.

The second part sets the constraints for your Marketing Plan— Section IV (Marketing Objective) and Section V (Budget).

The Plan.

The remainder of the marketing planning document, starting with Section VI (Marketing Strategy), is the plan itself.

This includes Section VII (Creative), Section VIII (Media), Section IX (Sales Promotion), Section X (MarCom, Section XI (Evaluation) and Section XII (Testing).

The Outline begins on the following page.

Follow it in preparing your Marketing Plan and your advertising campaign. The more detail you provide, the better the information.

If you can add a new segment or two, you will add dimension to the plan. Try to find new ways to communicate with your group.

You will notice that this outline follows the structure of the book. It is similar to the Table of Contents, but not identical.

When you begin to develop your presentation, you will also find that this outline is a useful structure for your presentation as well—though you will naturally need to condense and dramatize as necessary.

Marketing Planning Document Outline:

I. Situation Analysis
   A. Current Users
   B. Geographical Emphasis
   C. Seasonality
   D. Purchase Cycle
   E. Creative Requirements
   F. Competitive Sales
   G. Competitive Media

II. Research
   A. Objectives
   B. Strategies
   C. Methodology
   D. Summary of Findings

III. Problems & Opportunities

IV. Marketing Objective
   A. Number
   B. Rationale

V. Budget

VI. Marketing Strategy
   A. Promotion
      1. Advertising
         a. Creative
         b. Media
         c. Production
      2. Sales Promotion
         a. Consumer
         b. Trade
      3. Public Relations
         a. Publics
         b. Tactics

4. Direct Marketing
   a. Direct Response Media
   b. Telemarketing
5. Event Marketing
   a. Consumer Events
   b. Trade Events
6. Miscellaneous
   a. Personal Selling
   b. Packaging
   c. Merchandising
   d. Promotional Products
B. Product
C. Pricing
D. Distribution (Place)
E. People
F. Rationale

VII. Advertising Creative

A. Target Audience
B. Objective
C. Strategy
D. Support
E. Consideration
F. Tone
G. Rationale
H. Tactics

VIII. Advertising Media

A. Objectives
   1. Target Audience
   2. Geography
   3. Seasonality
   4. Continuity, Flighting
   5. Creative Constraints
   6. Reach versus Frequency
B. Strategies
   1. Media Mix and Types

      2. Media Format or Classes

      3. Geographic Use of Media

      4. Seasonal Use of Media

      5. Flighting versus Continuity

  C. Rationale

      1. Support of Strategy

      2. Support of Delivery and Efficiency

  D. Tactics

IX. Sales Promotion

  A. Consumer Promotion

      1. Current Situation

      2. Objectives

      3. Strategies

      4. Rationale

      5. Tactics (Events)

      6. Payout

  B. Trade Promotion

      1. Current Situation

      2. Objectives

      3. Strategies

      4. Rationale

      5. Tactics (Events)

      6. Payout

X. MarCom

  A. Public Relations

      1. Current Situation

      2. Objectives

      3. Publics

      4. Strategies

      5. Rationale

  B. Direct Markeing

      1. Current Situation

      2. Objectives

      3. Target Audience

      4. Strategies

      5. Rationale

C. Event Markeing
1. Current Situation
2. Objectives
3. Target Audience
4. Strategies
5. Rationale
D. Miscellaneous

XI. Evaluation (Research)
A. Current Situation
B. Objective
C. Strategy
D. Tactics (Methodology)

XII. Testing
A. Objective
B. Strategies
C. Tactics (Methodology)
D. Rationale
E. Evaluation

Additional Sections.
It is certainly appropriate to add a section. In Section VI, Marketing, you may wish to emphasize or delete as needed.

Example: Kellogg's Hispanic.
For example, if your Brand is Kellogg's Corn Flakes, it's likely that you will have a Hispanic Section. The Hispanic Section would have creative, media, and promotion within the one section.

It would also be acceptable to put a Hispanic Section in the creative section, in the media section, and in the promotion section.

There could be any number of other sections added to this outline, or you may choose to eliminate one of these sections.

Customize the Plan to Fit Your Brand.
This outline is intended to provide a view of the general marketing planning document. It is expected that each plan will be customized to fit that individual Brand.

Do not, however, construe this to give you permission to eliminate information—that could make this marketing planning document for your advertising campaign less valuable.

Get Started

*"The way to eat an elephant
is one bite at a time."*

—Unknown

Introduction.

Start Today.

Now you're ready to start. You have your systems and organization set, and you're anxious to get on with it.

You have a large task ahead. So you need to start today!

If you wait a week because you have other projects or classes to deal with, you'll be a week behind everyone else. Then, you'll have to find a way to make up that time.

The Marketing Planning Document.

How To Do It.

On the following pages we will start to track you through the writing of a Marketing Planning Document.

I have taken the time to write this guide because it did not exist anywhere else. There are several good textbooks on advertising campaigns, including *Strategic Advertising Campaigns* by Don Schultz and Beth E. Barnes.

Most of these books do a great job of educating you on what an advertising campaign is and expanding your advertising and marketing vocabulary. But none of them tell you how to do it. This one will.

First...

Get a pad and pencil. Next, sit down with this book and read.

Be ready to make notes on the pad and in the book. You will be reading most of this book more than once.

Follow the directions that start on the following page.

Take it one bite at a time.

Situation Analysis

"It may be that the race is not always to the swift, nor the battle to the strong. But that's the way to bet."

—Damon Runyon

Introduction.

The First Step—Know Where You Are.

The first step in advertising planning is to determine what you know.

Advertisers and students alike are often surprised to learn either how little they know at the beginning or how much knowledge they already have. You need to know where you are before you can determine where you'll need to take the business.

When all this information is assembled in one location, it's called a Situation Analysis.

If the Brand will be a new one, then there may be little or no information available concerning the history of the Brand or category.

This doesn't make the Situation Analysis impossible, it just provides a little challenge. You may have to rely on organizations such as trade associations or the government for the information you seek.

Either way, you'll have a better document, and you'll know what the challenges are ahead, if you get the information outlined here. You may become an expert in the use of the library. Sleuthing is good.

If you're a professional advertising agency pitching a new client, sometimes that client doesn't choose to share everything with you.

In this case, you'll win points—big time—if you're able to find information that isn't readily available. The best possible situation is if you're able to give that client (or even a current client) some piece of information they didn't already know.

MRA, a Kansas City advertising agency, refers to that as "the ah-ha!"

Also Known as "Background Review."

Writing this information down in one place is sometimes called a background review. As it expands to fill the formal outline, we undoubtedly learn something that we did not know.

The information for this background review, or Situation Analysis, will continue to be more and more important as time goes on.

Integrated Marketing Communications (IMC) endorses a program of reaching fewer and fewer people in a group. This narrowing of the target audience requires discipline in identifying specific groups of users.

These additional bits of information will help get us moving. It's necessary to formalize what we do know so we can ask the appropriate questions in the next section (Research) to get answers to the questions we currently do not know.

Seven Segments.

The purpose of the Situation (never situational) Analysis is to provide a complete outline of everything currently known that will contribute to the marketing of the Brand. It commonly has seven segments.

First Four Segments.

The first four segments deal with the people who use the product or, with a new product, the people we expect to use it.

These first four segments are:
- **Current Users**
- **Geographical Emphasis**
- **Seasonality**
- **Purchase Cycle**

Last Three Segments.

The last three segments of the background review give some detailed pieces of information about the history of the marketing of the Brand and of the category.

The last three segments are:
- **Creative Requirements**
- **Competitive Sales**
- **Competitive Media**

These seven segments make up the Situation Analysis and should address the current situation and any issues surrounding a given piece of information.

Example: Dannon Yogurt.

For example, in the first paragraph of the analysis labeled "Current Users," if the Brand is Dannon Yogurt, we will identify 18-to-49-year-old adults.

Only identify what is happening with the Brand at this point in time, never identify future opportunities in the writing of the Current User analysis. (Even if we may be giving consideration to a campaign designed to address women 50+ who are concerned about osteoporosis.)

Save Your New Ideas.

Take care not to reveal a new campaign idea or the key elements of the plan in this section. Only point out those issues that have been raised prior to the writing of the plan.

The new ideas should be saved for the strategy segments of your marketing plan, or they might be generated in the Problems & Opportunities section.

The New Idea File.

Most marketing plan authors have a file or a special yellow pad dedicated to new ideas.

Keep all your new ideas in the file or on the pad, but don't give the ideas to the reader of the Situation Analysis.

In the very beginning, it is likely that you have not had sufficient time or space to develop the right attitude to sell these new concepts. Wait until the segment dedicated to the subject for your recommendation, or for the presentation.

Convincing "The Keeper of the Money."

Remember, the reader of your Marketing Plan is usually the keeper of the money.

In a packaged goods company it will probably be a division president or a senior vice-president of marketing.

They are unlikely to approve the plan until they have been convinced that it will work.

Creating a Logical Flow of Information.

The discipline of revealing what we knew in the past (Situation Analysis) and what we learned this year (Research) before we reveal what we intend to do (Marketing Objectives) and how we intend to do it (Marketing Strategies) creates a logical flow of information.

If the author of the marketing planning document starts to tell what is intended for the coming year in the Situation Analysis, then the natural order of the plan is destroyed; therefore, there is no opportunity to build the proper environment to sell the plan. I hope I have made my point—save your new ideas for later.

"The Brand."

For multi-brand marketers, their advertising is most often for a given brand. For example, General Mills advertising is most often seen for Wheaties, Bisquick, or Betty Crocker Cake Mix.

In a very few cases, there may be more than one product in a Brand, such as Aunt Jemima Pancake Mix and Aunt Jemima Pancake Syrup, or the five sauces in the Ortega Sauce line.

It is even more rare to see advertising that features the manufacturer, like General Mills, and if there ever is this type of advertising, generally it will be found in the *Wall Street Journal,* not in the media directed to the end consumer.

Your Marketing Plan, including the Situation Analysis, will be on behalf of a brand, not the corporation that owns the brand.

It is common to refer to Bisquick, Wheaties, or Betty Crocker Pie Crust as the "Brand," in the the marketing document or plan.

When we are discussing brand work in general it is lowercase, but when we use Brand as a substitute for Bisquick, it is capitalized.
(This same general rule is followed for other topics. The situation analysis, in general, is not capitalized. Your Situation Analysis and your Marketing Plan are capitalized.)

We will also use the terms brand manager and product manager interchangeably, because some companies call them brand managers (Procter & Gamble, for example) while others call them product managers (General Mills or Kraft General Foods are two).

Other Businesses.

In most cases, services and retail businesses can be treated the same way as products. Banks have product managers in charge of credit cards, checking, and loans even though these are really more services than they are tangible products.

Major department stores have buyers who are in charge of a department in the same way a brand manager is responsible for the marketing of a brand.

In general, you will find the procedures for developing your Situation Analysis to be very similar whether you are working on the marketing of Dannon Yogurt, men's shoes at Bloomingdales, or checking accounts for First Interstate Bank.

A more detailed, step-by-step, how-to-do-it guide follows.

A. Current Users:

Understanding Who Buys the Product.

This portion of the situation analysis has historically been called the target audience section, but it is really a review of the current users. Understanding who buys the product is key to successful marketing, including the advertising.

If we can thoroughly understand who the current users are, then it's likely we can find new users similar to our current users.

This group could end up being our target audience, but we are not yet ready to make that decision. We will save that decision for the Marketing Strategy segment of your planning document.

In most cases it is safe to assume that users are knowledgeable about the product, its good points, and its weaknesses.

Knowledge about competing brands will aid this section as well.

Midas Muffler Shops' greatest competitor is probably CarX even though CarX is located in only a small portion of the United States. Both Midas and CarX sell replacement mufflers engineered to fit each car precisely, while Sears and Meineke sell mufflers that are universal, i.e., one muffler will fit several different car makes and models.

It is probably easier for Midas to compete with CarX, where the customers are similar, than it is for Midas to convert Meineke users where the primary reason for purchase motivation is price. Learning about the CarX user will aid the Midas marketing plan more than learning about the Meineke user.

Demographics and Psychographics.

The two key points to review about the current users are the demographics and the psychographics of the users.

1. Demographics:

There are two primary methods for verifying the demographics of the current users of the Brand and the category.

The first method is secondary research and the second method is primary research.

This may seem backward, to do secondary first and primary second, but it has to do with the root of the definitions.

Secondary research is information that has been gathered by someone else and published. You will want to search these sources first to find what knowledge aleady exists in order to avoid repeating someone else's work.

Then do your primary research, which is research that you conduct and pay for yourself to answer your specific questions. You are going directly to the user, or your target audience—you are asking the questions first or primarily.

a. **Secondary Research:**
   Mediamark Research, Inc. (MRI) and Simmons Market Research Bureau (SMRB) are good sources of secondary information concerning the demographics of the users of specific Brands and their respective categories. If neither of these companies audit the category in which your brand competes, then you will have to rely on primary research.

   Be sure to investigate both sources because while MRI and SMRB audit many of the same categories, there are some that each audit unto themselves. There are other sources of demographic information, but these two are the best places to start. See Note A for more detail.

b. **Primary Research:**
   The second method of determining or verifying information, such as the current user profile, is primary research.

   When you gain information for your marketing plan by asking direct questions to current and potential users of the Brand or category, you're doing primary research.

   This primary research can be used to determine usage patterns for those members of the target group who have acknowledged using the Brand.

   For example, if you wanted to know more about the demographics of your user base, ask demographic questions of respondents then correlate this information to the usage questions to get a grasp of the demographics of that user group.

Remember, however, that you will probably only interview a few hundred people in your primary research.

The information contained in MRI or SMRB has many times that in its sample. So if MRI tells you the demographic profile of the current user is Men 25 to 34, and your survey says it's Women, you better work very hard to convince me. Because to start with, I don't believe you.

It is also likely that primary research can be used to determine the factors that motivate purchase behavior in your category (what users use to make up their minds about which brand they will buy).

It can be the vehicle for identifying the demographic and psychographic characteristics of the current users. It can even be used to determine what the user group perceives to be unique about the Brand.

This will be discussed further in Chapter Two.

2. Psychographics:

The second key point to review in the Current Users is the psychographics of those key users.

There are a variety of companies that group consumers in typologies. VALS II, put out by SRI, uses eight typologies to classify Americans.

Prism, Kube, and LUVS are other systems that will provide equally useful information. Psychographics will provide information about the way your users and audience think.

This will allow you to write better, more targeted, harder hitting and, ultimately, more effective advertising.

The marketing director for a performing arts center once explained the value of psychographics to me with the following statement: *"If you tell me that my target audience is made of females between the ages of 25 and 54, earning over fifty thousand dollars a year, with at least a college education, I do not know as much about her as if you tell me she is likely to be a vegetarian."*

He convinced me that psychographics is important to understanding to whom you are writing the advertising.

B. Geographical Emphasis:

Find Out Where Current Users Live.

The purpose for this geography section of the Situation Analysis is to provide information on where the current users live.

In the Situation Analysis we are looking for general information, while we will be looking for a great deal of information for the Media section of this plan.

If, for example, we know that more mufflers are purchased in the area around the Great Lakes than are purchased in the Southwest, then we know something more about our customers.

If we know the geographic skew to our Brand sales, then we not only know where our customers live, but we also start to accumulate information about this important group of people.

For example, if you learn that the users skew to metro or urban areas, you understand something more about these people that buy and consume your product.

Past sales by district, region, state, DMA (Nielson's Designated Marketing Area) or ADI (Arbitron's Area of Dominate Influence) will give you a good start on where past users live.

This geographical information will not only generate information for the geographic section of the situation analysis, it will also provide the basis for the allocation of media dollars (to be discussed in Chapter Eight), and it will provide additional insight into the current user segment of the document.

Brand Development Index (BDI).

Brand Development Index (BDI) is the next step. BDI will give you a quantitative measure of the Brand's history of relative success for each marketing area. It will also require sales numbers for each of those marketing areas by geography: district, region, state, DMA, or ADI.

BDI is calculated using these geographic sales and the population for the area under consideration:

$$\text{Area BDI} = \frac{\%\text{ sales in this area} \times 100}{\%\text{ population in this area}}$$

BDI and BPI.

For example, there are quite a number of packaged goods companies that allocate media dollars based on where sales came from last year.

If the advertising case rate is one dollar, and the Brand sold 10,000 cases in the Casper/Riverton DMA, then the Brand will spend $10,000 in media in Casper/Riverton (less production of course).

The problem is that the Brand has been spending $10,000 in Casper/Riverton since it was introduced. Does the Brand sell the 10,000 cases because that is the proper potential of the Brand, or has it become a self-fulfilling prophesy as the advertising has created the market?

It could be that we'd have greater sales if some of the Casper/Riverton money was spent in Presque Isle, but we have no evidence of this.

A BDI profile will give you a picture of where the Brand's strong markets are, and which ones are weak.

This will become the basis for strategy—do you want a defensive strategy to spend where you are strong, or an offensive strategy to spend where you need help?

Most advertising dollars allocated in the marketplace are defensive dollars. There must be a reason why we've been able to sell 10,000 cases in Casper/Riverton. If we take that money and allocate it to Presque Isle, sales may increase in Maine, but decrease in Wyoming.

Most marketers would rather have the bird in the hand in Wyoming than gamble on the bird in the bush in Maine.

Determining the Greatest Sales Potential.
Later we will discuss how to determine sales potential.

This sales potential will allow us to know exactly where to allocate advertising media dollars.

If a brand development index is not available, then some regional information can be found in MRI or SMRB.

This may have to be enough if more exact information can't be found. See Note A at the end of Chapter Eight for more detail.

C. Seasonality:

Determining Key Selling Periods.
Sales in a given month when compared to other times of the year provide information about when marketing should take place.

This is a type of BDI, and could be construed to be a Seasonality Development Index, but it is usually simply called Seasonality.

This segment of the Situation Analysis will provide detail on when sales happen throughout the year. Christmas lights and other decorations may have the highest level of seasonality of any category of products.

Milk, at the other extreme, is used almost equally in every week of the year.

The Brand will have a seasonality to its sales, and that seasonality will impact your planning.

The Seasonality section of the Situation Analysis should define the key selling period, and there should be an exhibit that shows percent of sales per month and an index of that percent to the average month. (Usually this seasonality chart is found in the exhibits at the end of the media plan.)

Most packaged goods manufacturers skew advertising to those months when the greatest sales take place.

In fact, a great number of companies maintain a precise spending philosophy, i.e., if 13.2% of sales take place in March, then 13.2% of the advertising will be in March.

Make certain there should be 13.2% of sales in March, and that it's not a function of many years of advertising at high levels.

In other words, are the sales in March there because people want to consume the Brand at that time, or is it because the Brand has always advertised in March since that's when the annual sales meeting takes place?

If the Brand has been advertising for a long period of time, it is not always possible to determine which is taking place.

Offensive or Defensive.

This can also be construed to be an offensive versus a defensive issue. If you support each month as a function of the percent of sales in that month, you'll be using a defensive strategy because you're seeking to defend sales you've achieved in the past.

If you heavy-up spending in months when sales have been weak in the past, then you're using an offensive strategy.

Remember, as you did in the Geography segment of the plan, that you can only spend the money once.

If you spend it in an historically weak month you may not spend it to support a traditionally strong month.

D. Purchase Cycle:

How Often...

This section of your marketing document will help you understand how often your target group (or groups) use the brand.

It is useful because it helps you understand how much media weight is needed. Sometimes the media weight is simply a function of budget, but the levels can be adjusted through the use of flighting and pulsing.

Purchase cycle will aid the reader of the marketing document to put frequency into perspective—frequency of usage and frequency in media.

It helps to define how often the brand should be advertised.

Purchase cycle is defined as the number of days between the purchase of a standard unit in a given category.

In the Yogurt category, a cup is the standard unit. It can be calculated from the information in either MRI or SMRB. Look at MRI page167. (Look in Note A for detail on MRI and SMRB, page 61.)

Calculating Purchase Cycle.

Calculate the total number of cups of yogurt eaten and divide by the number of people. The number of cups in 30 days will be your answer. Set it up like this:

Yogurt Purchase Cycle:

Frequency	'000	Total Cups
10.0	4,561	45,610
8.0	893	7,144
7.0	2,198	15,386
6.0	2,756	16,536
5.0	2,138	10,690
4.0	3,895	15,580
3.0	3,343	10,029
2.0	4,920	9,840
1.0	3,565	3,565
	28,269	134,380

Now we know that 134 million cups of yogurt are eaten every seven days by 28 million female homemakers (or their families). That works out to 4.75 cups purchased in a seven day period, or seven-tenths of a cup every day.

If we compared this to the same information from ten years earlier (1988), we'd find that 49 million adults consumed 288 million cups of yogurt in that same 30-day period.

That would translate to a purchase of 5.88 cups and a purchase cycle of 5.1 days. The result is that fewer adults eat yogurt, but individually, they eat about the same amount of it and with about the same frequency.

Other Considerations.

The great majority of products can never use purchase cycle information because it is not possible to get sufficient exposures within the purchase cycle or because the purchase cycle is so long the numbers become meaningless. The average car owners replace their mufflers every 42 months.

The standard thinking calls for three exposures during a purchase cycle. However, if you are the marketing manager for Midas Muffler and Brake shops does that mean you advertise with a frequency of once per year? Of course not.

This information is valuable to most packaged good products. Even if it is not immediately actionable, it is still a good professional discipline to calculate purchase cycle.

Windows of Opportunity.

For other businesses, like restaurants or retailers, there are best times of the month, week, and year to place the advertising. Pay days, for example, are good days for advertising.

In Alaska, the state is a major employer and pays people every two-weeks on Friday, unlike most businesses, which pay employees twice a month. This change requires advertisers of some products, like mid-level restaurants or electronic appliances to schedule their advertising in line with when people are paid.

Following this line of thinking, most newspapers in the United States have developed a time when family purchasing agents look for grocery advertising in the newspaper.

This is called BFD—Best Food Day. Usually, it is either Wednesday or Thursday, but can vary by market in the United States.

Understanding the User.

Remember: this purchase cycle segment of the marketing planning document is part of our effort to understand the user.

We want to gain a grasp of how often the product is used.

A demographic and psychographic description of the user, where this user exists, when they use, and this last description of how often the user uses all contribute to the overall understanding of the consumer.

E. Creative Requirements:

Initial Input.

The purpose of this segment of the Situation Analysis is to outline what is needed. It is not likely at the initial writing of this document that you will be able to answer that question, but there is some initial input you can provide.

For example, if you are working on Bisquick, it is likely that the Brand will require print vehicles that provide very high quality appetite (visual) appeal of food cooked with the Brand.

Bisquick may also require a vehicle that will disperse coupons.

Look for Needs and Opportunities.

If the assignment is to write the Creative Requirements segment of the marketing document for a new ultra low-fat food, it may be that you want a medium and vehicle that will give a high level of credibility to the Brand.

In this case, you might eliminate outdoor and go with magazines dedicated to health or special-expert talk shows on television.

Try to Be Helpful, Not Confining.

This segment need not be long, but it should consider history and any expected future developments.

Take care not to give too much constraining information here.

While it is possible to write the plan so that you are required to use television, you should try not to write it in that fashion.

It is better to outline that the Brand will need strong visual support or to write whatever else might be important, than it is to restrict the thinking.

F. Competitive Sales:

What's Working? What's Not Working?

This is a review of the current business situation for both the Brand and for all the competitors in the category.

There are a number of analysis techniques available to determine good markets and poor markets, where advertising is working and where it isn't, where sales promotion is working and where it's not, and a variety of other parameters.

The goal is to learn which elements of both the Brand, and its competitors' marketing plans are working and those that aren't.

Analysis Techniques.

Here are a few analysis techniques to consider:

1. **Provide Brand sales as they relate to last year's plan, or the last two years if possible:**

    The more detail in which this information is presented will allow the Brand a greater capability to make good decisions. Ideally the sales figures should be presented by geographic area—ADI, DMA, state, sales region, etc.—provided on a quarterly basis. Be sure to show totals in both directions (across and down) if you are using a table.

    Once you have all the numbers in nice tidy columns showing sales this year versus last year for all 213 DMAs, this is a good place to use indices to show the increase of sales from one year to the next. The following is a format for this chart using DMAs as the basis for the geographic description.

Exhibit "A"

ABC Brand
Sales History FY 99
(Index versus year ago)

	Q1	Q2	1st Half	(Index)	Q3	Q4	2nd Half	(Index)	FY 99	(Index)
Abilene-Sweet	___	___	___	___	___	___	___	___	___	___
Albany, GA	___	___	___	___	___	___	___	___	___	___
Alb-Schen-Troy	___	___	___	___	___	___	___	___	___	___
Albuquerque	___	___	___	___	___	___	___	___	___	___
Alexandria, LA	___	___	___	___	___	___	___	___	___	___
Alexandria, MN	___	___	___	___	___	___	___	___	___	___
Alpena	___	___	___	___	___	___	___	___	___	___
Amarillo	___	___	___	___	___	___	___	___	___	___
Anniston	___	___	___	___	___	___	___	___	___	___
Total	___	___	___	___	___	___	___	___	___	___

This chart should be continued through the remaining 200+ DMAs.

Tracking Change.

You can look at the DMAs where the greatest change took place, either in a given six-month period, a quarter, or for the total year.

Then look at last year's plan to see what happened in those markets that was different from the other markets, which may explain the unusual increase in the year-to-year change in sales for whatever time period you've used.

If the Brand has one major competitor, you might want to show this same detail for the competition as well.

Factor Analysis.

You might also try separating the markets that received a given promotion or other element of the marketing plan.

For example, if you are working on Tide and you know that the Brand ran a trade allowance of $2.50 per case for a display allowance for a five-week period during the second quarter, and that this allowance was offered in St.Louis, Denver, Louisville, and Albany, then you might look at these markets as a total to determine the effect on sales.

Suppose that in total, these markets had an increase of 12.5% in the total year, and an increase of 4.4% last year.

Compare these market totals in the second quarter with similar markets that didn't have the trade allowance to determine the difference in sales.

If the non-allowance markets had an increase similar to the allowance markets in the year prior to the year when the allowance markets received the extra promotion monies, we can assume that the markets aren't usual for some other reason.

Then we need to record the percent change in sales in the non-allowance markets.

ABC Brand
Display Allowance Analysis
(percent change versus year ago)

	FY 1999	FY 1998
Display allowance areas	+12.5%	+4.4%
Areas w/o display allowance	+5.8	+4.7
Change attributable to allowance	+ 6.7%	-0.3%

The table above shows a useful format to illustrate the effect that the promotion actually had.

It is now safe to assume that the display allowance created an increase of 6.7% in sales.

Next, we need to know if this is enough to pay for the increase in funds allocated to the display allowance.

2. **Show sales for the total U.S. for all competitors in the category:**

Show these sales by quarter with totals for the year and for the six-month periods. This is another opportunity to use an index so the reader can quickly see the percentage increase for the period under consideration from the same time period a year ago.

The following is an example of how that chart might look:

Category Sales History FY 99
(Index versus year ago)

	Q1	Q2	1stHalf	(Index)	Q3	Q4	2ndHalf	(Index)	FY 99	(Index)
ABC Brand	__	__	__	__	__	__	__	__	__	__
Brand D	__	__	__	__	__	__	__	__	__	__
Brand E	__	__	__	__	__	__	__	__	__	__
Brand F	__	__	__	__	__	__	__	__	__	__
Brand G	__	__	__	__	__	__	__	__	__	__
Brand H	__	__	__	__	__	__	__	__	__	__
All others	__	__	__	__	__	__	__	__	__	__
Total	__	__	__	__	__	__	__	__	__	__

Take care to label these charts clearly. A continuation of these charts can be found in Chapter Eight; these two charts (Exhibits "A" and "C") will get you started.

Find Out Who Spent What.

This is a review of the funds spent on marketing the different brands in the category during the past year.

The media spending chart might look like the one below:

Exhibit "D"

ABC Brand
Category Media Review
(Index versus year ago)

| | Television | | | | | | | |
	Net	Spot	Cable	Radio	Mags	News	Outdr	Transt
Brand ABC								
- Dollars	—	—	—	—	—	—	—	—
- Index	—	—	—	—	—	—	—	—
Brand D								
- Dollars	—	—	—	—	—	—	—	—
- Index	—	—	—	—	—	—	—	—
Brand E								
- Dollars	—	—	—	—	—	—	—	—
- Index	—	—	—	—	—	—	—	—
Brand F								
- Dollars	—	—	—	—	—	—	—	—
- Index	—	—	—	—	—	—	—	—
Brand G								
- Dollars	—	—	—	—	—	—	—	—
- Index	—	—	—	—	—	—	—	—
All others								
- Dollars	—	—	—	—	—	—	—	—
- Index	—	—	—	—	—	—	—	—
Total								
- Dollars	—	—	—	—	—	—	—	—
- Index	—	—	—	—	—	—	—	—

The information above can be found in LNA (Leading National Advertisers—now known as Competitive Media Reporting).

Promotion Spending.

Information Resources, Inc. (IRI) is a source for information on promotional spending. You may give consideration to developing a chart to report promotion spending, or you might integrate the information into the chart above.

The spending can be analyzed to determine which brand is spending the most money and what impact that spending is making on sales. This is valuable information as you start to think of what tools you will use to market the Brand in the coming year.

Share of Expenditures and Share of Voice.

If you develop a chart showing the share of spending each competitor within a category has within a given time period, then this is called a Share of Expenditures chart.

If you go to the work to translate those expenditures into Gross Rating Points (GRPs) then the chart would be called a Share of Voice.

Share of Voice would be more useful than Share of Expenditures because your user group does not see dollars, they see GRPs and you are trying to ascertain your power in the marketplace.

However, as good as that idea is, the systems used to gather this information are not accurate enough to go to the work to translate this information from dollars to delivery.

While somewhat unlikely, an advertiser could be inefficient—resulting in a high share of expenditures and a low share of voice.

Most advertising agencies and their clients believe Share of Expenditures is good enough.

Usually you would like to have three years of history on these charts to determine the long-term effect of a spending strategy.

Case Rate and Percent of Sales.

Another consideration is a case rate or percent of sales analysis. There are many comparisons between this area and Chapter Eight. Percent of Sales is one example.

The case rate information is contained in Chapter Eight, but it could just as easily be presented here. A chart is usually helpful.

The case rate chart for the category will make it easy to recognize those brands that are spending the most on a per-unit basis.

Summary.

The outline that has just been presented will help the marketing plan author understand the people who will buy or use the brand.

If the business requires significant additional information, this outline should be altered to provide that input.

Part of the fun and part of the challenge is to find new ways to look at the information that reveal what others have not discovered.

For more information, please also read:

1. **Hitting the Sweet Spot**
   Fortini-Campbell, Lisa
   The Copy Workshop, Chicago, 1991.

   The total book is valuable for the situation analysis. Chapters Ten, Eleven, and Fourteen are particularly applicable.

2. **Strategic Advertising Campaigns**
   Schultz, Don E. and Barnes, Beth E.
   NTC Books, Chicago, 1994. Fourth Edition.

   Chapters One, Two, Three, and Sixteen are beneficial in developing your Situation Analysis.

Chapter One
Note A

MRI/SMRB

"Knowledge is Power."
—Francis Bacon

Introduction.

The Internet is quickly becoming the key source of information of all kinds. Advertising and marketing are not exceptions to this trend.

However, MRI and SMRB will contiue to be key sources of demographic and product usage information. This segment is intended to help you understand how to use that information.

Primary Sources for Secondary Research.

MRI and SMRB are in business to report consumption patterns of both products and media. That is, they report on how we use products and how we use the media.

Both services report consumption patterns for products (in the "P" books) and media (in the "M" books). Look in the "M" books to determine how a specific group of people consume magazines, radio, television, etc.

While there is a small difference in the way the information is gathered for the two companies, the key difference is in the product books. SMRB provides estimates of the number of users, while MRI includes volume estimates.

A. Category Demographics:

Number of Users and Incidence.

There is a variety of category demographic information to be gleaned from MRI and SMRB, so let's start with the number of users and the incidence of their usage.

The number of users can be found in column A. If there is an asterisk, then there are too few people for MRI or SMRB to stand by the numbers. Try to avoid those.

Look for the rows where the numbers are large in each demographic profile. In the chart at the end of this explanation (MRI page 178, Yogurt) is the demographic information for Yogurt users.

Notes on How to Do It.

Before you start, look at the top of the reprint of page 178 to understand who is being discussed. In this case, we are looking at female homemakers. Think about each number to see if it makes sense. (Is it smaller than a bread box or about the same?)

1. There are approximately 89,789,000 female homemakers in the U.S. You will notice that the number is identical for women and homemakers, but a little less for household heads. That makes sense.

2. There are 44,024,000 female homemakers that have used yogurt in the past six months (see the MRI reprint of page 175). Users represent 44.6% of all female homemakers.

3. There are 7,780,000 female homemakers between 18 and 24.

    Of those, 3,426,000 have used yogurt in the last 30 days.

4. Next, look for the incidence of usage in column C. It's labeled as Volume/Users Index

    This tells you that 44.0% of all female homemakers between the ages of 18 and 24 used yogurt in the past 30 days. This is less than the incidence of usage for female homemakers in total (44.6%) so it is an audience we will not consider because the incidence of usage is less than the national average.

5. Now look at female homemakers 35 to 44.

    There are over twenty million of them. 10,447,000 female homemakers between the ages of 35 and 44 have used yogurt in the past 30 days (Column A).

    That is 50.6% of all people in that age group (also called the incidence of usage) and is greater than the average at the top of the page (44.6%), so it is likely an age group of female homemakers we will consider to be in our target audience.

6. Now look over to column D opposite 35 to 44. That's the index.

    The index is 113. To understand this, remember that an index is a ratio of one number to another when the base is 100.

    So this 113 index shows us that a female homemaker between the ages of 35 and 44 has a 13% higher probability of eating yogurt than does the average female homemaker in the United States.

Sell Where Incidence is Highest.

Note we did not seek the target group with the absolute largest number of people. We sought the demographic with the highest incidence of usage.

If you were going to try to sell twenty-five sweatshirts that had "   " silkscreened across the chest, would you go downtown where there are a lot of people, or would you sit in front of the Tri-Delt sorority house at the university where you might only see a hundred people all day? The answer should be obvious—go to the university. It is easiest to sell where the incidence of users, or potential users, is highest.

Now that you understand what to look for in the age parameter, the next issue is how much spread in age should there be. There is no rule.

Look for where the similarities end, and when you add a new age segment, be certain they are more alike than they are different. In the yogurt example, the age parameter is likely 25 to 44, or even 54.

Next, you need to do the same thing for education, employment, professional status, marital status, race, income, household size, and anything else you can find.

B. Brand Demographics:

Discovering Differentiation.

We have been looking at category information, but there is also information available for the Brand. This time, turn to the MRI page on yogurt (reprint of Yogurt page 183).

You will notice in the far left column that there are still 88,789,000 female homemakers in the U.S., but there are only 21,717,000 female homemakers who consume low fat yogurt. This is 24.2% of total homemakers instead of the 44.6% of homemakers who consume any kind of yogurt.

This helps us to understand more about the current users, and consequently, about our target group.

Keep looking at that 'All Female Homemakers' row. In column C, incidence of usage, it shows 13.3% for nonfat/fat-free yogurt.

That makes a total of 37.5% who consume nonfat or fat-free yogurt. There go your plans for a high-fat yogurt—it doesn't look like anyone is interested.

Keep going. Now look at 'Brands.' Only 1.8% of users use Borden, while 4.1% use Breyers Blended, and 6.3% use Dannon Fruit-on-the-Bottom (MRI reprint page 185). This is good competitive information

Now we can check on the differences between the demographics of those different brand users. Notice that 18-to-24-year-olds are 12% more likely to use Borden than the average Borden user, but that 18-to-24-year-olds are 12% less likely to use Dannon Fruit-on-the-Bottom, than the average Dannon Fruit-on-the-Bottom user.

Again, the number of people is relatively unimportant, how much they use is more important.

Similar information is available in Simmons.

What Differentiates Users of Your Brand?
The goal of this analysis is to learn what differentiates the users of your Brand from other brands within the category.

Skip down to race. Notice that Black Americans consume more of the Bordens brand, while professional/managerial types prefer Dannon's Fruit-on-the-Bottom.

C. Printed vs. CD:

Both MRI and Simmons (SMRB) information have been available in printed paperbound volumes in the past. This is coming to an end. Simmons is only available on CD. MRI published their last volume in 1998. The 1999 information will only be on CD.

When you pull up the information on CD, make sure you understand which are columns and which are rows. It can be slightly confusing. We have included MRI from the paperbound version and Simmons from the CD so you can see the difference.

In the case of the examples, the product books, shown here via MRI are printed with the subject headings at the top with the parameters of that subject in the far left column.

The media books, illustrated by Simmons information, are the other way. Age demographics for magazine consumption are at the top of the page.

Be sure you are clear which way the information is running before you conduct an analysis.

D. Media Consumption:

How to Reach "Reach."

MRI and SMRB both report media consumption information by product users and by demographics unrelated to product consumption information.

1. **Product Related:**

   Look first at the MRI information from the 'P' books (for product) this time on page 71 (MRI page 180 Yogurt). Note that regular female homemakers who use yogurt have a higher incidence of usage among readers of *Fortune* and *Forbes* than they do among the users (readers) of *Family Circle*.

   To be included on this page the respondent must both use Yogurt and the magazines listed.

2. **Product Unrelated:**

   This time turn to the SMRB information on media on page 94 of this book. Note that at the top of the page that we are reading information relating only to females so it is obvious that the numbers will be higher than for female homemakers.

   There are 101,169,000 females in the United States.

   a.   There are 7,659,000 females who read *Cosmopolitan*.

   b.   That is 7.57% of total U.S. females.

   This number is reach.

   There are 12,404,000 females between the ages of 18 and 24 in the United States.

   a.   There are 2,390,000 females between the ages of 18 and 24 who read *Cosmopolitan*.

   b.   This creates a reach of 19.26% among females 18 to 24 for *Cosmopolitan*.

   c.   In this case, the index is 417, which means 18-to-24-year-olds are 317% more likely to read *Cosmopolitan* than the average female reader. This makes sense since the magazine targets young women.

   Similar information is available in MRI.

D. Analysis:

Category Review and Trend Analysis.

Your analysis of this MRI or SMRB (or both) information should include a review of the category, including heavy and light users, and the Brand.

This is also a good opportunity to conduct a trend analysis. Show three years history of MRI or SMRB to show how consumption is changing.

The pages that follow are used by permission of Simmons Market Research Bureau and Mediamark Research, Inc.

List of Materials:

Here are the materials provided for your review:

MRI/Spring 1998 (pages 67–80)
- Yogurt – pages 175–176
- Yogurt – pages 178–189

Simmons Market Research Bureau (pages 81–95)
- Yogurt/Demographics – pages 1–10
- Yogurt/TV Radio – pages 1–3
- Yogurt/Magazines – pages 1–2

These pages were provided courtesy of Mediamark Research, Inc. and Simmons Market Research Bureau.

BASE: FEMALE HOMEMAKERS (89,789,000)	ALL			SHARE OF USERS	SHARE OF VOLUME	VOLUME/ USERS INDEX	MALE HOMEMAKERS (31,714,000)		
	'000	%	UNWGT				'000	%	UNWGT
Total Used in Last 6 Months	40024	44.6	5059				9968	31.4	1426
Types:									
With Fruit - premixed	22013	24.5	2559						
With Fruit - not premixed	9043	10.1	1163						
Other Flavor	7088	7.9	831						
Plain (Unflavored)	5137	5.7	677						
Kinds:									
Low Fat	21717	24.2	2522						
Non Fat/Fat Free	11940	13.3	1489						
Brands:									
Borden	1639	1.8	166	2.0	1.4	70			
Breyers Blended	3645	4.1	443	4.4	3.6	82			
Breyers Fruit On the Bottom	3955	4.4	483	4.8	4.1	85			
Breyers Light	2293	2.6	273	2.8	2.4	86			
Colombo	2749	3.1	411	3.3	3.1	94			
Dannon Chunky Fruit	3776	4.2	498	4.6	5.7	124			
Dannon Classic Flavors	3882	4.3	470	4.7	4.1	87			
Dannon Danimals	1331	1.5	151	1.6	1.4	88			
Dannon Double Delights	2560	2.9	304	3.1	3.2	103			
Dannon Fruit on the Bottom	5612	6.3	701	6.8	6.6	97			
Dannon Light	8187	9.1	1092	9.9	11.2	113			
Dannon Light & Crunchy	1293	1.4	146	1.6	1.8	113			
Dannon Light Duets	750	.8	99	.9	.6	67			
Dannon Sprinkl'ins	1183	1.3	156	1.4	1.0	71			
Jell-O Jiggles & Bits	747	.8	85	.9	.7	78			
Jell-O Kid Pack	1993	2.2	245	2.4	2.0	83			
La Yogurt	1138	1.3	157	1.4	1.6	114			
Light 'n Lively	2355	2.6	272	2.9	3.0	103			
Snackwell's	1517	1.7	175	1.8	1.2	67			
Stonyfield Farm	1076	1.2	166	1.3	1.0	77			
Trix	2385	2.7	247	2.9	3.0	103			
Yoplait Crunch 'N Yogurt	963	1.1	127	1.2	.7	58			
Yoplait Fat Free	3229	3.6	376	3.9	4.2	108			
Yoplait Fat Free Fruit on the Bottom	2509	2.8	268	3.0	3.0	100			
Yoplait Fat Free Light	2137	2.4	252	2.6	2.5	96			
Yoplait Original	4310	4.8	513	5.2	6.3	121			
Yoplait Custard Style	3128	3.5	371	3.8	3.4	89			
Yoplait Light	2042	2.3	254	2.5	1.9	76			
Store's Own Brand	6961	7.8	778	8.4	10.4	124			
Other	3049	3.4	399	3.7	4.9	132			
Containers/Last 7 Days									
L None	11753	13.1	1376						
L 1	3565	4.0	465						
M 2	4920	5.5	619						
M 3	3343	3.7	501						
H 4	3895	4.3	502						
H 5	2138	2.4	271						
H 6	2756	3.1	365						
H 7	2198	2.4	279						
H 8	893	1.0	115						
H 9 or more	4561	5.1	566						
L Total	15318	17.1	1841	38.3	2.3				
M Total	8263	9.2	1120	20.6	13.0				
H Total	16443	18.3	2098	41.1	84.7				

Spring 1998

67

	ALL			SHARE OF USERS	SHARE OF VOLUME	VOLUME/ USERS INDEX
BASE: TOTAL HOMEMAKERS (121,504,000)	'000	%	UNWGT			
Total Used in Last 6 Months	49992	41.1	6485			
Types:						
With Fruit - premixed	26859	22.1	3206			
With Fruit - not premixed	11092	9.1	1469			
Other Flavor	8322	6.8	1007			
Plain (Unflavored)	6445	5.3	830			
Kinds:						
Low Fat	26623	21.9	3196			
Non Fat/Fat Free	14207	11.7	1817			
Brands:						
Borden	2116	1.7	224	2.1	1.7	81
Breyers Blended	4304	3.5	546	4.4	3.8	86
Breyers Fruit On the Bottom	4572	3.8	599	4.6	4.0	87
Breyers Light	2678	2.2	342	2.7	2.3	85
Colombo	3228	2.7	502	3.3	3.1	94
Dannon Chunky Fruit	4725	3.9	629	4.8	5.7	119
Dannon Classic Flavors	4790	3.9	605	4.9	4.1	84
Dannon Danimals	1546	1.3	185	1.6	1.3	81
Dannon Double Delights	2954	2.4	356	3.0	3.0	100
Dannon Fruit on the Bottom	6741	5.5	872	6.8	6.9	101
Dannon Light	10168	8.4	1397	10.3	11.2	109
Dannon Light & Crunchy	1386	1.1	170	1.4	1.5	107
Dannon Light Duets	816	.7	113	.8	.5	63
Dannon Sprinkl'ins	1443	1.2	196	1.5	1.1	73
Jell-O Jiggles & Bits	844	.7	94	.9	.6	67
Jell-O Kid Pack	2269	1.9	280	2.3	2.1	91
La Yogurt	1474	1.2	200	1.5	2.2	147
Light 'n Lively	2509	2.1	314	2.5	2.5	100
Snackwell's	1704	1.4	211	1.7	1.3	76
Stonyfield Farm	1265	1.0	205	1.3	.9	69
Trix	2605	2.1	282	2.6	2.9	112
Yoplait Crunch 'N Yogurt	1077	.9	156	1.1	.7	64
Yoplait Fat Free	3899	3.2	461	4.0	4.3	108
Yoplait Fat Free Fruit on the Bottom	3150	2.6	342	3.2	2.9	91
Yoplait Fat Free Light	2578	2.1	314	2.6	2.4	92
Yoplait Original	5438	4.5	654	5.5	5.9	107
Yoplait Custard Style	3567	2.9	431	3.6	3.0	83
Yoplait Light	2368	1.9	296	2.4	2.2	92
Store's Own Brand	8498	7.0	1005	8.6	10.8	126
Other	3777	3.1	491	3.8	5.1	134
Containers/Last 7 Days						
L None	14434	11.9	1766			
L 1	4992	4.1	650			
M 2	6106	5.0	794			
M 3	4074	3.4	621			
H 4	4615	3.8	625			
H 5	2556	2.1	330			
H 6	3594	3.0	465			
H 7	2609	2.1	359			
H 8	1229	1.0	162			
H 9 or more	5783	4.8	713			
L Total	19426	16.0	2416	38.9	2.6	
M Total	10181	8.4	1415	20.4	12.7	
H Total	20386	16.8	2654	40.8	84.7	

Spring 1998

178 YOGURT

BASE: FEMALE HOMEMAKERS	TOTAL U.S. '000	ALL A '000	ALL B % DOWN	ALL C % ACROSS	ALL D INDEX	CONTAINERS/LAST 7 DAYS HEAVY MORE THAN 3 A '000	HEAVY B % DOWN	HEAVY C % ACROSS	HEAVY D INDEX	MEDIUM 2 - 3 A '000	MEDIUM B % DOWN	MEDIUM C % ACROSS	MEDIUM D INDEX	LIGHT LESS THAN 2 A '000	LIGHT B % DOWN	LIGHT C % ACROSS	LIGHT D INDEX
All Female Homemakers	89789	40024	100.0	44.6	100	16443	100.0	18.3	100	8263	100.0	9.2	100	15318	100.0	17.1	100
Men	-	-	-	-	-	-	-	-	-	-	-	-	-	-	-	-	-
Women	89789	40024	100.0	44.6	100	16443	100.0	18.3	100	8263	100.0	9.2	100	15318	100.0	17.1	100
Household Heads	39088	16122	40.3	41.2	93	6323	38.5	16.2	88	3808	46.1	9.7	106	5991	39.1	15.3	90
Homemakers	89789	40024	100.0	44.6	100	16443	100.0	18.3	100	8263	100.0	9.2	100	15318	100.0	17.1	100
Graduated College	18398	10918	27.3	59.3	133	4387	26.7	23.8	130	2348	28.4	12.8	139	4183	27.3	22.7	133
Attended College	24064	11839	29.6	49.2	110	4935	30.0	20.5	112	2484	30.1	10.3	112	4421	28.9	18.4	108
Graduated High School	31577	12415	31.0	39.3	88	5207	31.7	16.5	90	2363	28.6	7.5	81	4845	31.6	15.3	90
Did not Graduate High School	15751	4852	12.1	30.8	69	1913	11.6	12.1	66	1069	12.9	6.8	74	1870	12.2	11.9	70
18-24	7780	3426	8.6	44.0	99	1412	8.6	18.2	99	743	9.0	9.6	104	1270	8.3	16.3	96
25-34	18631	8714	21.8	46.8	105	3754	22.8	20.1	110	1738	21.0	9.3	101	3222	21.0	17.3	101
35-44	20651	10447	26.1	50.6	113	4506	27.4	21.8	119	1775	21.5	8.6	93	4165	27.2	20.2	118
45-54	15603	7789	19.5	49.9	112	3079	18.7	19.7	108	1722	20.8	11.0	120	2988	19.5	19.2	112
55-64	10181	4190	10.5	41.2	92	1824	11.1	17.9	98	788	9.5	7.7	84	1579	10.3	15.5	91
65 or over	16943	5459	13.6	32.2	72	1867	11.4	11.0	60	1498	18.1	8.8	96	2093	13.7	12.4	72
18-34	26410	12140	30.3	46.0	103	5166	31.4	19.6	107	2481	30.0	9.4	102	4493	29.3	17.0	100
18-49	55960	27212	68.0	48.6	109	11588	70.5	20.7	113	5212	63.1	9.3	101	10413	68.0	18.6	109
25-54	54886	26950	67.3	49.1	110	11339	69.0	20.7	113	5235	63.3	9.5	104	10376	67.7	18.9	111
Employed Full Time	41154	20014	50.0	48.6	109	8406	51.1	20.4	112	3763	45.5	9.1	99	7844	51.2	19.1	112
Part-time	11398	5738	14.3	50.3	113	2435	14.8	21.4	117	1316	15.9	11.5	125	1987	13.0	17.4	102
Sole Wage Earner	14006	5944	14.9	42.4	95	2269	13.8	16.2	88	1421	17.2	10.1	110	2254	14.7	16.1	94
Not Employed	37237	14273	35.7	38.3	86	5602	34.1	15.0	82	3184	38.5	8.6	93	5487	35.8	14.7	86
Professional	9642	5737	14.3	59.5	133	2509	15.3	26.0	142	1092	13.2	11.3	123	2135	13.9	22.1	130
Executive/Admin./Managerial	7128	3920	9.8	55.0	123	1556	9.5	21.8	119	771	9.3	10.8	117	1593	10.4	22.3	131
Clerical/Sales/Technical	20870	9991	25.0	47.9	107	4157	25.3	19.9	109	2054	24.9	9.8	107	3781	24.7	18.1	106
Precision/Crafts/Repair	1102	419	1.0	38.0	85	*150	0.9	13.6	74	*92	1.1	8.4	91	*176	1.2	16.0	94
Other Employed	13810	5685	14.2	41.2	92	2469	15.0	17.9	98	1071	13.0	7.8	84	2145	14.0	15.5	91
H/D Income $75,000 or More	15443	9164	22.9	59.3	133	4005	24.4	25.9	142	1590	19.2	10.3	112	3569	23.3	23.1	135
$60,000 - 74,999	8775	4618	11.5	52.6	118	2138	13.0	24.4	133	894	10.8	10.2	111	1586	10.4	18.1	106
$50,000 - 59,999	7850	4220	10.5	53.8	121	1612	9.8	20.5	112	939	11.4	12.0	130	1669	10.9	21.3	125
$40,000 - 49,999	9648	4586	11.5	47.5	107	1894	11.5	19.6	107	906	11.0	9.4	102	1785	11.7	18.5	108
$30,000 - 39,999	11493	4988	12.5	43.4	97	2051	12.5	17.8	97	971	11.7	8.4	92	1966	12.8	17.1	100
$20,000 - 29,999	12298	4716	11.8	38.3	86	1619	9.8	13.2	72	1193	14.4	9.7	105	1905	12.4	15.5	91
$10,000 - 19,999	14330	4890	12.2	34.1	77	1966	12.0	13.7	75	1160	14.0	8.1	88	1764	11.5	12.3	72
Less than $10,000	9953	2843	7.1	28.6	64	1158	7.0	11.6	64	610	7.4	6.1	67	1075	7.0	10.8	63
Census Region: North East	18074	9417	23.5	52.1	117	4002	24.3	22.1	121	1902	23.0	10.5	114	3513	22.9	19.4	114
North Central	20967	9097	22.7	43.4	97	3714	22.6	17.7	97	1881	22.8	9.0	97	3502	22.9	16.7	98
South	32182	12077	30.2	37.5	84	4745	28.9	14.7	81	2517	30.5	7.8	85	4816	31.4	15.0	88
West	18567	9432	23.6	50.8	114	3981	24.2	21.4	117	1964	23.8	10.6	115	3487	22.8	18.8	110
Marketing Reg.: New England	4705	2660	6.6	56.5	127	1165	7.1	24.8	135	533	6.4	11.3	123	963	6.3	20.5	120
Middle Atlantic	15444	7633	19.1	49.4	111	3309	20.1	21.4	117	1522	18.4	9.9	107	2802	18.3	18.1	106
East Central	11580	5082	12.7	43.9	98	1956	11.9	16.9	92	1159	14.0	10.0	109	1967	12.8	17.0	100
West Central	13616	6017	15.0	44.2	99	2381	14.5	17.5	95	1194	14.4	8.8	95	2443	15.9	17.9	105
South East	18271	6831	17.1	37.4	84	2374	14.4	13.0	71	1361	16.5	7.4	81	3096	20.2	16.9	99
South West	10224	3804	9.5	37.2	83	1757	10.7	17.2	94	846	10.2	8.3	90	1201	7.8	11.7	69
Pacific	15950	7997	20.0	50.1	112	3502	21.3	22.0	120	1648	19.9	10.3	112	2847	18.6	17.9	105
County Size A	35658	18126	45.3	50.8	114	8347	50.8	23.4	128	3594	43.5	10.1	110	6185	40.4	17.3	102
County Size B	27101	12284	30.7	45.3	102	4880	29.7	18.0	98	2297	27.8	8.5	92	5108	33.3	18.8	110
County Size C	13387	5326	13.3	39.8	89	1923	11.7	14.4	78	1307	15.8	9.8	106	2096	13.7	15.7	92
County Size D	13644	4289	10.7	31.4	71	1293	7.9	9.5	52	1066	12.9	7.8	85	1929	12.6	14.1	83
MSA Central City	29169	13452	33.6	46.1	103	5458	33.2	18.7	102	2759	33.4	9.5	103	5235	34.2	17.9	105
MSA Suburban	42524	20473	51.2	48.1	108	9097	55.3	21.4	117	3948	47.8	9.3	101	7428	48.5	17.5	102
Non-MSA	18096	6099	15.2	33.7	76	1887	11.5	10.4	57	1557	18.8	8.6	93	2656	17.3	14.7	86
Single	14479	6448	16.1	44.5	100	2617	15.9	18.1	99	1384	16.7	9.6	104	2448	16.0	16.9	99
Married	51935	24956	62.4	48.1	108	10407	63.3	20.0	109	4801	58.1	9.2	100	9748	63.6	18.8	110
Other	23376	8620	21.5	36.9	83	3418	20.8	14.6	80	2079	25.2	8.9	97	3122	20.4	13.4	78
Parents	35881	17885	44.7	49.8	112	8062	49.0	22.5	123	3063	37.1	8.5	93	6760	44.1	18.8	110
Working Parents	24725	12941	32.3	52.3	117	5838	35.5	23.6	129	2282	27.6	9.2	100	4821	31.5	19.5	114
Household Size: 1 Person	15017	5687	14.2	37.9	85	1819	11.1	12.1	66	1563	18.9	10.4	113	2305	15.1	15.4	90
2 Persons	28950	12019	30.0	41.5	93	4674	28.4	16.1	88	2931	35.5	10.1	110	4414	28.8	15.2	89
3 or More	45822	22319	55.8	48.7	109	9950	60.5	21.7	119	3770	45.6	8.2	89	8599	56.1	18.8	110
Any Child in Household	39070	19277	48.2	49.3	111	8733	53.1	22.4	122	3203	38.8	8.2	89	7341	47.9	18.8	110
Under 2 Years	6763	3301	8.2	48.8	109	1555	9.5	23.0	126	587	7.1	8.7	94	1159	7.6	17.1	100
2-5 Years	14794	7084	17.7	47.9	107	3320	20.2	22.4	123	1232	14.9	8.3	91	2531	16.5	17.1	100
6-11 Years	18719	9179	22.9	49.0	110	4183	25.4	22.3	122	1459	17.7	7.8	85	3538	23.1	18.9	111
12-17 Years	17576	8642	21.6	49.2	110	3793	23.1	21.6	118	1333	16.1	7.6	82	3515	22.9	20.0	117
White	75919	34683	86.7	45.7	102	14255	86.7	18.8	103	7222	87.4	9.5	103	13205	86.2	17.4	102
Black	10706	3616	9.0	33.8	76	1423	8.7	13.3	73	673	8.1	6.3	68	1521	9.9	14.2	83
Spanish Speaking	8317	3692	9.2	44.4	100	1856	11.3	22.3	122	693	8.4	8.3	91	1143	7.5	13.7	81
Home Owned	60568	27980	69.9	46.2	104	11279	68.6	18.6	102	5817	70.4	9.6	104	10883	71.0	18.0	105
Daily Newspapers: Read Any	45840	21781	54.4	47.5	107	9203	56.0	20.1	110	4545	55.0	9.9	108	8033	52.4	17.5	103
Read One Daily	38270	17739	44.3	46.4	104	7371	44.8	19.3	105	3821	46.2	10.0	109	6547	42.7	17.1	100
Read Two or More Dailies	7570	4041	10.1	53.4	120	1832	11.1	24.2	132	723	8.8	9.6	104	1486	9.7	19.6	115
Sunday Newspapers: Read Any	56265	27005	67.5	48.0	108	11687	71.1	20.8	113	5520	66.8	9.8	107	9799	64.0	17.4	102
Read One Sunday	50043	23624	59.0	47.2	106	10208	62.1	20.4	111	4926	59.6	9.8	107	8490	55.4	17.0	99
Read Two or More Sundays	6222	3381	8.4	54.3	122	1478	9.0	23.8	130	594	7.2	9.6	104	1309	8.5	21.0	123
Quintile I - Outdoor	18125	8508	21.3	46.9	105	3504	21.3	19.3	106	1776	21.5	9.8	106	3228	21.1	17.8	104
Quintile II	18373	8864	22.1	48.2	108	3906	23.8	21.3	116	1755	21.2	9.6	104	3203	20.9	17.4	102
Quintile III	18047	8033	20.1	44.5	100	3358	20.4	18.6	102	1615	19.5	8.9	97	3060	20.0	17.0	99
Quintile IV	17944	8060	20.1	44.9	101	3179	19.3	17.7	97	1845	22.3	10.3	112	3036	19.8	16.9	99
Quintile V	17301	6560	16.4	37.9	85	2496	15.2	14.4	79	1272	15.4	7.4	80	2792	18.2	16.1	95
Quintile I - Magazines	17661	8705	21.7	49.3	111	3952	24.0	22.4	122	1691	20.5	9.6	104	3062	20.0	17.3	102
Quintile II	18263	9216	23.0	50.5	113	3853	23.4	21.1	115	2079	25.2	11.4	124	3284	21.4	18.0	105
Quintile III	18067	7884	19.7	43.6	98	3185	19.4	17.6	96	1594	19.3	8.8	96	3105	20.3	17.2	101
Quintile IV	18091	7534	18.8	41.6	93	2973	18.1	16.4	90	1466	17.7	8.1	88	3095	20.2	17.1	100
Quintile V	17707	6684	16.7	37.7	85	2480	15.1	14.0	76	1433	17.3	8.1	88	2771	18.1	15.7	92
Quintile I - Newspapers	18091	9068	22.7	50.1	112	4165	25.3	23.0	126	1658	20.1	9.2	100	3245	21.2	17.9	105
Quintile II	18456	8741	21.8	47.4	106	3573	21.7	19.4	106	2037	24.7	11.0	120	3130	20.4	17.0	99
Quintile III	17894	7984	19.9	44.6	100	3039	18.5	17.0	93	1753	21.2	9.8	106	3193	20.8	17.8	105
Quintile IV	17581	7657	19.1	43.6	98	3157	19.2	18.0	98	1678	20.3	9.5	104	2822	18.4	16.1	94
Quintile V	17768	6574	16.4	37.0	83	2508	15.3	14.1	77	1137	13.8	6.4	70	2929	19.1	16.5	97
Quintile I - Radio	17547	8288	20.7	47.2	106	3447	21.0	19.6	107	1483	17.9	8.5	92	3358	21.9	19.1	112
Quintile II	17611	8519	21.3	48.4	109	4033	24.5	22.9	125	1631	19.7	9.3	101	2855	18.6	16.2	95
Quintile III	18471	8177	20.4	44.3	99	3450	21.0	18.7	102	1671	20.2	9.0	98	3056	19.9	16.5	97
Quintile IV	18117	8167	20.4	45.1	101	3150	19.2	17.4	95	1691	20.5	9.3	101	3326	21.7	18.4	108
Quintile V	18043	6873	17.2	38.1	85	2362	14.4	13.1	71	1788	21.6	9.9	108	2724	17.8	15.1	88

BASE: FEMALE HOMEMAKERS	TOTAL U.S. '000	ALL A '000	ALL B % DOWN	ALL C % ACROSS	ALL D INDEX	CONTAINERS/LAST 7 DAYS: HEAVY MORE THAN 3 A '000	HEAVY B % DOWN	HEAVY C % ACROSS	HEAVY D INDEX	MEDIUM 2 - 3 A '000	MEDIUM B % DOWN	MEDIUM C % ACROSS	MEDIUM D INDEX	LIGHT LESS THAN 2 A '000	LIGHT B % DOWN	LIGHT C % ACROSS	LIGHT D INDEX
All Female Homemakers	89789	40024	100.0	44.6	100	16443	100.0	18.3	100	8263	100.0	9.2	100	15318	100.0	17.1	100
Quintile I - TV (Total)	18184	6678	16.7	36.7	82	2794	17.0	15.4	84	1312	15.9	7.2	78	2572	16.8	14.1	83
Quintile II	18448	7944	19.8	43.1	97	3468	21.1	18.8	103	1698	20.5	9.2	100	2777	18.1	15.1	88
Quintile III	17812	7941	19.8	44.6	100	3504	21.3	19.7	107	1645	19.9	9.2	100	2792	18.2	15.7	92
Quintile IV	17544	8562	21.4	48.8	109	3377	20.5	19.2	105	1815	22.0	10.3	112	3370	22.0	19.2	113
Quintile V	17802	8900	22.2	50.0	112	3300	20.1	18.5	101	1794	21.7	10.1	109	3807	24.9	21.4	125
Tercile I - Yellow Pages	14032	7287	18.2	51.9	117	2989	18.2	21.3	116	1324	16.0	9.4	103	2975	19.4	21.2	124
Tercile II	14086	7123	17.8	50.6	113	3080	18.7	21.9	119	1520	18.4	10.8	117	2524	16.5	17.9	105
Tercile III	14348	6313	15.8	44.0	99	2583	15.7	18.0	98	1369	16.6	9.5	104	2362	15.4	16.5	96
Radio Wkday: 6-10:00 am Cume	49471	23231	58.0	47.0	105	10026	61.0	20.3	111	4365	52.8	8.8	96	8839	57.7	17.9	105
10:00 am - 3:00 pm	30552	14487	36.2	47.4	106	5889	35.8	19.3	105	2916	35.3	9.5	104	5682	37.1	18.6	109
3:00 pm - 7:00 pm	36623	18139	45.3	49.5	111	7762	47.2	21.2	116	3496	42.3	9.5	104	6880	44.9	18.8	110
7:00 pm - Midnight	11595	5477	13.7	47.2	106	2292	13.9	19.8	108	1121	13.6	9.7	105	2065	13.5	17.8	104
Radio Average Weekday Cume	66936	31209	78.0	46.6	105	13230	80.5	19.8	108	6012	72.8	9.0	98	11967	78.1	17.9	105
Radio Avg. Weekend Day Cume	53806	24962	62.4	46.4	104	10514	63.9	19.5	107	4978	60.2	9.3	101	9470	61.8	17.6	103
Radio Formats: Adult Contemp	19969	10297	25.7	51.6	116	4520	27.5	22.6	124	1924	23.3	9.6	105	3852	25.1	19.3	113
All News	4162	2538	6.3	61.0	137	1029	6.3	24.7	135	495	6.0	11.9	129	1015	6.6	24.4	143
All Sports	5462	2701	6.7	49.5	111	1258	7.7	23.0	126	518	6.3	9.5	103	925	6.0	16.9	99
AOR/Progressive Rock	6126	3200	8.0	52.2	117	1329	8.1	21.7	118	527	6.4	8.6	94	1344	8.8	21.9	129
CHR/Rock	11669	5930	14.8	50.8	114	2617	15.9	22.4	122	1142	13.8	9.8	106	2172	14.2	18.6	109
Classic Rock	6153	3068	7.7	49.9	112	1399	8.5	22.7	124	508	6.1	8.3	90	1161	7.6	18.9	111
Classical	2032	1257	3.1	61.9	139	579	3.5	28.5	156	239	2.9	11.8	128	439	2.9	21.6	127
Country	16825	6873	17.2	40.8	92	2852	17.3	17.0	93	1386	16.8	8.2	89	2635	17.2	15.7	92
Golden Oldies	11620	6032	15.1	51.9	116	2468	15.0	21.2	116	1337	16.2	11.5	125	2228	14.5	19.2	112
Jazz	4359	2465	6.2	56.6	127	1182	7.2	27.1	148	631	7.6	14.5	157	653	4.3	15.0	88
Modern Rock	2603	1494	3.7	57.4	129	652	4.0	25.0	137	*230	2.8	8.8	96	613	4.0	23.5	138
MOR/Nostalgia	2173	1058	2.6	48.7	109	461	2.8	21.2	116	*193	2.3	8.9	97	404	2.6	18.6	109
News/Talk	12583	6618	16.5	52.6	118	3042	18.5	24.2	132	1298	15.7	10.3	112	2278	14.9	18.1	106
Religious/Gospel	5266	2419	6.0	45.9	103	1163	7.1	22.1	121	360	4.4	6.8	74	895	5.8	17.0	100
Urban Contemporary	6386	2584	6.5	40.5	91	1271	7.7	19.9	109	385	4.7	6.0	65	929	6.1	14.5	85
Radio Networks:ABC Advantage	5854	3026	7.6	51.7	116	1184	7.2	20.2	110	716	8.7	12.2	133	1127	7.4	19.2	113
ABC ESPN	1684	872	2.2	51.8	116	390	2.4	23.1	126	*184	2.2	10.9	119	*298	1.9	17.7	104
ABC Genesis	5292	2394	6.0	45.2	101	988	6.0	18.7	102	438	5.3	8.3	90	968	6.3	18.3	107
ABC Platinum	7513	3728	9.3	49.6	111	1637	10.0	21.8	119	666	8.1	8.9	96	1425	9.3	19.0	111
ABC Prime	13747	6058	15.1	44.1	99	2574	15.7	18.7	102	1134	13.7	8.3	90	2350	15.3	17.1	100
AM/FM Adult	6610	3152	7.9	47.7	107	1416	8.6	21.4	117	648	7.8	9.8	107	1088	7.1	16.5	96
AM/FM Youth	5721	2730	6.8	47.7	107	1326	8.1	23.2	127	504	6.1	8.8	96	901	5.9	15.8	92
Bloomberg Network	1441	801	2.0	55.6	125	323	2.0	22.4	123	*209	2.5	14.5	157	269	1.8	18.7	109
CBS	6034	3168	7.9	52.5	118	1524	9.3	25.3	138	604	7.3	10.0	109	1041	6.8	17.2	101
CBS Spectrum	8699	4600	11.5	52.9	119	2113	12.8	24.3	133	823	10.0	9.5	103	1665	10.9	19.1	112
Dow Jones/Wall Street Netw.	4470	2250	5.6	50.3	113	1031	6.3	23.1	126	452	5.5	10.1	110	767	5.0	17.2	101
Interep	35094	17713	44.3	50.5	113	7790	47.4	22.2	121	3623	43.8	10.3	112	6301	41.1	18.0	105
Katz Radio Group	37623	17982	44.9	47.8	107	7901	48.1	21.0	115	3595	43.5	9.6	104	6486	42.3	17.2	101
NPR	2796	1858	4.6	66.4	149	703	4.3	25.1	137	405	4.9	14.5	157	749	4.9	26.8	157
Wall Street Journal Network	3508	1754	4.4	50.0	112	728	4.4	20.7	113	366	4.4	10.4	114	660	4.3	18.8	110
Westwood CNN+	6540	3288	8.2	50.3	113	1367	8.3	20.9	114	763	9.2	11.7	127	1158	7.6	17.7	104
Westwood NBC	9221	4614	11.5	50.0	112	2117	12.9	23.0	125	937	11.3	10.2	110	1561	10.2	16.9	99
Westwood Next	5628	2694	6.7	47.9	107	1240	7.5	22.0	120	396	4.8	7.0	76	1057	6.9	18.8	110
Westwood The Source	3570	1743	4.4	48.8	110	712	4.3	19.9	109	*277	3.4	7.8	84	754	4.9	21.1	124
Westwood Variety	6870	3295	8.2	48.0	108	1360	8.3	19.8	108	713	8.6	10.4	113	1222	8.0	17.8	104
America Online	7088	4072	10.2	57.4	129	1711	10.4	24.1	132	823	10.0	11.6	126	1538	10.0	21.7	127
Compuserve	631	393	1.0	62.3	140	*202	1.2	32.0	175	*40	0.5	6.3	68	*151	1.0	24.0	141
Microsoft	1801	934	2.3	51.9	116	*389	2.4	21.6	118	*144	1.7	8.0	87	*402	2.6	22.3	131
Prodigy	508	*301	0.8	59.3	133	*139	0.8	27.3	149	*89	1.1	17.4	189	*74	0.5	14.6	86
TV Wkday Av 1/2 Hr:7-9:00am	8839	3751	9.4	42.4	95	1493	9.1	16.9	92	623	7.5	7.0	77	1636	10.7	18.5	108
9:00 am - 4:00 pm	11532	3880	9.7	33.6	75	1540	9.4	13.4	73	779	9.4	6.8	73	1561	10.2	13.5	79
4:00 pm - 7:30 pm	21044	8174	20.4	38.8	87	3448	21.0	16.4	89	1563	18.9	7.4	81	3163	20.6	15.0	88
7:30 pm - 8:00 pm	32195	12634	31.6	39.2	88	5595	34.0	17.4	95	2525	30.6	7.8	85	4514	29.5	14.0	82
8:00 pm - 11:00 pm	38073	16070	40.1	42.2	95	7025	42.7	18.5	101	3432	41.5	9.0	98	5613	36.6	14.7	86
11:00 pm - 11:30 pm	23089	9850	24.6	42.7	96	4561	27.7	19.8	108	2145	26.0	9.3	101	3144	20.5	13.6	80
11:30 pm - 1:00 am	7270	3095	7.7	42.6	96	1369	8.3	18.8	103	707	8.6	9.7	106	1019	6.7	14.0	82
TV Prime Time Cume	70405	30735	76.8	43.7	98	12926	78.6	18.4	100	6467	78.3	9.2	100	11342	74.0	16.1	94
Program-Types:Adv/West-Prime	5631	2315	5.8	41.1	92	871	5.3	15.5	84	487	5.9	8.7	94	957	6.2	17.0	100
Early Eve. Netwk News - M-F	11513	4939	12.3	42.9	96	2198	13.4	19.1	104	1030	12.5	8.9	97	1711	11.2	14.9	87
Feature Films - Prime	6926	3158	7.9	45.6	102	1262	7.7	18.2	99	584	7.1	8.4	92	1312	8.6	18.9	111
General Drama - Prime	8488	3635	9.1	42.8	96	1613	9.8	19.0	104	720	8.7	8.5	92	1302	8.5	15.3	90
Police Docudrama	5857	2224	5.6	38.0	85	1118	6.8	19.1	104	*343	4.2	5.9	64	763	5.0	13.0	76
Pvt Det/Susp/Myst/Pol.-Prime	6834	2850	7.1	41.7	94	1196	7.3	17.5	96	503	6.1	7.4	80	1151	7.5	16.8	99
Situation Comedies - Prime	5620	2718	6.8	48.4	108	1135	6.9	20.2	110	606	7.3	10.8	117	977	6.4	17.4	102
Cable TV	58050	26640	66.6	45.9	103	10947	66.6	18.9	103	5573	67.4	9.6	104	10119	66.1	17.4	102
Pay TV	27985	13512	33.8	48.3	108	5686	34.6	20.3	111	2574	31.1	9.2	100	5252	34.3	18.8	110
Heavy Cable Viewing (15+ Hr)	35554	15331	38.3	43.1	97	6013	36.6	16.9	92	3111	37.7	8.8	95	6206	40.5	17.5	102
Cable Networks:																	
A&E (Arts & Entertainment)	21255	10197	25.5	48.0	108	3955	24.1	18.6	102	2100	25.4	9.9	107	4142	27.0	19.5	114
AMC (Amer. Movie Classics)	14430	6216	15.5	43.1	97	2243	13.6	15.5	85	1400	16.9	9.7	105	2573	16.8	17.8	105
Animal Planet	5720	2604	6.5	45.5	102	1001	6.1	17.5	96	592	7.2	10.3	112	1010	6.6	17.7	104
Cartoon Network	6543	2876	7.2	44.0	99	1282	7.8	19.6	107	586	7.1	9.0	97	1009	6.6	15.4	90
CNBC	9908	5231	13.1	52.8	118	2214	13.5	22.3	122	1045	12.6	10.5	115	1972	12.9	19.9	117
CNN	29356	14069	35.2	47.9	108	5818	35.4	19.8	108	2888	34.9	9.8	107	5363	35.0	18.3	107
Comedy Central	6252	3244	8.1	51.9	116	1286	7.8	20.6	112	640	7.7	10.2	111	1318	8.6	21.1	124
The Discovery Channel	29211	13498	33.7	46.2	104	5488	33.4	18.8	103	2917	35.3	10.0	109	5093	33.2	17.4	102
E! Entertainment Television	7299	3716	9.3	50.9	114	1489	9.1	20.4	111	677	8.2	9.3	101	1550	10.1	21.2	124
ESPN	13889	6352	15.9	45.7	103	2482	15.1	17.9	98	1388	16.8	10.0	109	2482	16.2	17.9	105
ESPN2	3864	1987	5.0	51.4	115	819	5.0	21.2	116	364	4.4	9.4	102	804	5.3	20.8	122
The Family Channel	21633	8841	22.1	40.9	92	3335	20.3	15.4	84	1656	20.0	7.7	83	3850	25.1	17.8	104
FX	5253	2258	5.6	43.0	96	845	5.1	16.1	88	485	5.9	9.2	100	928	6.1	17.7	104
Fox News Network	9231	4338	10.8	47.0	105	1919	11.7	20.8	114	706	8.5	7.6	83	1712	11.2	18.6	109
Headline News	12720	5967	14.9	46.9	105	2337	14.2	18.4	100	1225	14.8	9.6	105	2405	15.7	18.9	111
History Channel	7270	3346	8.4	46.0	103	1243	7.6	17.1	93	606	7.3	8.3	91	1497	9.8	20.6	121
Home & Garden Television	6668	3339	8.3	50.1	112	1257	7.6	18.9	103	630	7.6	9.5	103	1451	9.5	21.8	128
Lifetime	25627	11196	28.0	43.7	98	4773	29.0	18.6	102	2096	25.4	8.2	89	4327	28.2	16.9	99
MTV	6480	3078	7.7	47.5	107	1199	7.3	18.5	101	643	7.8	9.9	108	1236	8.1	19.1	112
Nick at Nite	9437	4346	10.9	46.1	103	1881	11.4	19.9	109	807	9.8	8.5	93	1658	10.8	17.6	103
Nickelodeon	10503	4817	12.0	45.9	103	1945	11.8	18.5	101	972	11.8	9.3	101	1901	12.4	18.1	106
Prevue Channel	6588	3362	8.4	51.0	114	1336	8.1	20.3	111	640	7.7	9.7	106	1386	9.0	21.0	123
Sci-Fi Channel	4840	2310	5.8	47.7	107	1051	6.4	21.7	119	*338	4.1	7.0	76	922	6.0	19.0	112
TBS	20445	8483	21.2	41.5	93	3265	19.9	16.0	87	1866	22.6	9.1	99	3351	21.9	16.4	96
TLC: The Learning Channel	10854	5374	13.4	49.5	111	2132	13.0	19.6	107	1139	13.8	10.5	114	2102	13.7	19.4	114
TNN: The Nashville Network	11952	4273	10.7	35.8	80	1619	9.8	13.5	74	980	11.9	8.2	89	1674	10.9	14.0	82
TNT	18577	8014	20.0	43.1	97	3166	19.3	17.0	93	1692	20.5	9.1	99	3156	20.6	17.0	100
USA Network	22142	8958	22.4	40.5	91	3649	22.2	16.5	90	1916	23.2	8.7	94	3393	22.2	15.3	90
VH1	5610	2829	7.1	50.4	113	1112	6.8	19.8	108	582	7.0	10.4	113	1135	7.4	20.2	119
The Weather Channel	26297	11998	30.0	45.6	102	5016	30.5	19.1	104	2405	29.1	9.1	99	4577	29.9	17.4	102
WGN-TV	8230	3276	8.2	39.8	89	1188	7.2	14.4	79	617	7.5	7.5	81	1471	9.6	17.9	105

Spring 1998

70

180 YOGURT

						-------------------- CONTAINERS/LAST 7 DAYS --------------------											
		ALL				HEAVY MORE THAN 3				MEDIUM 2 - 3				LIGHT LESS THAN 2			
BASE: FEMALE HOMEMAKERS	TOTAL U.S. '000	A '000	B % DOWN	C % ACROSS	D INDEX	A '000	B % DOWN	C % ACROSS	D INDEX	A '000	B % DOWN	C % ACROSS	D INDEX	A '000	B % DOWN	C % ACROSS	D INDEX
All Female Homemakers	89789	40024	100.0	44.6	100	16443	100.0	18.3	100	8263	100.0	9.2	100	15318	100.0	17.1	100
Allure	1767	987	2.5	55.9	125	459	2.8	26.0	142	*270	3.3	15.3	166	*258	1.7	14.6	86
American Baby	3886	1760	4.4	45.3	102	766	4.7	19.7	108	*380	4.6	9.8	106	614	4.0	15.8	93
American Health for Women	2399	1355	3.4	56.5	127	587	3.6	24.5	134	*304	3.7	12.7	138	464	3.0	19.3	113
American Homestyle/Gardening	2175	984	2.5	45.2	101	394	2.4	18.1	99	*203	2.5	9.3	101	*387	2.5	17.8	104
American Hunter	*610	*237	0.6	-	-	*98	0.6	-	-	*45	0.5	-	-	*94	0.6	-	-
American Legion	1137	443	1.1	39.0	87	*98	0.6	8.6	47	*166	2.0	14.6	159	*179	1.2	15.8	92
American Rifleman	*572	*193	0.5	-	-	*122	0.7	-	-	-	-	-	-	*70	0.5	-	-
American Way	414	*229	0.6	55.2	124	*84	0.5	20.3	111	*98	1.2	23.6	256	*47	0.3	11.4	67
Architectural Digest	2543	1591	4.0	62.6	140	682	4.1	26.8	146	*279	3.4	11.0	119	630	4.1	24.8	145
Atlantic Monthly	642	488	1.2	76.0	171	*189	1.1	29.5	161	*110	1.3	17.1	186	*189	1.2	29.4	172
Audubon	733	438	1.1	59.7	134	*195	1.2	26.7	146	*87	1.0	11.8	129	*156	1.0	21.2	124
Automobile	*293	*140	0.3	-	-	*67	0.4	-	-	*2	0.0	-	-	*70	0.5	-	-
Baby Talk	2317	986	2.5	42.6	95	*447	2.7	19.3	105	*100	1.2	4.3	47	*440	2.9	19.0	111
Barron's	289	*132	0.3	45.7	102	*36	0.2	12.5	68	*47	0.6	16.1	175	*49	0.3	17.0	100
Bassmaster	*540	*222	0.6	-	-	*79	0.5	-	-	*33	0.4	-	-	*110	0.7	-	-
Beckett Baseball Card Mnthly	*454	*220	0.5	-	-	*97	0.6	-	-	*36	0.4	-	-	*87	0.6	-	-
Better Homes & Gardens	24188	11668	29.2	48.2	108	4764	29.0	19.7	108	2400	29.0	9.9	108	4504	29.4	18.6	109
Black Enterprise	1276	501	1.3	39.2	88	*200	1.2	15.7	86	*156	1.9	12.3	133	*144	0.9	11.3	66
Bon Appetit	3361	1835	4.6	54.6	123	837	5.1	24.9	136	361	4.4	10.7	117	638	4.2	19.0	111
Bridal Guide	1684	733	1.8	43.6	98	*274	1.7	16.3	89	*174	2.1	10.3	112	*285	1.9	16.9	99
Bride's	3110	1301	3.3	41.8	94	527	3.2	16.9	93	*229	2.8	7.4	80	544	3.6	17.5	103
Business Week	1484	704	1.8	47.5	106	364	2.2	24.5	134	*166	2.0	11.2	121	*174	1.1	11.8	69
Byte	*162	*126	0.3	-	-	*92	0.6	-	-	*18	0.2	-	-	*15	0.1	-	-
Cable Guide	4780	1993	5.0	41.7	94	1061	6.4	22.2	121	316	3.8	6.6	72	616	4.0	12.9	76
Car and Driver	786	*424	1.1	53.9	121	*154	0.9	19.5	107	*82	1.0	10.4	113	*188	1.2	24.0	140
Car Craft	*205	*117	0.3	-	-	*13	0.1	-	-	*34	0.4	-	-	*69	0.5	-	-
Catholic Digest	1767	752	1.9	42.6	95	*451	2.7	25.5	139	*151	1.8	8.5	93	*150	1.0	8.5	50
Child	2434	1108	2.8	45.5	102	424	2.6	17.4	95	*194	2.3	8.0	87	*491	3.2	20.1	118
Colonial Homes	1820	932	2.3	51.2	115	*407	2.5	22.4	122	*178	2.2	9.8	106	*347	2.3	19.1	112
Computer Shopper	483	*232	0.6	48.0	108	*124	0.8	25.7	140	*7	0.1	1.5	16	*100	0.7	20.8	122
Conde Nast Package (Gr)	42869	22397	56.0	52.2	117	10311	62.7	24.1	131	4673	56.5	10.9	118	7413	48.4	17.3	101
Conde Nast Traveler	1129	599	1.5	53.0	119	*288	1.8	25.5	139	*111	1.3	9.8	107	*200	1.3	17.7	104
Consumers Digest	2499	1402	3.5	56.1	126	545	3.3	21.8	119	*272	3.3	10.9	118	585	3.8	23.4	137
Cooking Light	4213	2432	6.1	57.7	129	1085	6.6	25.7	141	633	7.7	15.0	163	714	4.7	16.9	99
Cosmopolitan	11351	5647	14.1	49.8	112	2639	16.1	23.2	127	1292	15.6	11.4	124	1716	11.2	15.1	89
Country America	1570	581	1.5	37.0	83	*165	1.0	10.5	57	*178	2.2	11.4	123	*238	1.6	15.1	89
Country Home	5742	2757	6.9	48.0	108	1015	6.2	17.7	97	572	6.9	10.0	108	1170	7.6	20.4	119
Country Living	7586	3594	9.0	47.4	106	1254	7.6	16.5	90	748	9.0	9.9	107	1592	10.4	21.0	123
Country Music	3101	1278	3.2	41.2	92	660	4.0	21.3	116	*201	2.4	6.5	71	*416	2.7	13.4	79
Delta's SKY Magazine	894	522	1.3	58.5	131	*203	1.2	22.7	124	*47	0.6	5.3	57	*272	1.8	30.4	178
Discover	2098	1055	2.6	50.3	113	440	2.7	21.0	115	*126	1.5	6.0	65	489	3.2	23.3	136
Easyriders	*418	*203	0.5	-	-	*91	0.6	-	-	*48	0.6	-	-	*64	0.4	-	-
Eating Well	2034	1114	2.8	54.8	123	458	2.8	22.5	123	*340	4.1	16.7	182	*316	2.1	15.5	91
Ebony	5823	2128	5.3	36.6	82	912	5.5	15.7	86	459	5.6	7.9	86	757	4.9	13.0	76
Elle	2950	1612	4.0	54.6	123	635	3.9	21.5	117	*375	4.5	12.7	138	602	3.9	20.4	120
Endless Vacation	629	*317	0.8	50.5	113	*151	0.9	24.1	131	*42	0.5	6.7	73	*124	0.8	19.8	116
Entertainment Weekly	3651	1726	4.3	47.3	106	870	5.3	23.8	130	358	4.3	9.8	107	498	3.3	13.6	80
Entrepreneur	958	425	1.1	44.4	99	*209	1.3	21.8	119	*105	1.3	11.0	119	*111	0.7	11.6	68
Esquire	813	*316	0.8	38.9	87	*166	1.0	20.5	112	*44	0.5	5.4	59	*106	0.7	13.0	76
Essence	4101	1478	3.7	36.0	81	704	4.3	17.2	94	*282	3.4	6.9	75	493	3.2	12.0	70
Family Circle	18303	8491	21.2	46.4	104	3565	21.7	19.5	106	1651	20.0	9.0	98	3275	21.4	17.9	105
Family Fun	1306	742	1.9	56.8	127	352	2.1	26.9	147	*92	1.1	7.1	77	*298	1.9	22.8	134
Family Handyman	1130	509	1.3	45.0	101	*274	1.7	24.3	133	*66	0.8	5.8	63	*169	1.1	14.9	88
Field & Stream	2269	1083	2.7	47.7	107	*263	1.6	11.6	63	*167	2.0	7.4	80	*652	4.3	28.8	169
Field & Strm/Outdr Life (Gr)	3439	1665	4.2	48.4	109	*467	2.8	13.6	74	*338	4.1	9.8	107	859	5.6	25.0	146
Financial World	*270	*151	0.4	-	-	*53	0.3	-	-	*42	0.5	-	-	*56	0.4	-	-
First For Women	3228	1737	4.3	53.8	121	784	4.8	24.3	133	*268	3.2	8.3	90	686	4.5	21.2	124
Fitness	2770	1445	3.6	52.2	117	547	3.3	19.7	108	*341	4.1	12.3	134	557	3.6	20.1	118
Flower & Garden	3727	1776	4.4	47.7	107	809	4.9	21.7	119	*354	4.3	9.5	103	613	4.0	16.4	96
Food & Wine	2417	1365	3.4	56.4	127	542	3.3	22.4	123	*297	3.6	12.3	134	525	3.4	21.7	127
Forbes	1302	766	1.9	58.8	132	*328	2.0	25.2	137	*149	1.8	11.4	124	*289	1.9	22.2	130
Fortune	1523	833	2.1	54.7	123	428	2.6	28.1	154	*142	1.7	9.3	101	*263	1.7	17.3	101
4 Wheel & Off Road	*269	*95	0.2	-	-	*32	0.2	-	-	*16	0.2	-	-	*47	0.3	-	-
Four Wheeler	*280	*96	0.2	-	-	*66	0.4	-	-	*2	0.0	-	-	*28	0.2	-	-
Glamour	9619	4807	12.0	50.0	112	2196	13.4	22.8	125	1091	13.2	11.3	123	1519	9.9	15.8	93
Golf Digest	1198	543	1.4	45.3	102	*248	1.5	20.7	113	*121	1.5	10.1	110	*174	1.1	14.5	85
Golf Magazine	1047	503	1.3	48.0	108	*171	1.0	16.3	89	*103	1.3	9.9	107	*229	1.5	21.9	128
Golf World	*193	*85	0.2	-	-	*34	0.2	-	-	*18	0.2	-	-	*34	0.2	-	-
Good Housekeeping	20099	9047	22.6	45.0	101	3784	23.0	18.8	103	1937	23.4	9.6	105	3325	21.7	16.5	97
Gourmet	3091	1729	4.3	56.0	126	678	4.1	21.9	120	423	5.1	13.7	149	628	4.1	20.3	119
GQ (Gentlemen's Quarterly)	1400	563	1.4	40.2	90	*198	1.2	14.1	77	*137	1.7	9.8	106	*228	1.5	16.3	95
Guns & Ammo	732	*238	0.6	32.5	73	*86	0.5	11.7	64	*74	0.9	10.1	110	*78	0.5	10.7	63
Hachette Magazine Ntwk (Gr)	31881	16119	40.3	50.6	113	6599	40.1	20.7	113	3540	42.8	11.1	121	5979	39.0	18.8	110
Hachette Men's Package (Gr)	3396	1847	4.6	54.4	122	668	4.1	19.7	107	*420	5.1	12.4	134	760	5.0	22.4	131
Harper's Bazaar	2177	1143	2.9	52.5	118	491	3.0	22.5	123	*300	3.6	13.8	150	*353	2.3	16.2	95
Health	3669	2083	5.2	56.8	127	891	5.4	24.3	133	410	5.0	11.2	122	782	5.1	21.3	125
Hearst Magazine Group (Gr)	65990	31907	79.7	48.4	108	13930	84.7	21.1	115	6579	79.6	10.0	108	11398	74.4	17.3	101
Hemispheres (United)	560	368	0.9	65.7	147	*190	1.2	33.8	185	*58	0.7	10.4	113	*120	0.8	21.4	126
Home	2779	1272	3.2	45.8	103	453	2.8	16.3	89	*276	3.3	9.9	108	543	3.5	19.5	115
Home Office Computing	449	*171	0.4	38.0	85	*55	0.3	12.3	67	*23	0.3	5.2	56	*92	0.6	20.5	120
Hot Rod	693	*322	0.8	46.5	104	*142	0.9	20.5	112	*39	0.5	5.6	61	*142	0.9	20.4	120
House Beautiful	5745	2856	7.1	49.7	112	1303	7.9	22.7	124	564	6.8	9.8	107	989	6.5	17.2	101
Hunting	*236	*68	0.2	-	-	*61	0.4	-	-	*6	0.1	-	-	-	-	-	-
Inc.	660	322	0.8	48.7	109	*80	0.5	12.1	66	*149	1.8	22.6	245	*93	0.6	14.0	82
Inside Sports	565	*224	0.6	39.6	89	*93	0.6	16.5	90	*30	0.4	5.3	57	*101	0.7	17.9	105
Jet	4279	1375	3.4	32.1	72	639	3.9	14.9	82	*276	3.3	6.5	70	460	3.0	10.7	63
Kiplinger's Personal Finance	973	648	1.6	66.6	149	*374	2.3	38.5	210	*94	1.1	9.7	105	*179	1.2	18.4	108
Ladies' Home Journal	13995	6722	16.8	48.0	108	2931	17.8	20.9	114	1290	15.6	9.2	100	2501	16.3	17.9	105
Life	7327	3546	8.9	48.4	109	1378	8.4	18.8	103	767	9.3	10.5	114	1402	9.2	19.1	112
Los Angeles Times Magazine	1441	819	2.0	56.8	128	*343	2.1	23.8	130	*188	2.3	13.0	142	*288	1.9	20.0	117
Macworld	851	557	1.4	65.4	147	*188	1.1	22.1	121	*116	1.4	13.7	149	*252	1.6	29.6	173
Mademoiselle	3984	2124	5.3	53.3	120	1064	6.5	26.7	146	383	4.6	9.6	104	677	4.4	17.0	100
Martha Stewart Living	7310	4100	10.2	56.1	126	1694	10.3	23.2	127	939	11.4	12.8	140	1466	9.6	20.1	118
McCall's	12348	5710	14.3	46.2	104	2659	16.2	21.5	118	1165	14.1	9.4	103	1885	12.3	15.3	89
Men's Fitness	489	*319	0.8	65.2	146	*187	1.1	38.2	209	*13	0.2	2.6	28	*119	0.8	24.4	143
Men's Health	963	622	1.6	64.6	145	*350	2.1	36.4	199	*49	0.6	5.1	55	*223	1.5	23.1	136
Men's Journal	*189	*87	0.2	-	-	*14	0.1	-	-	*30	0.4	-	-	*43	0.3	-	-
Metropolitan Home	1485	913	2.3	61.5	138	331	2.0	22.3	122	*252	3.1	17.0	185	329	2.1	22.2	130
Metro-Puck Comics Network	40845	20171	50.4	49.4	111	9185	55.9	22.5	123	3871	46.8	9.5	103	7115	46.4	17.4	102
Midwest Living	1660	908	2.3	54.7	123	373	2.3	22.4	123	*224	2.7	13.5	147	*312	2.0	18.8	110
Mirabella	1256	700	1.7	55.7	125	*255	1.6	20.3	111	*135	1.6	10.7	117	*310	2.0	24.7	145
Modern Bride	2293	1006	2.5	43.9	98	*337	2.1	14.7	80	*149	1.8	6.5	71	519	3.4	22.6	133
Modern Maturity	10059	4611	11.5	45.8	103	1759	10.7	17.5	95	1155	14.0	11.5	125	1697	11.1	16.9	99
Money	2923	1724	4.3	59.0	132	848	5.2	29.0	158	360	4.4	12.3	134	515	3.4	17.6	103

Spring 1998

BASE: FEMALE HOMEMAKERS	TOTAL U.S. '000	ALL A '000	ALL B % DOWN	ALL C % ACROSS	ALL D INDEX	HEAVY MORE THAN 3 A '000	HEAVY B % DOWN	HEAVY C % ACROSS	HEAVY D INDEX	MEDIUM 2 - 3 A '000	MEDIUM B % DOWN	MEDIUM C % ACROSS	MEDIUM D INDEX	LIGHT LESS THAN 2 A '000	LIGHT B % DOWN	LIGHT C % ACROSS	LIGHT D INDEX
						CONTAINERS/LAST 7 DAYS											
All Female Homemakers	89789	40024	100.0	44.6	100	16443	100.0	18.3	100	8263	100.0	9.2	100	15318	100.0	17.1	100
Motor Trend	*431	*258	0.6	-	-	*121	0.7	-	-	*60	0.7	-	-	*77	0.5	-	-
Muscle & Fitness	1290	675	1.7	52.3	117	*267	1.6	20.7	113	*101	1.2	7.8	85	*307	2.0	23.8	140
National Enquirer	8328	3482	8.7	41.8	94	1573	9.6	18.9	103	738	8.9	8.9	96	1171	7.6	14.1	82
National Geographic	12447	6545	16.4	52.6	118	2652	16.1	21.3	116	1332	16.1	10.7	116	2562	16.7	20.6	121
National Geographic Traveler	1684	876	2.2	52.1	117	306	1.9	18.2	99	*199	2.4	11.8	128	371	2.4	22.0	129
Natural History	648	440	1.1	67.9	152	*113	0.7	17.5	95	*101	1.2	15.6	170	*226	1.5	34.9	204
Newsweek	8478	4591	11.5	54.2	121	1870	11.4	22.1	120	1019	12.3	12.0	131	1703	11.1	20.1	118
New Woman	3372	1615	4.0	47.9	107	751	4.6	22.3	122	*303	3.7	9.0	97	562	3.7	16.7	98
New York Magazine	644	316	0.8	49.0	110	*97	0.6	15.0	82	*85	1.0	13.2	144	*134	0.9	20.8	122
New York Times (Daily)	1396	965	2.4	69.1	155	361	2.2	25.8	141	*176	2.1	12.6	137	429	2.8	30.7	180
New York Times Magazine	2024	1280	3.2	63.2	142	393	2.4	19.4	106	305	3.7	15.1	164	581	3.8	28.7	168
The New Yorker	1363	877	2.2	64.3	144	299	1.8	21.9	120	*132	1.6	9.7	105	446	2.9	32.7	192
North American Fisherman	*564	*226	0.6	-	-	*132	0.8	-	-	*16	0.2	-	-	*77	0.5	-	-
North American Hunter	*478	*210	0.5	-	-	*51	0.3	-	-	*18	0.2	-	-	*141	0.9	-	-
N. American Outdoor Grp (Gr)	1042	*435	1.1	41.8	94	*183	1.1	17.6	96	*34	0.4	3.3	36	*218	1.4	20.9	123
Northwest World Traveler	502	*238	0.6	47.4	106	*134	0.8	26.8	146	*23	0.3	4.6	50	*81	0.5	16.1	94
Organic Gardening	2437	1392	3.5	57.1	128	572	3.5	23.5	128	*362	4.4	14.8	161	*458	3.0	18.8	110
Outdoor Life	1169	*582	1.5	49.8	112	*204	1.2	17.5	95	*171	2.1	14.6	159	*207	1.4	17.7	104
Outside	556	*347	0.9	62.5	140	*121	0.7	21.8	119	*83	1.0	14.9	162	*143	0.9	25.8	151
Parade	38339	18422	46.0	48.0	108	8249	50.2	21.5	117	3672	44.4	9.6	104	6501	42.4	17.0	99
Parenting	5083	2486	6.2	48.9	110	1115	6.8	21.9	120	453	5.5	8.9	97	918	6.0	18.1	106
Parents' Magazine	8536	4186	10.5	49.0	110	1887	11.5	22.1	121	817	9.9	9.6	104	1482	9.7	17.4	102
PC Computing	1156	649	1.6	56.2	126	*223	1.4	19.3	105	*145	1.8	12.5	136	*281	1.8	24.3	143
PC Magazine	1630	805	2.0	49.4	111	254	1.5	15.6	85	*114	1.4	7.0	76	436	2.8	26.7	157
PC World	1677	934	2.3	55.7	125	341	2.1	20.3	111	*156	1.9	9.3	101	*438	2.9	26.1	153
Penthouse	*351	*200	0.5	-	-	*77	0.5	-	-	*26	0.3	-	-	*96	0.6	-	-
People	21758	10720	26.8	49.3	111	5139	31.3	23.6	129	2118	25.6	9.7	106	3463	22.6	15.9	93
Petersen Magazine Netwk (Gr)	4312	1847	4.6	42.8	96	796	4.8	18.5	101	*414	5.0	9.6	104	637	4.2	14.8	87
Playboy	1561	704	1.8	45.1	101	*251	1.5	16.1	88	*128	1.6	8.2	89	*325	2.1	20.8	122
Popular Hot Rodding	*311	*166	0.4	-	-	*105	0.6	-	-	*9	0.1	-	-	*52	0.3	-	-
Popular Mechanics	1126	587	1.5	52.1	117	*279	1.7	24.8	136	*136	1.6	12.1	131	*172	1.1	15.2	89
Popular Science	910	503	1.3	55.3	124	*179	1.1	19.7	108	*153	1.8	16.8	182	*171	1.1	18.8	110
Premiere	692	*300	0.7	43.4	97	*162	1.0	23.4	128	*50	0.6	7.3	79	*88	0.6	12.7	74
Prevention	7501	4091	10.2	54.5	122	1810	11.0	24.1	132	919	11.1	12.2	133	1362	8.9	18.2	106
Psychology Today	2111	1152	2.9	54.6	122	363	2.2	17.2	94	*273	3.3	12.9	140	516	3.4	24.4	143
Reader's Digest	26825	12197	30.5	45.5	102	4963	30.2	18.5	101	2477	30.0	9.2	100	4756	31.0	17.7	104
Redbook	9290	4559	11.4	49.1	110	2035	12.4	21.9	120	825	10.0	8.9	96	1699	11.1	18.3	107
Road & Track	412	*227	0.6	55.1	124	*128	0.8	31.1	170	*60	0.7	14.7	159	*38	0.3	9.3	55
Rodale Active Network (Gr)	2560	1672	4.2	65.3	146	812	4.9	31.7	173	*200	2.4	7.8	85	660	4.3	25.8	151
Rolling Stone	2394	1250	3.1	52.2	117	567	3.4	23.7	129	*326	3.9	13.6	148	*357	2.3	14.9	87
Runner's World	660	364	0.9	55.1	124	*143	0.9	21.7	119	*92	1.1	13.9	151	*129	0.8	19.5	114
Saturday Evening Post	2041	928	2.3	45.5	102	466	2.8	22.8	125	*111	1.3	5.4	59	*351	2.3	17.2	101
Scientific American	595	394	1.0	66.2	148	*153	0.9	25.7	140	*55	0.7	9.3	101	*185	1.2	31.2	183
Self	3492	1998	5.0	57.2	128	956	5.8	27.4	149	408	4.9	11.7	127	634	4.1	18.1	106
Sesame Street Parents	3508	1633	4.1	46.5	104	611	3.7	17.4	95	*274	3.3	7.8	85	747	4.9	21.3	125
Seventeen	4289	2149	5.4	50.1	112	961	5.8	22.4	122	*298	3.6	7.0	76	889	5.8	20.7	122
Shape	2342	1442	3.6	61.6	138	576	3.5	24.6	134	*320	3.9	13.7	148	546	3.6	23.3	137
Sierra	473	*324	0.8	68.6	154	*121	0.7	25.6	140	*57	0.7	12.0	130	*147	1.0	31.0	182
Ski	458	*339	0.8	74.0	166	*217	1.3	47.4	259	*49	0.6	10.7	117	*73	0.5	15.9	93
Skiing	422	*289	0.7	68.5	154	*158	1.0	37.4	204	*68	0.8	16.0	174	*63	0.4	15.0	88
Ski/Skiing (Gr)	880	628	1.6	71.4	160	*375	2.3	42.6	233	*117	1.4	13.3	144	*136	0.9	15.5	91
Smart Money	1004	647	1.6	64.5	145	428	2.6	42.6	233	*77	0.9	7.7	84	*142	0.9	14.2	83
Smithsonian	3483	1989	5.0	57.1	128	766	4.7	22.0	120	448	5.4	12.9	140	774	5.1	22.2	130
Soap Opera Digest	5278	2186	5.5	41.4	93	967	5.9	18.3	100	422	5.1	8.0	87	798	5.2	15.1	89
Soap Opera Weekly	3349	1333	3.3	39.8	89	607	3.7	18.1	99	*289	3.5	8.6	94	*437	2.9	13.0	76
Southern Accents	1119	504	1.3	45.0	101	*205	1.2	18.3	100	*109	1.3	9.8	106	*190	1.2	17.0	99
Southern Living	8754	3572	8.9	40.8	92	1319	8.0	15.1	82	676	8.2	7.7	84	1577	10.3	18.0	106
Southwest Spirit	456	*309	0.8	67.8	152	*53	0.3	11.7	64	*61	0.7	13.4	146	*194	1.3	42.6	250
Spin	594	*329	0.8	55.5	125	*117	0.7	19.7	107	*112	1.4	18.9	206	*100	0.7	16.9	99
Sport	486	*195	0.5	40.1	90	*134	0.8	27.5	150	*21	0.3	4.4	48	*40	0.3	8.2	48
The Sporting News	*250	*84	0.2	-	-	*30	0.2	-	-	*29	0.3	-	-	*25	0.2	-	-
Sports Afield	*342	*106	0.3	-	-	*36	0.2	-	-	*18	0.2	-	-	*52	0.3	-	-
Sports Illustrated	4693	2321	5.8	49.5	111	1076	6.5	22.9	125	405	4.9	8.6	94	840	5.5	17.9	105
Star	4597	1931	4.8	42.0	94	1021	6.2	22.2	121	337	4.1	7.3	80	573	3.7	12.5	73
Success	488	*235	0.6	48.2	108	*107	0.7	21.9	120	*43	0.5	8.8	95	*86	0.6	17.5	103
Sunday Mag/Net	13172	6912	17.3	52.5	118	3069	18.7	23.3	127	1394	16.9	10.6	115	2449	16.0	18.6	109
Sunset	2610	1727	4.3	66.2	148	672	4.1	25.8	141	359	4.3	13.8	149	696	4.5	26.7	156
Teen	2426	1087	2.7	44.8	100	*387	2.4	15.9	87	*129	1.6	5.3	58	*571	3.7	23.5	138
Tennis	521	*259	0.6	49.7	111	*138	0.8	26.5	145	*22	0.3	4.2	46	*99	0.6	18.9	111
Texas Monthly	949	354	0.9	37.3	84	*185	1.1	19.5	106	*85	1.0	9.0	98	*84	0.5	8.8	52
This Old House	1458	741	1.9	50.8	114	*428	2.6	29.3	160	*104	1.3	7.1	77	*210	1.4	14.4	84
Time	10097	5053	12.6	50.0	112	2135	13.0	21.1	115	1046	12.7	10.4	113	1872	12.2	18.5	109
Times Mirror A-List (Gr)	2171	1286	3.2	59.2	133	593	3.6	27.3	149	*282	3.4	13.0	141	411	2.7	19.0	111
Town & Country	1808	957	2.4	52.9	119	437	2.7	24.1	132	*115	1.4	6.4	69	405	2.6	22.4	131
Traditional Home	2027	1054	2.6	52.0	117	441	2.7	21.8	119	*142	1.7	7.0	76	471	3.1	23.2	136
Travel & Leisure	2209	1197	3.0	54.2	122	494	3.0	22.4	122	*217	2.6	9.8	107	486	3.2	22.0	129
True Story	3022	1045	2.6	34.6	78	*424	2.6	14.0	77	*160	1.9	5.3	58	*461	3.0	15.3	89
TV Guide	17688	7648	19.1	43.2	97	3220	19.6	18.2	99	1605	19.4	9.1	99	2823	18.4	16.0	94
U.S. News & World Report	4158	2160	5.4	51.9	117	983	6.0	23.6	129	380	4.6	9.2	99	796	5.2	19.2	112
Us	2089	1007	2.5	48.2	108	546	3.3	26.2	143	*163	2.0	7.8	85	*298	1.9	14.3	84
USA Today	1140	506	1.3	44.3	99	*289	1.8	25.4	139	*58	0.7	5.1	55	*158	1.0	13.9	81
USA Today Baseball Weekly	*206	*122	0.3	-	-	*42	0.3	-	-	*20	0.2	-	-	*61	0.4	-	-
USA Weekend	19300	9257	23.1	48.0	108	4010	24.4	20.8	113	1902	23.0	9.9	107	3346	21.8	17.3	102
Vanity Fair	2963	1624	4.1	54.8	123	792	4.8	26.7	146	*279	3.4	9.4	102	553	3.6	18.6	109
VFW Magazine	815	*240	0.6	29.5	66	*53	0.3	6.4	35	*72	0.9	8.9	96	*116	0.8	14.2	83
Vibe	1158	393	1.0	34.0	76	*223	1.4	19.3	105	*69	0.8	6.0	65	*101	0.7	8.7	51
Victoria	2395	1255	3.1	52.4	118	579	3.5	24.2	132	286	3.5	12.0	130	389	2.5	16.3	95
Vogue	6410	3238	8.1	50.5	113	1634	9.9	25.5	139	700	8.5	10.9	119	905	5.9	14.1	83
Walking Magazine	1246	619	1.5	49.7	111	*267	1.6	21.5	117	*160	1.9	12.9	140	*191	1.2	15.4	90
Wall Street Journal	1207	745	1.9	61.7	138	341	2.1	28.2	154	*126	1.5	10.4	113	*278	1.8	23.1	135
Washington Post (Sunday)	1082	613	1.5	56.7	127	335	2.0	31.0	169	*96	1.2	8.9	97	*182	1.2	16.8	99
Weight Watchers	3471	1716	4.3	49.4	111	819	5.0	23.6	129	*301	3.6	8.7	94	597	3.9	17.2	101
Windows	758	429	1.1	56.6	127	*262	1.6	34.5	188	*79	1.0	10.5	114	*88	0.6	11.7	68
Woman's Day	17290	8361	20.9	48.4	108	3638	22.1	21.0	115	1691	20.5	9.8	106	3031	19.8	17.5	103
Woman's World	6215	2956	7.4	47.6	107	1397	8.5	22.5	123	540	6.5	8.7	94	1019	6.7	16.4	96
Workbench	562	*211	0.5	37.5	84	*90	0.5	16.1	88	*19	0.2	3.4	37	*102	0.7	18.1	106
Working Mother	2129	1164	2.9	54.6	123	476	2.9	22.3	122	*194	2.3	9.1	99	494	3.2	23.2	136
Working Woman	2843	1632	4.1	57.4	129	887	5.4	31.2	170	*265	3.2	9.3	101	480	3.1	16.9	99
Worth	358	*192	0.5	53.7	120	*131	0.8	36.6	200	*35	0.4	9.7	105	*27	0.2	7.4	44
WWF Magazine	551	*232	0.6	42.1	94	*106	0.6	19.2	105	*22	0.3	4.0	44	*104	0.7	18.9	111
Yankee	1013	572	1.4	56.5	127	*331	2.0	32.7	179	*95	1.2	9.4	102	*146	1.0	14.4	84
YM	2057	1130	2.8	55.0	123	*387	2.4	18.8	103	*257	3.1	12.5	136	*487	3.2	23.7	139
Your Money	637	*302	0.8	47.5	107	*110	0.7	17.3	94	*59	0.7	9.3	101	*133	0.9	20.9	122

Spring 1998

72

182 YOGURT

BASE: FEMALE HOMEMAKERS	TOTAL U.S. '000	WITH FRUIT - PREMIXED A '000	B % DOWN	C % ACROSS	D INDEX	WITH FRUIT - NOT PREMIXED A '000	B % DOWN	C % ACROSS	D INDEX	OTHER FLAVOR A '000	B % DOWN	C % ACROSS	D INDEX	PLAIN (UNFLAVORED) A '000	B % DOWN	C % ACROSS	D INDEX
All Female Homemakers	89789	22013	100.0	24.5	100	9043	100.0	10.1	100	7088	100.0	7.9	100	5137	100.0	5.7	100
Men	-	-	-	-	-	-	-	-	-	-	-	-	-	-	-	-	-
Women	89789	22013	100.0	24.5	100	9043	100.0	10.1	100	7088	100.0	7.9	100	5137	100.0	5.7	100
Household Heads	39088	8529	38.7	21.8	89	3341	36.9	8.5	85	2646	37.3	6.8	86	2003	39.0	5.1	90
Homemakers	89789	22013	100.0	24.5	100	9043	100.0	10.1	100	7088	100.0	7.9	100	5137	100.0	5.7	100
Graduated College	18398	5647	25.7	30.7	125	2916	32.2	15.8	157	1992	28.1	10.8	137	1776	34.6	9.7	169
Attended College	24064	6771	30.8	28.1	115	2514	27.8	10.4	104	2346	33.1	9.7	123	1422	27.7	5.9	103
Graduated High School	31577	7039	32.0	22.3	91	2709	30.0	8.6	85	1861	26.3	5.9	75	1420	27.7	4.5	79
Did not Graduate High School	15751	2555	11.6	16.2	66	904	10.0	5.7	57	889	12.5	5.6	71	*519	10.1	3.3	58
18-24	7780	1933	8.8	24.8	101	643	7.1	8.3	82	752	10.6	9.7	123	*468	9.1	6.0	105
25-34	18631	4892	22.2	26.3	107	1986	22.0	10.7	106	1476	20.8	7.9	100	1001	19.5	5.4	94
35-44	20651	6120	27.8	29.6	121	2384	26.4	11.5	115	2141	30.2	10.4	131	1193	23.2	5.8	101
45-54	15603	4367	19.8	28.0	114	2150	23.8	13.8	137	1393	19.7	8.9	113	1034	20.1	6.6	116
55-64	10181	2177	9.9	21.4	87	983	10.9	9.7	96	560	7.9	5.5	70	559	10.9	5.5	96
65 or over	16943	2524	11.5	14.9	61	897	9.9	5.3	53	765	10.8	4.5	57	882	17.2	5.2	91
18-34	26410	6825	31.0	25.8	105	2629	29.1	10.0	99	2229	31.4	8.4	107	1469	28.6	5.6	97
18-49	55960	15564	70.7	27.8	113	6419	71.0	11.5	114	5206	73.5	9.3	118	3351	65.2	6.0	105
25-54	54886	15379	69.9	28.0	114	6520	72.1	11.9	118	5011	70.7	9.1	116	3228	62.8	5.9	103
Employed Full Time	41154	11097	50.4	27.0	110	4586	50.7	11.1	111	3588	50.6	8.7	110	2413	47.0	5.9	103
Part-time	11398	3353	15.2	29.4	120	1500	16.6	13.2	131	1307	18.4	11.5	145	680	13.2	6.0	104
Sole Wage Earner	14006	2802	12.7	20.0	82	1147	12.7	8.2	81	963	13.6	6.9	87	766	14.9	5.5	96
Not Employed	37237	7563	34.4	20.3	83	2957	32.7	7.9	79	2193	30.9	5.9	75	2043	39.8	5.5	96
Professional	9642	3077	14.0	31.9	130	1647	18.2	17.1	170	1273	18.0	13.2	167	846	16.5	8.8	153
Executive/Admin./Managerial	7128	2155	9.8	30.2	123	845	9.3	11.9	118	689	9.7	9.7	122	567	11.0	8.0	139
Clerical/Sales/Technical	20870	5722	26.0	27.4	112	2347	26.0	11.2	112	1973	27.8	9.5	120	1115	21.7	5.3	93
Precision/Crafts/Repair	1102	*302	1.4	27.4	112	*115	1.3	10.5	104	*60	0.9	5.5	69	*70	1.4	6.4	112
Other Employed	13810	3194	14.5	23.1	94	1131	12.5	8.2	81	900	12.7	6.5	83	495	9.6	3.6	63
H/D Income $75,000 or More	15443	4502	20.5	29.2	119	2545	28.1	16.5	164	1591	22.5	10.3	131	1370	26.7	8.9	155
$60,000 - 74,999	8775	2892	13.1	33.0	134	1213	13.4	13.8	137	978	13.8	11.1	141	549	10.7	6.3	109
$50,000 - 59,999	7850	2642	12.0	33.6	137	992	11.0	12.6	126	818	11.5	10.4	132	572	11.1	7.3	127
$40,000 - 49,999	9648	2707	12.3	28.1	114	832	9.2	8.6	86	703	9.9	7.3	92	495	9.6	5.1	90
$30,000 - 39,999	11493	2871	13.0	25.0	102	932	10.3	8.1	80	838	11.8	7.3	92	636	12.4	5.5	97
$20,000 - 29,999	12298	2505	11.4	20.4	83	1032	11.4	8.4	83	901	12.7	7.3	93	679	13.2	5.5	96
$10,000 - 19,999	14330	2424	11.0	16.9	69	937	10.4	6.5	65	873	12.3	6.1	77	505	9.8	3.5	62
Less than $10,000	9953	1471	6.7	14.8	60	561	6.2	5.6	56	*386	5.4	3.9	49	*332	6.5	3.3	58
Census Region: North East	18074	4585	20.8	25.4	103	2704	29.9	15.0	149	1607	22.7	8.9	113	1096	21.3	6.1	106
North Central	20967	5634	25.6	26.9	110	2017	22.3	9.6	96	1629	23.0	7.8	98	1159	22.6	5.5	97
South	32182	6395	29.1	19.9	81	2402	26.6	7.5	74	2205	31.1	6.9	87	1480	28.8	4.6	80
West	18567	5398	24.5	29.1	119	1919	21.2	10.3	103	1647	23.2	8.9	112	1402	27.3	7.6	132
Marketing Reg.: New England	4705	1386	6.3	29.5	120	734	8.1	15.6	155	422	6.0	9.0	114	358	7.0	7.6	133
Middle Atlantic	15444	3654	16.6	23.7	97	2170	24.0	14.0	140	1375	19.4	8.9	113	847	16.5	5.5	96
East Central	11580	3133	14.2	27.1	110	1209	13.4	10.4	104	919	13.0	7.9	100	694	13.5	6.0	105
West Central	13616	3661	16.6	26.9	110	1266	14.0	9.3	92	1040	14.7	7.6	97	932	18.1	6.8	120
South East	18271	3789	17.2	20.7	85	1305	14.4	7.1	71	1294	18.3	7.1	90	764	14.9	4.2	73
South West	10224	1754	8.0	17.2	70	774	8.6	7.6	75	611	8.6	6.0	76	*437	8.5	4.3	75
Pacific	15950	4636	21.1	29.1	119	1585	17.5	9.9	99	1427	20.1	8.9	113	1106	21.5	6.9	121
County Size A	35658	9129	41.5	25.6	104	4497	49.7	12.6	125	2893	40.8	8.1	103	2217	43.2	6.2	109
County Size B	27101	6891	31.3	25.4	104	2712	30.0	10.0	99	2339	33.0	8.6	109	1774	34.5	6.5	114
County Size C	13387	3173	14.4	23.7	97	928	10.3	6.9	69	889	12.5	6.6	84	630	12.3	4.7	82
County Size D	13644	2820	12.8	20.7	84	906	10.0	6.6	66	967	13.6	7.1	90	*516	10.0	3.8	66
MSA Central City	29169	7106	32.3	24.4	99	2824	31.2	9.7	96	2131	30.1	7.3	93	1905	37.1	6.5	114
MSA Suburban	42524	10689	49.3	25.5	104	4959	54.8	11.7	116	3725	52.6	8.8	111	2467	48.0	5.8	101
Non-MSA	18096	4057	18.4	22.4	91	1260	13.9	7.0	69	1232	17.4	6.8	86	764	14.9	4.2	74
Single	14479	3316	15.1	22.9	93	1266	14.0	8.7	87	1188	16.8	8.2	104	881	17.1	6.1	106
Married	51935	14616	66.4	28.1	115	6154	68.1	11.9	118	4604	65.0	8.9	112	3162	61.6	6.1	106
Other	23376	4081	18.5	17.5	71	1623	17.9	6.9	69	1295	18.3	5.5	70	1094	21.3	4.7	82
Parents	35881	10686	48.5	29.8	121	4707	52.1	13.1	130	3433	48.4	9.6	121	2100	40.9	5.9	102
Working Parents	24725	7740	35.2	31.3	128	3422	37.8	13.8	137	2512	35.4	10.2	129	1442	28.1	5.8	102
Household Size: 1 Person	15017	2511	11.4	16.7	68	1099	12.1	7.3	73	749	10.6	5.0	63	798	15.5	5.3	93
2 Persons	28950	6172	28.0	21.3	87	2502	27.7	8.6	86	1961	27.7	6.8	86	1773	34.5	6.1	107
3 or More	45822	13330	60.6	29.1	119	5442	60.2	11.9	118	4379	61.8	9.6	121	2566	50.0	5.6	98
Any Child in Household	39070	11515	52.3	29.5	120	5054	55.9	12.9	128	3746	52.9	9.6	121	2223	43.3	5.7	99
Under 2 Years	6763	2100	9.5	31.1	127	754	8.3	11.2	111	595	8.4	8.8	112	513	10.0	7.7	134
2-5 Years	14794	4500	20.4	30.4	124	1849	20.5	12.5	124	1357	19.1	9.2	116	713	13.9	4.8	84
6-11 Years	18719	5304	24.1	28.3	116	2298	25.4	12.3	122	1822	25.7	9.7	123	1070	20.8	5.7	100
12-17 Years	17576	5247	23.8	29.9	122	2421	26.8	13.8	137	1813	25.6	10.3	131	905	17.6	5.1	90
White	75919	19224	87.3	25.3	103	7877	87.1	10.4	103	6285	88.7	8.3	105	4636	90.3	6.1	107
Black	10706	1801	8.2	16.8	69	853	9.4	8.0	79	493	7.0	4.6	58	*295	5.8	2.8	48
Spanish Speaking	8317	2029	9.2	24.4	100	649	7.2	7.8	77	613	8.6	7.4	93	*539	10.5	6.5	113
Home Owned	60568	15620	71.0	25.8	105	6451	71.3	10.7	106	5115	72.2	8.4	107	3687	71.8	6.1	106

Spring 1998

	TOTAL U.S. '000	LOW FAT A '000	B % DOWN	C % ACROSS	D INDEX	NON FAT/FAT FREE A '000	B % DOWN	C % ACROSS	D INDEX	BORDEN A '000	B % DOWN	C % ACROSS	D INDEX	BREYERS BLENDED A '000	B % DOWN	C % ACROSS	D INDEX
BASE: FEMALE HOMEMAKERS																	
All Female Homemakers	89789	21717	100.0	24.2	100	11940	100.0	13.3	100	1639	100.0	1.8	100	3645	100.0	4.1	100
Men	89789	21717	100.0	24.2	100	11940	100.0	13.3	100	1639	100.0	1.8	100	3645	100.0	4.1	100
Women	39088	7856	36.2	20.1	83	4891	41.0	12.5	94	755	46.1	1.9	106	1554	42.6	4.0	98
Household Heads	89789	21717	100.0	24.2	100	11940	100.0	13.3	100	1639	100.0	1.8	100	3645	100.0	4.1	100
Homemakers	89789	21717	100.0	24.2	100	11940	100.0	13.3	100	1639	100.0	1.8	100	3645	100.0	4.1	100
Graduated College	18398	6013	27.7	32.7	135	3474	29.1	18.9	142	*311	19.0	1.7	93	844	23.2	4.6	113
Attended College	24064	6421	29.6	26.7	110	3679	30.8	15.3	115	*395	24.1	1.6	90	1162	31.9	4.8	119
Graduated High School	31577	6742	31.0	21.4	88	3564	29.8	11.3	85	663	40.5	2.1	115	1233	33.8	3.9	96
Did not Graduate High School	15751	2541	11.7	16.1	67	1223	10.2	7.8	58	*270	16.4	1.7	94	*407	11.2	2.6	64
18-24	7780	1821	8.4	23.4	97	979	8.2	12.6	95	*159	9.7	2.0	112	*414	11.3	5.3	131
25-34	18631	5201	23.9	27.9	115	2217	18.6	11.9	90	*403	24.6	2.2	119	877	24.1	4.7	116
35-44	20651	5969	27.5	28.9	120	3252	27.2	15.7	118	*438	26.7	2.1	116	871	23.9	4.2	104
45-54	15603	4149	19.1	26.6	110	2797	23.4	17.9	135	*295	18.0	1.9	104	802	22.0	5.1	127
55-64	10181	2200	10.1	21.6	89	1284	10.8	12.6	95	*110	6.7	1.1	59	*312	8.6	3.1	76
65 or over	16943	2378	11.0	14.0	58	1411	11.8	8.3	63	*234	14.3	1.4	76	370	10.1	2.2	54
18-34	26410	7021	32.3	26.6	110	3197	26.8	12.1	91	562	34.3	2.1	116	1291	35.4	4.9	120
18-49	55960	15698	72.3	28.1	116	8227	68.9	14.7	111	1158	70.6	2.1	113	2604	71.4	4.7	115
25-54	54886	15318	70.5	27.9	115	8266	69.2	15.1	113	1136	69.3	2.1	113	2550	69.9	4.6	114
Employed Full Time	41154	10925	50.3	26.5	110	6424	53.8	15.6	117	819	50.0	2.0	109	1802	49.4	4.4	108
Part-time	11398	3367	15.5	29.5	122	1652	13.8	14.5	109	*171	10.4	1.5	82	608	16.7	5.3	131
Sole Wage Earner	14006	2717	12.5	19.4	80	1770	14.8	12.6	95	*289	17.7	2.1	113	503	13.8	3.6	88
Not Employed	37237	7426	34.2	19.9	82	3864	32.4	10.4	78	649	39.6	1.7	95	1234	33.9	3.3	82
Professional	9642	3045	14.0	31.6	131	2033	17.0	21.1	159	*183	11.1	1.9	104	442	12.1	4.6	113
Executive/Admin./Managerial	7128	2262	10.4	31.7	131	1366	11.4	19.2	144	*103	6.3	1.4	79	*396	10.9	5.6	137
Clerical/Sales/Technical	20870	5597	25.8	26.8	111	3050	25.5	14.6	110	*495	30.2	2.4	130	951	26.1	4.6	112
Precision/Crafts/Repair	1102	*285	1.3	25.8	107	*162	1.4	14.7	110	–	–	–	–	*35	1.0	3.2	79
Other Employed	13810	3103	14.3	22.5	93	1466	12.3	10.6	80	*210	12.8	1.5	83	586	16.1	4.2	104
H/D Income $75,000 or More	15443	4874	22.4	31.6	130	3090	25.9	20.0	150	*242	14.8	1.6	86	644	17.7	4.2	103
$60,000 - 74,999	8775	2681	12.3	30.6	126	1545	12.9	17.6	132	*172	10.5	2.0	108	596	16.3	6.8	167
$50,000 - 59,999	7850	2507	11.5	31.9	132	1390	11.6	17.7	133	*130	7.9	1.7	90	393	10.8	5.0	123
$40,000 - 49,999	9648	2671	12.3	27.7	114	1160	9.7	12.0	90	*206	12.6	2.1	117	579	15.9	6.0	148
$30,000 - 39,999	11493	2699	12.4	23.5	97	1516	12.7	13.2	99	*218	13.3	1.9	103	470	12.9	4.1	99
$20,000 - 29,999	12298	2619	12.1	21.3	88	1173	9.8	9.5	72	*208	12.7	1.7	93	486	13.3	3.4	83
$10,000 - 19,999	14330	2311	10.6	16.1	67	1256	10.5	8.8	66	*252	15.4	1.8	97	473	13.0	3.3	81
Less than $10,000	9953	1355	6.2	13.6	56	811	6.8	8.1	61	*209	12.8	2.1	115	*264	7.2	2.7	65
Census Region: North East	18074	4761	21.9	26.3	109	2676	22.4	14.8	111	*199	12.1	1.1	60	1293	35.5	7.2	176
North Central	20967	5367	24.7	25.6	106	2712	22.7	12.9	97	*358	21.8	1.7	93	837	23.0	4.0	98
South	32182	6259	28.8	19.4	80	3594	30.1	11.2	84	835	50.9	2.6	142	1397	38.3	4.3	107
West	18567	5330	24.5	28.7	119	2958	24.8	15.9	120	*247	15.1	1.3	73	*118	3.2	0.6	16
Marketing Reg.: New England	4705	1371	6.3	29.1	121	902	7.6	19.2	144	*8	0.5	0.2	10	*360	9.9	7.6	188
Middle Atlantic	15444	3746	17.3	24.3	100	2045	17.1	13.2	100	*214	13.1	1.4	76	1061	29.1	6.9	169
East Central	11580	3057	14.1	26.4	109	1480	12.4	12.8	96	*184	11.2	1.6	87	471	12.9	4.1	100
West Central	13616	3627	16.7	26.6	110	1697	14.2	12.5	94	*185	11.3	1.4	74	407	11.2	3.0	74
South East	18271	3914	18.0	21.4	89	2095	17.5	11.5	86	*511	31.2	2.8	153	907	24.9	5.0	122
South West	10224	1627	7.5	15.9	66	1075	9.0	10.5	79	*300	18.3	2.9	161	*329	9.0	3.2	79
Pacific	15950	4373	20.1	27.4	113	2646	22.2	16.6	125	*237	14.4	1.5	81	*111	3.0	0.7	17
County Size A	35658	8930	41.1	25.0	104	5411	45.3	15.2	114	629	38.4	1.8	97	1598	43.8	4.5	110
County Size B	27101	7190	33.1	26.5	110	3738	31.3	13.8	104	*500	30.5	1.8	101	1122	30.8	4.1	102
County Size C	13387	2882	13.3	21.5	89	1553	13.0	11.6	87	*263	16.0	2.0	108	*573	15.7	4.3	105
County Size D	13644	2715	12.5	19.9	82	1238	10.4	9.1	68	*247	15.1	1.8	99	*353	9.7	2.6	64
MSA Central City	29169	7005	32.3	24.0	99	3677	30.8	12.6	95	547	33.4	1.9	103	1150	31.6	3.9	97
MSA Suburban	42524	10815	49.8	25.4	105	6489	54.3	15.3	115	756	46.2	1.8	97	1790	49.1	4.2	104
Non-MSA	18096	3897	17.9	21.5	89	1775	14.9	9.8	74	*336	20.5	1.9	102	705	19.3	3.9	96
Single	14479	3036	14.0	21.0	87	1859	15.6	12.8	97	*303	18.5	2.1	115	682	18.7	4.7	116
Married	51935	14692	67.7	28.3	117	7911	66.3	15.2	115	934	57.0	1.8	99	2345	64.3	4.5	111
Other	23376	3989	18.4	17.1	71	2171	18.2	9.3	70	401	24.5	1.7	94	618	16.9	2.6	65
Parents	35881	10910	50.2	30.4	126	5161	43.2	14.4	108	817	49.9	2.3	125	1588	43.6	4.4	109
Working Parents	24725	7848	36.1	31.7	131	3868	32.4	15.6	118	702	42.8	2.8	155	1107	30.4	4.5	110
Household Size: 1 Person	15017	2548	11.7	17.0	70	1602	13.4	10.7	80	*211	12.9	1.4	77	513	14.1	3.4	84
2 Persons	28950	6192	28.5	21.4	88	3927	32.9	13.6	102	488	29.8	1.7	92	1211	33.2	4.2	103
3 or More	45822	12978	59.8	28.3	117	6411	53.7	14.0	105	940	57.3	2.1	112	1922	52.7	4.2	103
Any Child in Household	39070	11531	53.1	29.5	122	5542	46.4	14.2	107	835	50.9	2.1	117	1768	48.5	4.5	111
Under 2 Years	6763	1909	8.8	28.2	117	861	7.2	12.7	96	*97	5.9	1.4	79	*391	10.7	5.8	142
2-5 Years	14794	4425	20.4	29.9	124	1742	14.6	11.8	89	*235	14.3	1.6	87	625	17.1	4.2	104
6-11 Years	18719	5498	25.3	29.4	121	2525	21.1	13.5	101	*435	26.6	2.3	127	787	21.6	4.2	104
12-17 Years	17576	5090	23.4	29.0	120	2858	23.9	16.3	122	*473	28.8	2.7	147	806	22.1	4.6	113
White	75919	19032	87.6	25.1	104	10626	89.0	14.0	105	1213	74.0	1.6	87	3216	88.2	4.2	104
Black	10706	1533	7.1	14.3	59	980	8.2	9.2	69	*377	23.0	3.5	193	*317	8.7	3.0	73
Spanish Speaking	8317	2052	9.5	24.7	102	842	7.1	10.1	76	*170	10.4	2.0	110	*354	9.7	4.3	105
Home Owned	60568	15662	72.1	25.9	107	8715	73.0	14.4	108	1124	68.6	1.9	102	2537	69.6	4.2	103

Spring 1998

184 YOGURT

BASE: FEMALE HOMEMAKERS	TOTAL U.S. '000	BREYERS FRUIT ON THE BOTTOM A '000	B % DOWN	C % ACROSS	D INDEX	BREYERS LIGHT A '000	B % DOWN	C % ACROSS	D INDEX	COLOMBO A '000	B % DOWN	C % ACROSS	D INDEX	DANNON CHUNKY FRUIT A '000	B % DOWN	C % ACROSS	D INDEX
All Female Homemakers	89789	3955	100.0	4.4	100	2293	100.0	2.6	100	2749	100.0	3.1	100	3776	100.0	4.2	100
Men	–	–	–	–	–	–	–	–	–	–	–	–	–	–	–	–	–
Women	89789	3955	100.0	4.4	100	2293	100.0	2.6	100	2749	100.0	3.1	100	3776	100.0	4.2	100
Household Heads	39088	1707	43.1	4.4	99	735	32.1	1.9	74	1054	38.3	2.7	88	1727	45.7	4.4	105
Homemakers	89789	3955	100.0	4.4	100	2293	100.0	2.6	100	2749	100.0	3.1	100	3776	100.0	4.2	100
Graduated College	18398	984	24.9	5.4	121	514	22.4	2.8	109	808	29.4	4.4	143	730	19.3	4.0	94
Attended College	24064	1085	27.4	4.5	102	760	33.2	3.2	124	873	31.8	3.6	119	1200	31.8	5.0	119
Graduated High School	31577	1372	34.7	4.3	99	790	34.4	2.5	98	860	31.3	2.7	89	1357	35.9	4.3	102
Did not Graduate High School	15751	515	13.0	3.3	74	*229	10.0	1.5	57	*207	7.5	1.3	43	489	12.9	3.1	74
18-24	7780	*343	8.7	4.4	100	*223	9.7	2.9	112	*203	7.4	2.6	85	*252	6.7	3.2	77
25-34	18631	624	15.8	3.3	76	*439	19.2	2.4	92	610	22.2	3.3	107	745	19.7	4.0	95
35-44	20651	892	22.6	4.3	98	651	28.4	3.2	123	670	24.4	3.2	106	1090	28.9	5.3	126
45-54	15603	1059	26.8	6.8	154	490	21.4	3.1	123	649	23.6	4.2	136	840	22.2	5.4	128
55-64	10181	455	11.5	4.5	101	*213	9.3	2.1	82	*157	5.7	1.5	50	371	9.8	3.6	87
65 or over	16943	583	14.7	3.4	78	*277	12.1	1.6	64	459	16.7	2.7	89	478	12.7	2.8	67
18-34	26410	966	24.4	3.7	83	663	28.9	2.5	98	813	29.6	3.1	101	996	26.4	3.8	90
18-49	55960	2512	63.5	4.5	102	1692	73.8	3.0	118	1879	68.4	3.4	110	2666	70.6	4.8	113
25-54	54886	2575	65.1	4.7	106	1580	68.9	2.9	113	1929	70.2	3.5	115	2675	70.8	4.9	116
Employed Full Time	41154	1770	44.7	4.3	98	1276	55.6	3.1	121	1363	49.6	3.3	108	1762	46.7	4.3	102
Part-time	11398	595	15.1	5.2	119	*261	11.4	2.3	90	496	18.0	4.4	142	571	15.1	5.0	119
Sole Wage Earner	14006	458	11.6	3.3	74	287	12.5	2.1	80	439	16.0	3.1	102	428	11.3	3.1	73
Not Employed	37237	1590	40.2	4.3	97	756	33.0	2.0	80	890	32.4	2.4	78	1442	38.2	3.9	92
Professional	9642	593	15.0	6.1	140	*390	17.0	4.0	158	545	19.8	5.7	185	359	9.5	3.7	89
Executive/Admin./Managerial	7128	*329	8.3	4.6	105	*170	7.4	2.4	94	*257	9.3	3.6	118	*209	5.5	2.9	70
Clerical/Sales/Technical	20870	875	22.1	4.2	95	553	24.1	2.6	104	648	23.6	3.1	102	1066	28.2	5.1	121
Precision/Crafts/Repair	1102	*42	1.1	3.8	86	*9	0.4	0.8	32	*16	0.6	1.5	48	*66	1.8	6.0	143
Other Employed	13810	527	13.3	3.8	87	*415	18.1	3.0	118	*392	14.3	2.8	93	634	16.8	4.6	109
H/D Income $75,000 or More	15443	805	20.4	5.2	118	*447	19.5	2.9	113	847	30.8	5.5	179	777	20.6	5.0	120
$60,000 - 74,999	8775	548	13.9	6.2	142	*304	13.3	3.5	136	338	12.3	3.9	126	363	9.6	4.1	98
$50,000 - 59,999	7850	395	10.0	5.0	114	*351	15.3	4.5	175	*199	7.2	2.5	83	407	10.8	5.2	123
$40,000 - 49,999	9648	*428	10.8	4.4	101	*253	11.0	2.6	103	331	12.0	3.4	112	461	12.2	4.8	114
$30,000 - 39,999	11493	414	10.5	3.6	82	*249	10.8	2.2	85	296	10.8	2.6	84	480	12.7	4.2	99
$20,000 - 29,999	12298	581	14.7	4.7	107	*194	8.5	1.6	62	*327	11.9	2.7	87	451	11.9	3.7	87
$10,000 - 19,999	14330	524	13.3	3.7	83	*365	15.9	2.5	100	*311	11.3	2.2	71	572	15.2	4.0	95
Less than $10,000	9953	*259	6.6	2.6	59	*130	5.7	1.3	51	*99	3.6	1.0	33	*266	7.0	2.7	64
Census Region: North East	18074	1466	37.1	8.1	184	675	29.4	3.7	146	1397	50.8	7.7	252	1038	27.5	5.7	137
North Central	20967	725	18.3	3.5	78	504	22.2	2.4	95	591	21.5	2.8	92	700	18.5	3.3	79
South	32182	1550	39.2	4.8	109	958	41.8	3.0	117	356	12.9	1.1	36	1233	32.6	3.8	91
West	18567	*215	5.4	1.2	26	*152	6.6	0.8	32	*405	14.7	2.2	71	806	21.3	4.3	103
Marketing Reg.: New England	4705	*234	5.9	5.0	113	*171	7.5	3.6	143	554	20.1	11.8	385	*199	5.3	4.2	101
Middle Atlantic	15444	1333	33.7	8.6	196	563	24.6	3.6	143	970	35.3	6.3	205	999	26.5	6.5	154
East Central	11580	538	13.6	4.6	105	*265	11.6	2.3	90	*207	7.5	1.8	58	385	10.2	3.3	79
West Central	13616	339	8.6	2.5	57	*306	13.3	2.2	88	411	14.9	3.0	99	*348	9.2	2.6	61
South East	18271	1068	27.0	5.8	133	704	30.7	3.9	151	*135	4.9	0.7	24	630	16.7	3.4	82
South West	10224	*256	6.5	2.5	57	*139	6.1	1.4	53	*94	3.4	0.9	30	448	11.9	4.4	104
Pacific	15950	*187	4.7	1.2	27	*145	6.3	0.9	36	*378	13.8	2.4	77	766	20.3	4.8	114
County Size A	35658	1768	44.7	5.0	113	1120	48.9	3.1	123	1430	52.0	4.0	131	2228	59.0	6.2	149
County Size B	27101	1462	37.0	5.4	122	807	35.2	3.0	117	873	31.8	3.2	105	878	23.3	3.2	77
County Size C	13387	502	12.7	3.7	85	*208	9.1	1.6	61	*387	14.1	2.9	95	447	11.8	3.3	79
County Size D	13644	*222	5.6	1.6	37	*158	6.9	1.2	45	*58	2.1	0.4	14	*223	5.9	1.6	39
MSA Central City	29169	1456	36.8	5.0	113	876	38.2	3.0	118	713	25.9	2.4	80	1316	34.9	4.5	107
MSA Suburban	42524	2088	52.8	4.9	111	1189	51.8	2.8	109	1728	62.9	4.1	133	2026	53.7	4.8	113
Non-MSA	18096	*411	10.4	2.3	52	*228	9.9	1.3	49	*308	11.2	1.7	56	*434	11.5	2.4	57
Single	14479	558	14.1	3.9	87	353	15.4	2.4	96	519	18.9	3.6	117	558	14.8	3.9	92
Married	51935	2557	64.6	4.9	112	1579	68.8	3.0	119	1773	64.5	3.4	112	2286	60.5	4.4	105
Other	23376	841	21.3	3.6	82	361	15.7	1.5	60	457	16.6	2.0	64	932	24.7	4.0	95
Parents	35881	1680	42.5	4.7	106	887	38.7	2.5	97	1042	37.9	2.9	95	1665	44.1	4.6	110
Working Parents	24725	1193	30.2	4.8	109	675	29.4	2.7	107	772	28.1	3.1	102	1179	31.2	4.8	113
Household Size: 1 Person	15017	467	11.8	3.1	71	264	11.5	1.8	69	416	15.1	2.8	91	523	13.8	3.5	83
2 Persons	28950	1305	33.0	4.5	102	794	34.6	2.7	107	841	30.6	2.9	95	1116	29.6	3.9	92
3 or More	45822	2183	55.2	4.8	108	1235	53.9	2.7	106	1491	54.3	3.3	106	2138	56.6	4.7	111
Any Child in Household	39070	1842	46.6	4.7	107	932	40.6	2.4	93	1212	44.1	3.1	101	1864	49.4	4.8	113
Under 2 Years	6763	*214	5.4	3.2	72	*163	7.1	2.4	94	*106	3.9	1.6	51	*223	5.9	3.3	78
2-5 Years	14794	738	18.7	5.0	113	*299	13.1	2.0	79	*458	16.7	3.1	101	459	12.2	3.1	74
6-11 Years	18719	930	23.5	5.0	113	574	25.0	3.1	120	607	22.1	3.2	106	866	22.9	4.6	110
12-17 Years	17576	784	19.8	4.5	101	*543	23.7	3.1	121	582	21.2	3.3	108	970	25.7	5.5	131
White	75919	3181	80.4	4.2	95	1913	83.4	2.5	99	2468	89.8	3.3	106	3083	81.7	4.1	97
Black	10706	565	14.3	5.3	120	*259	11.3	2.4	95	*173	6.3	1.6	53	*499	13.2	4.7	111
Spanish Speaking	8317	*365	9.2	4.4	100	*222	9.7	2.7	105	*181	6.6	2.2	71	633	16.8	7.6	181
Home Owned	60568	2758	69.7	4.6	103	1575	68.7	2.6	102	1966	71.5	3.2	106	2575	68.2	4.3	101

Spring 1998

BASE: FEMALE HOMEMAKERS	TOTAL U.S. '000	DANNON CLASSIC FLAVORS A '000	B % DOWN	C % ACROSS	D INDEX	DANNON DANIMALS A '000	B % DOWN	C % ACROSS	D INDEX	DANNON DOUBLE DELIGHTS A '000	B % DOWN	C % ACROSS	D INDEX	DANNON FRUIT ON THE BOTTOM A '000	B % DOWN	C % ACROSS	D INDEX
All Female Homemakers	89789	3882	100.0	4.3	100	1331	100.0	1.5	100	2560	100.0	2.9	100	5612	100.0	6.3	100
Men	-	-	-	-	-	-	-	-	-	-	-	-	-	-	-	-	-	-
Women	89789	3882	100.0	4.3	100	1331	100.0	1.5	100	2560	100.0	2.9	100	5612	100.0	6.3	100
Household Heads	39088	1521	39.2	3.9	90	574	43.1	1.5	99	950	37.1	2.4	85	2366	42.2	6.1	97
Homemakers	89789	3882	100.0	4.3	100	1331	100.0	1.5	100	2560	100.0	2.9	100	5612	100.0	6.3	100
Graduated College	18398	930	24.0	5.1	117	477	35.9	2.6	175	563	22.0	3.1	107	1475	26.3	8.0	128
Attended College	24064	1244	32.1	5.2	120	*325	24.4	1.4	91	886	34.6	3.7	129	1698	30.3	7.1	113
Graduated High School	31577	1198	30.9	3.8	88	*356	26.8	1.1	76	753	29.4	2.4	84	1844	32.9	5.8	93
Did not Graduate High School	15751	*510	13.1	3.2	75	*173	13.0	1.1	74	*358	14.0	2.3	80	596	10.6	3.8	61
18-24	7780	*442	11.4	5.7	131	*38	2.9	0.5	33	*249	9.7	3.2	112	*427	7.6	5.5	88
25-34	18631	652	16.8	3.5	81	*527	39.6	2.8	191	565	22.1	3.0	106	1124	20.0	6.0	97
35-44	20651	1271	32.7	6.2	142	506	38.0	2.5	165	754	29.5	3.7	128	1340	23.9	6.5	104
45-54	15603	803	20.7	5.1	119	*189	14.2	1.2	82	528	20.6	3.4	119	1417	25.3	9.1	145
55-64	10181	*336	8.6	3.3	76	*22	1.6	0.2	14	*218	8.5	2.1	75	568	10.1	5.6	89
65 or over	16943	378	9.7	2.2	52	*50	3.7	0.3	20	*247	9.6	1.5	51	735	13.1	4.3	69
18-34	26410	1094	28.2	4.1	96	565	42.4	2.1	144	813	31.8	3.1	108	1552	27.6	5.9	94
18-49	55960	2886	74.4	5.2	119	1174	88.2	2.1	141	1911	74.6	3.4	120	3832	68.3	6.8	110
25-54	54886	2726	70.2	5.0	115	1222	91.8	2.2	150	1847	72.1	3.4	118	3881	69.2	7.1	113
Employed Full Time	41154	1842	47.5	4.5	104	647	48.6	1.6	106	1462	57.1	3.6	125	2849	50.8	6.9	111
Part-time	11398	546	14.1	4.8	111	*259	19.4	2.3	153	*261	10.2	2.3	80	945	16.8	8.3	133
Sole Wage Earner	14006	490	12.6	3.5	81	*140	10.5	1.0	67	436	17.0	3.1	109	764	13.6	5.5	87
Not Employed	37237	1493	38.5	4.0	93	425	31.9	1.1	77	837	32.7	2.2	79	1818	32.4	4.9	78
Professional	9642	553	14.2	5.7	133	*169	12.7	1.8	118	*328	12.8	3.4	119	923	16.4	9.6	153
Executive/Admin./Managerial	7128	*309	7.9	4.3	100	*185	13.9	2.6	175	*142	5.5	2.0	70	*445	7.9	6.2	100
Clerical/Sales/Technical	20870	961	24.8	4.6	107	*350	26.3	1.7	113	837	32.7	4.0	141	1611	28.7	7.7	123
Precision/Crafts/Repair	1102	*77	2.0	7.0	161	*50	3.8	4.6	309	*6	0.2	0.5	19	*118	2.1	10.7	172
Other Employed	13810	489	12.6	3.5	82	*152	11.4	1.1	74	*409	16.0	3.0	104	697	12.4	5.0	81
H/D Income $75,000 or More	15443	766	19.7	5.0	115	*339	25.4	2.2	148	597	23.3	3.9	136	1410	25.1	9.1	146
$60,000 - 74,999	8775	569	14.7	6.5	150	*179	13.4	2.0	137	*306	11.9	3.5	122	647	11.5	7.4	118
$50,000 - 59,999	7850	*385	9.9	4.9	113	*125	9.4	1.6	107	*254	9.9	3.2	112	544	9.7	6.9	111
$40,000 - 49,999	9648	557	14.3	5.8	133	*201	15.1	2.1	140	*231	9.0	2.4	84	713	12.7	7.4	118
$30,000 - 39,999	11493	441	11.4	3.8	89	*222	16.7	1.9	130	*322	12.6	2.8	98	608	10.8	5.3	85
$20,000 - 29,999	12298	449	11.6	3.7	84	*93	7.0	0.8	51	*326	12.7	2.7	93	701	12.5	5.7	91
$10,000 - 19,999	14330	*423	10.9	3.0	68	*133	10.0	0.9	62	*347	13.6	2.4	85	647	11.5	4.5	72
Less than $10,000	9953	*292	7.5	2.9	68	*41	3.0	0.4	27	*180	7.0	1.8	63	*343	6.1	3.4	55
Census Region: North East	18074	931	24.0	5.2	119	350	26.3	1.9	131	523	20.4	2.9	102	1386	24.7	7.7	123
North Central	20967	1275	32.8	6.1	141	*309	23.2	1.5	99	904	35.3	4.3	151	1450	25.8	6.9	111
South	32182	747	19.2	2.3	54	*439	33.0	1.4	92	679	26.5	2.1	74	1741	31.0	5.4	87
West	18567	929	23.9	5.0	116	*233	17.5	1.3	85	453	17.7	2.4	86	1035	18.4	5.6	89
Marketing Reg.: New England	4705	*201	5.2	4.3	99	*156	11.7	3.3	224	*85	3.3	1.8	63	*306	5.5	6.5	104
Middle Atlantic	15444	871	22.4	5.6	130	*244	18.3	1.6	107	520	20.3	3.4	118	1244	22.2	8.1	129
East Central	11580	681	17.5	5.9	136	*185	13.9	1.6	108	602	23.5	5.2	182	878	15.6	7.6	121
West Central	13616	731	18.8	5.4	124	*124	9.3	0.9	62	*367	14.3	2.7	94	906	16.2	6.7	107
South East	18271	*371	9.5	2.0	47	*351	26.4	1.9	130	*262	10.2	1.4	50	929	16.6	5.1	81
South West	10224	*240	6.2	2.3	54	*37	2.8	0.4	25	*313	12.2	3.1	108	533	9.5	5.2	83
Pacific	15950	787	20.3	4.9	114	*233	17.5	1.5	99	411	16.1	2.6	90	816	14.5	5.1	82
County Size A	35658	1645	42.4	4.6	107	655	49.2	1.8	124	1214	47.4	3.4	119	2538	45.2	7.1	114
County Size B	27401	1402	36.1	5.2	120	*499	37.5	1.8	124	888	34.7	3.3	115	1721	30.7	6.4	102
County Size C	13387	*414	10.7	3.1	72	*131	9.9	1.0	66	*288	11.2	2.1	75	700	12.5	5.2	84
County Size D	13644	*420	10.8	3.1	71	*46	3.4	0.3	23	*170	6.6	1.2	44	653	11.6	4.8	77
MSA Central City	29169	1293	33.3	4.4	103	*491	36.8	1.7	113	1083	42.3	3.7	130	1902	33.9	6.5	104
MSA Suburban	42524	1987	51.2	4.7	108	718	54.0	1.7	114	1237	48.3	2.9	102	2801	49.9	6.6	105
Non-MSA	18096	*602	15.5	3.3	77	*122	9.2	0.7	46	*240	9.4	1.3	46	909	16.2	5.0	80
Single	14479	708	18.2	4.9	113	*51	3.8	0.4	24	487	19.0	3.4	118	919	16.4	6.3	102
Married	51935	2473	63.7	4.8	110	1006	75.6	1.9	131	1547	60.4	3.0	105	3574	63.7	6.9	110
Other	23376	701	18.1	3.0	69	*274	20.6	1.2	79	525	20.5	2.2	79	1120	19.9	4.8	77
Parents	35881	2012	51.8	5.6	130	1107	83.1	3.1	208	1343	52.5	3.7	131	2589	46.1	7.2	115
Working Parents	24725	1408	36.3	5.7	132	769	57.7	3.1	210	993	38.8	4.0	141	1996	35.6	8.1	129
Household Size: 1 Person	15017	381	9.8	2.5	59	*19	1.4	0.1	8	315	12.3	2.1	74	772	13.8	5.1	82
2 Persons	28950	1010	26.0	3.5	81	*119	8.9	0.4	28	670	26.2	2.3	81	1742	31.0	6.0	96
3 or More	45822	2491	64.2	5.4	126	1194	89.7	2.6	176	1575	61.5	3.4	121	3098	55.2	6.8	108
Any Child in Household	39070	2209	56.9	5.7	131	1207	90.7	3.1	208	1415	55.3	3.6	127	2755	49.1	7.1	113
Under 2 Years	6763	*368	9.5	5.4	126	*187	14.1	2.8	187	*188	7.3	2.8	97	*286	5.1	4.2	68
2-5 Years	14794	*779	20.1	5.3	122	579	43.5	3.9	264	469	18.3	3.2	111	1070	19.1	7.2	116
6-11 Years	18719	1090	28.1	5.8	135	656	49.3	3.5	236	701	27.4	3.7	131	1379	24.6	7.4	118
12-17 Years	17576	1151	29.7	6.5	151	*479	36.0	2.7	184	763	29.8	4.3	152	1333	23.7	7.6	121
White	75919	3243	83.5	4.3	99	1174	88.2	1.5	104	2065	80.7	2.7	95	4769	85.0	6.3	100
Black	10706	*360	9.3	3.4	78	*97	7.3	0.9	62	*400	15.6	3.7	131	680	12.1	6.4	102
Spanish Speaking	8317	*347	8.9	4.2	97	*176	13.2	2.1	143	*243	9.5	2.9	102	*412	7.3	5.0	79
Home Owned	60568	2679	69.0	4.4	102	992	74.5	1.6	110	1790	69.9	3.0	104	3996	71.2	6.6	106

Spring 1998

186 YOGURT

BASE: FEMALE HOMEMAKERS	TOTAL U.S. '000	DANNON LIGHT A '000	B % DOWN	C % ACROSS	D INDEX	DANNON SPRINKL'INS A '000	B % DOWN	C % ACROSS	D INDEX	JELL-O KID PACK A '000	B % DOWN	C % ACROSS	D INDEX	LA YOGURT A '000	B % DOWN	C % ACROSS	D INDEX
All Female Homemakers	89789	8187	100.0	9.1	100	1183	100.0	1.3	100	1993	100.0	2.2	100	1138	100.0	1.3	100
Men	-	-	-	-	-	-	-	-	-	-	-	-	-	-	-	-	-
Women	89789	8187	100.0	9.1	100	1183	100.0	1.3	100	1993	100.0	2.2	100	1138	100.0	1.3	100
Household Heads	39088	3197	39.1	8.2	90	508	42.9	1.3	99	840	42.1	2.1	97	480	42.2	1.2	97
Homemakers	89789	8187	100.0	9.1	100	1183	100.0	1.3	100	1993	100.0	2.2	100	1138	100.0	1.3	100
Graduated College	18398	2518	30.8	13.7	150	363	30.7	2.0	150	376	18.9	2.0	92	292	25.6	1.6	125
Attended College	24064	2571	31.4	10.7	117	*258	21.8	1.1	81	556	27.9	2.3	104	*293	25.8	1.2	96
Graduated High School	31577	2344	28.6	7.4	81	*416	35.2	1.3	100	747	37.5	2.4	107	369	32.4	1.2	92
Did not Graduate High School	15751	754	9.2	4.8	53	*147	12.4	0.9	71	*313	15.7	2.0	90	*184	16.2	1.2	92
18-24	7780	621	7.6	8.0	88	*51	4.3	0.7	50	*121	6.1	1.6	70	*69	6.1	0.9	70
25-34	18631	1559	19.0	8.4	92	*341	28.8	1.8	139	683	34.3	3.7	165	*371	32.6	2.0	157
35-44	20651	2124	25.9	10.3	113	386	32.7	1.9	142	674	33.8	3.3	147	*255	22.4	1.2	98
45-54	15603	1753	21.4	11.2	123	*237	20.0	1.5	115	*304	15.3	1.9	88	*227	20.0	1.5	115
55-64	10181	1052	12.8	10.3	113	*36	3.1	0.4	27	*88	4.4	0.9	39	*108	9.5	1.1	84
65 or over	16943	1077	13.2	6.4	70	*131	11.1	0.8	59	*123	6.2	0.7	33	*107	9.4	0.6	50
18-34	26410	2181	26.6	8.3	91	*392	33.1	1.5	113	804	40.4	3.0	137	*440	38.7	1.7	132
18-49	55960	5463	66.7	9.8	107	928	78.4	1.7	126	1642	82.4	2.9	132	829	72.8	1.5	117
25-54	54886	5436	66.4	9.9	109	965	81.5	1.8	133	1662	83.4	3.0	136	854	75.0	1.6	123
Employed Full Time	41154	4466	54.6	10.9	119	541	45.7	1.3	100	806	40.5	2.0	88	620	54.5	1.5	119
Part-time	11398	1054	12.9	9.2	101	*198	16.8	1.7	132	*321	16.1	2.8	127	*142	12.5	1.2	99
Sole Wage Earner	14006	1134	13.8	8.1	89	*129	10.9	0.9	70	*229	11.5	1.6	74	*267	23.5	1.9	151
Not Employed	37237	2666	32.6	7.2	79	444	37.5	1.2	90	865	43.4	2.3	105	376	33.0	1.0	80
Professional	9642	1401	17.1	14.5	159	*228	19.3	2.4	180	*189	9.5	2.0	88	*197	17.3	2.0	161
Executive/Admin./Managerial	7128	1101	13.4	15.4	169	*110	9.3	1.5	117	*150	7.5	2.1	95	*72	6.3	1.0	79
Clerical/Sales/Technical	20870	1907	23.3	9.1	100	*240	20.3	1.1	87	506	25.4	2.4	109	*250	22.0	1.2	95
Precision/Crafts/Repair	1102	*82	1.0	7.5	82	*6	0.5	0.6	42	*29	1.5	2.7	120	*6	0.5	0.5	40
Other Employed	13810	1029	12.6	7.5	82	*155	13.1	1.1	85	*253	12.7	1.8	83	*238	20.9	1.7	136
H/D Income $75,000 or More	15443	2297	28.1	14.9	163	*319	27.0	2.1	157	*372	18.6	2.4	108	*168	14.8	1.1	86
$60,000 - 74,999	8775	1015	12.4	11.6	127	*202	17.1	2.3	175	*241	12.1	2.7	124	*156	13.7	1.8	141
$50,000 - 59,999	7850	941	11.5	12.0	131	*101	8.5	1.3	97	*195	9.8	2.5	112	*125	10.9	1.6	125
$40,000 - 49,999	9648	805	9.8	8.3	91	*118	9.9	1.2	93	*194	9.7	2.0	90	*259	22.8	2.7	212
$30,000 - 39,999	11493	949	11.6	8.3	91	*147	12.4	1.3	97	*227	11.4	2.0	89	*76	6.7	0.7	52
$20,000 - 29,999	12298	930	11.4	7.6	83	*108	9.1	0.9	67	*302	15.2	2.5	111	*75	6.6	0.6	48
$10,000 - 19,999	14330	760	9.3	5.3	58	*125	10.6	0.9	66	*243	12.2	1.7	76	*209	18.3	1.5	115
Less than $10,000	9953	491	6.0	4.9	54	*63	5.3	0.6	48	*219	11.0	2.2	99	*70	6.2	0.7	56
Census Region: North East	18074	2210	27.0	12.2	134	*180	15.2	1.0	75	493	24.7	2.7	123	752	66.1	4.2	328
North Central	20967	1977	24.2	9.4	103	332	28.0	1.6	120	638	32.0	3.0	137	*22	1.9	0.1	8
South	32182	2350	28.7	7.3	80	*337	28.5	1.0	80	631	31.7	2.0	88	*264	23.2	0.8	65
West	18567	1649	20.1	8.9	97	*335	28.3	1.8	137	*231	11.6	1.2	56	*100	8.8	0.5	43
Marketing Reg.: New England	4705	496	6.1	10.5	116	*14	1.2	0.3	23	*154	7.7	3.3	148	*42	3.7	0.9	70
Middle Atlantic	15444	1972	24.1	12.8	140	*201	17.0	1.3	99	355	17.8	2.3	103	777	68.3	5.0	397
East Central	11580	912	11.1	7.9	86	*153	13.0	1.3	101	376	18.9	3.2	146	*8	0.7	0.1	5
West Central	13616	1491	18.2	11.0	120	*216	18.3	1.6	121	*276	13.8	2.0	91	*14	1.2	0.1	8
South East	18271	1434	17.5	7.9	86	*239	20.2	1.3	99	*469	23.5	2.6	116	*180	15.8	1.0	78
South West	10224	593	7.2	5.8	64	*62	5.3	0.6	46	*133	6.7	1.3	59	*18	1.6	0.2	14
Pacific	15950	1288	15.7	8.1	89	*297	25.1	1.9	141	*231	11.6	1.4	65	*100	8.8	0.6	50
County Size A	35658	4207	51.4	11.8	129	680	57.5	1.9	145	981	49.2	2.8	124	877	77.1	2.5	194
County Size B	27101	2335	28.5	8.6	95	*284	24.0	1.0	80	539	27.1	2.0	90	*86	7.6	0.3	25
County Size C	13387	867	10.6	6.5	71	*120	10.1	0.9	68	*217	10.9	1.6	73	*77	10.3	0.9	69
County Size D	13644	778	9.5	5.7	63	*99	8.4	0.7	55	*255	12.8	1.9	84	*58	5.1	0.4	33
MSA Central City	29169	2755	33.7	9.4	104	378	31.9	1.3	98	622	31.2	2.1	96	*325	28.6	1.1	88
MSA Suburban	42524	4385	53.6	10.3	113	649	54.9	1.5	116	1000	50.2	2.4	106	704	61.9	1.7	131
Non-MSA	18096	1047	12.8	5.8	63	*157	13.2	0.9	66	*371	18.6	2.0	92	*108	9.5	0.6	47
Single	14479	1315	16.1	9.1	100	*107	9.1	0.7	56	*235	11.8	1.6	73	*247	21.7	1.7	134
Married	51935	5230	63.9	10.1	110	818	69.1	1.6	120	1370	68.7	2.6	119	621	54.6	1.2	94
Other	23376	1642	20.1	7.0	77	*258	21.8	1.1	84	387	19.4	1.7	75	270	23.7	1.2	91
Parents	35881	3158	38.6	8.8	97	889	75.1	2.5	188	1446	72.6	4.0	182	679	59.7	1.9	149
Working Parents	24725	2358	28.8	9.5	105	616	52.1	2.5	189	883	44.3	3.6	161	507	44.6	2.1	162
Household Size: 1 Person	15017	1160	14.2	7.7	85	*64	5.4	0.4	32	*74	3.7	0.5	22	*116	10.2	0.8	61
2 Persons	28950	2952	36.1	10.2	112	*136	11.5	0.5	36	350	17.6	1.2	55	*239	21.0	0.8	65
3 or More	45822	4074	49.8	8.9	98	983	83.1	2.1	163	1568	78.7	3.4	154	783	68.8	1.7	135
Any Child in Household	39070	3282	40.1	8.4	92	957	80.9	2.5	186	1587	79.7	4.1	183	748	65.8	1.9	151
Under 2 Years	6763	*428	5.2	6.3	69	*30	2.6	0.4	34	*219	11.0	3.2	146	*198	17.4	2.9	232
2-5 Years	14794	866	10.6	5.9	64	484	40.9	3.3	248	780	39.1	5.3	238	*258	22.7	1.7	138
6-11 Years	18719	1403	17.1	7.5	82	560	47.4	3.0	227	915	45.9	4.9	220	*287	25.2	1.5	121
12-17 Years	17576	1890	23.1	10.8	118	394	33.3	2.2	167	473	23.7	2.7	121	*373	32.8	2.1	167
White	75919	7302	89.2	9.6	105	979	82.8	1.3	98	1581	79.4	2.1	94	728	64.0	1.0	76
Black	10706	590	7.2	5.5	60	*185	15.6	1.7	131	*292	14.6	2.7	123	*315	27.7	2.9	232
Spanish Speaking	8317	398	4.9	4.8	52	*62	5.3	0.7	56	*217	10.9	2.6	117	*196	17.2	2.4	186
Home Owned	60568	5838	71.3	9.6	106	925	78.2	1.5	116	1297	65.1	2.1	96	690	60.7	1.1	90

BASE: FEMALE HOMEMAKERS	TOTAL U.S. '000	LIGHT 'N LIVELY A '000	B % DOWN	C % ACROSS	D INDEX	SNACKWELL'S A '000	B % DOWN	C % ACROSS	D INDEX	STONYFIELD FARM A '000	B % DOWN	C % ACROSS	D INDEX	TRIX A '000	B % DOWN	C % ACROSS	D INDEX
All Female Homemakers	89789	2355	100.0	2.6	100	1517	100.0	1.7	100	1076	100.0	1.2	100	2385	100.0	2.7	100
Men	89789	2355	100.0	2.6	100	1517	100.0	1.7	100	1076	100.0	1.2	100	2385	100.0	2.7	100
Women	39088	960	40.8	2.5	94	610	40.2	1.6	92	386	35.9	1.0	82	1007	42.2	2.6	97
Household Heads	89088	2355	100.0	2.5	100												
Homemakers	89789	2355	100.0	2.6	100	1517	100.0	1.7	100	1076	100.0	1.2	100	2385	100.0	2.7	100
Graduated College	18398	375	15.9	2.0	88	*308	20.3	1.7	99	570	52.9	3.1	258	558	23.4	3.0	114
Attended College	24064	818	34.7	3.4	130	442	29.2	1.8	109	*231	21.5	1.0	80	652	27.3	2.7	102
Graduated High School	31577	974	41.4	3.1	118	524	34.5	1.7	98	*218	20.3	0.7	58	763	32.0	2.4	91
Did not Graduate High School	15751	*188	8.0	1.2	46	*243	16.0	1.5	91	*57	5.3	0.4	30	*411	17.2	2.6	98
18-24	7780	*180	7.7	2.3	88	*131	8.7	1.7	100	*71	6.6	0.9	76	*280	11.7	3.6	135
25-34	18631	*406	17.3	2.2	83	*316	20.8	1.7	100	*215	20.0	1.2	96	852	35.7	4.6	172
35-44	20651	559	23.7	2.7	103	482	31.8	2.3	138	284	26.4	1.4	115	928	38.9	4.5	169
45-54	15603	513	21.8	3.3	125	*336	22.1	2.2	127	*231	21.4	1.5	123	*197	8.3	1.3	48
55-64	10181	*394	16.7	3.9	148	*70	4.6	0.7	41	*113	10.5	1.1	93	*23	1.0	0.2	8
65 or over	16943	*302	12.8	1.8	68	*182	12.0	1.1	64	*162	15.1	1.0	80	*105	4.4	0.6	23
18-34	26410	587	24.9	2.2	85	*447	29.5	1.7	100	*286	26.6	1.1	90	1132	47.5	4.3	161
18-49	55960	1435	61.0	2.6	98	1179	77.7	2.1	125	710	65.9	1.3	106	2173	91.1	3.9	146
25-54	54886	1479	62.8	2.7	103	1133	74.7	2.1	122	730	67.8	1.3	111	1978	82.9	3.6	136
Employed Full Time	41154	1132	48.1	2.7	105	837	55.2	2.0	120	575	53.4	1.4	116	1277	53.5	3.1	117
Part-time	11398	*272	11.6	2.4	91	*214	14.1	1.9	111	*137	12.7	1.2	100	*389	16.3	3.4	128
Sole Wage Earner	14006	380	16.2	2.7	104	*205	13.5	1.5	87	*155	14.4	1.1	92	*208	8.7	1.5	56
Not Employed	37237	951	40.4	2.6	97	466	30.7	1.3	74	365	33.9	1.0	82	720	30.2	1.9	73
Professional	9642	*254	10.8	2.6	101	*170	11.2	1.8	104	*198	18.4	2.1	171	*261	10.9	2.7	102
Executive/Admin./Managerial	7128	*263	11.2	3.7	140	*164	10.8	2.3	136	*177	16.4	2.5	207	*258	10.8	3.6	136
Clerical/Sales/Technical	20870	526	22.3	2.5	96	*380	25.0	1.8	108	*248	23.1	1.2	99	732	30.7	3.5	132
Precision/Crafts/Repair	1102	*12	0.5	1.1	42	*24	1.6	2.1	126					*67	2.8	6.1	229
Other Employed	13810	*349	14.8	2.5	96	*314	20.7	2.3	134	*89	8.3	0.6	54	*348	14.6	2.5	95
H/D Income $75,000 or More	15443	*286	12.1	1.9	71	*308	20.3	2.0	118	*372	34.6	2.4	201	540	22.7	3.5	132
$60,000 - 74,999	8775	*329	14.0	3.7	143	*221	14.5	2.5	149	*148	13.7	1.7	140	*259	10.9	3.0	111
$50,000 - 59,999	7850	*365	15.5	4.7	178	*143	9.4	1.8	108	*140	13.0	1.8	149	*213	8.9	2.7	102
$40,000 - 49,999	9648	*217	9.2	2.2	86	*95	6.3	1.0	59	*81	7.5	0.8	70	*317	13.3	3.3	124
$30,000 - 39,999	11493	*267	11.4	2.3	89	*142	9.4	1.2	73	*119	11.0	1.0	86	*314	13.2	2.7	103
$20,000 - 29,999	12298	*346	14.7	2.8	107	*88	5.8	0.7	43	*85	7.9	0.7	58	*333	13.9	2.7	102
$10,000 - 19,999	14330	*363	15.4	2.5	97	*420	27.7	2.9	174	*85	7.9	0.6	50	*288	12.1	2.0	76
Less than $10,000	9953	*182	7.7	1.8	70	*100	6.6	1.0	59	*45	4.2	0.5	38	*121	5.1	1.2	46
Census Region: North East	18074	596	25.3	3.3	126	438	28.9	2.4	143	829	77.0	4.6	383	517	21.7	2.9	108
North Central	20967	564	24.0	2.7	103	383	25.2	1.8	108	*5	0.5	0.0	2	649	27.2	3.1	117
South	32182	1151	48.9	3.6	136	520	34.2	1.6	96	*140	13.0	0.4	36	712	29.9	2.2	83
West	18567	*44	1.9	0.2	9	*177	11.7	1.0	56	*102	9.5	0.6	46	*507	21.3	2.7	103
Marketing Reg.: New England	4705	*245	10.4	5.2	199	*85	5.6	1.8	107	337	31.3	7.2	597	*227	9.5	4.8	182
Middle Atlantic	15444	395	16.8	2.6	97	*379	25.0	2.5	145	515	47.8	3.3	278	338	14.2	2.2	82
East Central	11580	*346	14.7	3.0	114	*16	1.5	0.1	7	*16	1.5	0.1	12	*371	15.6	3.2	121
West Central	13616	*312	13.2	2.3	87	*155	10.2	1.1	67	*12	1.1	0.1	7	*286	12.0	2.1	79
South East	18271	790	33.5	4.3	165	*292	19.2	1.6	94	*87	8.1	0.5	40	*463	19.4	2.5	95
South West	10224	*224	9.5	2.2	83	*191	12.6	1.9	111	*17	1.6	0.2	14	*201	8.4	2.0	74
Pacific	15950	*44	1.9	0.3	10	*177	11.7	1.1	66	*93	8.7	0.6	49	*499	20.9	3.1	118
County Size A	35658	797	33.8	2.2	85	650	42.8	1.8	107	628	58.1	1.8	146	949	39.8	2.7	100
County Size B	27104	771	32.8	2.8	109	*491	32.4	1.8	107	*313	29.1	1.2	96	933	39.1	3.4	130
County Size C	13387	*423	18.0	3.2	120	*270	17.8	2.0	120	*137	12.8	1.0	86	*355	14.9	2.6	100
County Size D	13644	*364	15.4	2.7	102	*106	7.0	0.8	46					*149	6.2	1.1	41
MSA Central City	29169	726	30.8	2.5	95	557	36.7	1.9	113	*268	24.9	0.9	77	770	32.3	2.6	99
MSA Suburban	42524	1030	43.7	2.4	92	752	49.5	1.8	105	726	67.4	1.7	142	1277	53.5	3.0	113
Non-MSA	18096	*598	25.4	3.3	126	*209	13.8	1.2	68	*83	7.7	0.5	38	*338	14.2	1.9	70
Single	14479	*287	12.2	2.0	76	*215	14.2	1.5	88	*185	17.2	1.3	107	*339	14.2	2.3	88
Married	51935	1509	64.1	2.9	111	1039	68.5	2.0	118	725	67.4	1.4	116	1619	67.9	3.1	117
Other	23376	559	23.7	2.4	91	*263	17.4	1.1	67	*166	15.4	0.7	59	427	17.9	1.8	69
Parents	35881	1045	44.4	2.9	111	849	56.0	2.4	140	379	35.2	1.1	88	1947	81.6	5.4	204
Working Parents	24725	717	30.4	2.9	111	625	41.2	2.5	150	*249	23.2	1.0	84	1422	59.6	5.8	216
Household Size: 1 Person	15017	354	15.0	2.4	90	*151	9.9	1.0	57	*149	13.9	1.0	83	*75	3.2	0.5	19
2 Persons	28950	756	32.1	2.6	100	495	32.6	1.7	101	410	38.1	1.4	118	*201	8.4	0.7	26
3 or More	45822	1245	52.9	2.7	100	871	57.4	1.9	113	517	48.0	1.1	94	2109	88.4	4.6	173
Any Child in Household	39070	1153	49.0	3.0	113	857	56.5	2.2	130	*409	38.0	1.0	87	2070	86.8	5.3	199
Under 2 Years	6763	*97	4.1	1.4	55	*137	9.0	2.0	120	*89	8.2	1.3	109	*328	13.8	4.9	183
2-5 Years	14794	*349	14.8	2.4	90	*303	20.0	2.1	121	*179	16.6	1.2	101	1001	42.0	6.8	255
6-11 Years	18710	715	30.4	3.8	146	*424	28.0	2.3	134	*162	15.1	0.9	72	1300	54.5	6.9	261
12-17 Years	17576	*591	25.1	3.4	128	*421	27.7	2.4	142	*143	13.3	0.8	68	673	28.2	3.8	144
White	75919	1946	82.7	2.6	98	1226	80.8	1.6	96	976	90.6	1.3	107	2032	85.2	2.7	101
Black	10706	*373	15.8	3.5	133	*221	14.6	2.1	122	*84	7.8	0.8	65	*155	6.5	1.4	54
Spanish Speaking	8317	*80	3.4	1.0	37	*119	7.8	1.4	84	*54	5.0	0.7	54	*467	19.6	5.6	211
Home Owned	60568	1817	77.1	3.0	114	929	61.3	1.5	91	758	70.4	1.3	104	1574	66.0	2.6	98

Spring 1998

188 YOGURT

BASE: FEMALE HOMEMAKERS	TOTAL U.S. '000	YOPLAIT FAT FREE A '000	B % DOWN	C % ACROSS	D INDEX	YOPLAIT FAT FREE FRUIT ON THE BOTTOM A '000	B % DOWN	C % ACROSS	D INDEX	YOPLAIT FAT FREE LIGHT A '000	B % DOWN	C % ACROSS	D INDEX	YOPLAIT ORIGINAL A '000	B % DOWN	C % ACROSS	D INDEX
All Female Homemakers	89789	3229	100.0	3.6	100	2509	100.0	2.8	100	2137	100.0	2.4	100	4310	100.0	4.8	100
Men																	
Women	89789	3229	100.0	3.6	100	2509	100.0	2.8	100	2137	100.0	2.4	100	4310	100.0	4.8	100
Household Heads	39088	1303	40.4	3.3	93	1133	45.2	2.9	104	1004	47.0	2.6	108	1722	39.9	4.4	92
Homemakers	89789	3229	100.0	3.6	100	2509	100.0	2.8	100	2137	100.0	2.4	100	4310	100.0	4.8	100
Graduated College	18398	888	27.5	4.8	134	*461	18.4	2.5	90	723	33.8	3.9	165	1287	29.9	7.0	146
Attended College	24064	970	30.0	4.0	112	660	26.3	2.7	98	535	25.0	2.2	93	1463	34.0	6.1	127
Graduated High School	31577	1004	31.1	3.2	88	910	36.3	2.9	103	602	28.2	1.9	80	1015	23.6	3.2	67
Did not Graduate High School	15751	*367	11.4	2.3	65	*478	19.0	3.0	109	*278	13.0	1.8	74	*544	12.6	3.5	72
18-24	7780	*336	10.4	4.3	120	*355	14.1	4.6	163	*230	10.8	3.0	124	*458	10.6	5.9	123
25-34	18631	509	15.8	2.7	76	*286	11.4	1.5	55	*331	15.5	1.8	75	1268	29.4	6.8	142
35-44	20651	994	30.8	4.8	134	647	25.8	3.1	112	622	29.1	3.0	127	1126	26.1	5.5	114
45-54	15603	668	20.7	4.3	119	*436	17.4	2.8	100	*401	18.8	2.6	108	725	16.8	4.6	97
55-64	10181	361	11.2	3.5	99	*245	9.8	2.4	86	*164	7.7	1.6	68	*333	7.7	3.3	68
65 or over	16943	*361	11.2	2.1	59	540	21.5	3.2	114	*388	18.1	2.3	96	399	9.3	2.4	49
18-34	26410	845	26.2	3.2	89	641	25.6	2.4	87	562	26.3	2.1	89	1726	40.1	6.5	136
18-49	55960	2187	67.7	3.9	109	1574	62.7	2.8	101	1381	64.6	2.5	104	3353	77.8	6.0	125
25-54	54886	2171	67.2	4.0	110	1370	54.6	2.5	89	1355	63.4	2.5	104	3119	72.4	5.7	118
Employed Full Time	41154	1754	54.3	4.3	119	976	38.9	2.4	85	1266	59.3	3.1	129	2263	52.5	5.5	115
Part-time	11398	*400	12.4	3.5	98	*359	14.3	3.2	113	*168	7.9	1.5	62	823	19.1	7.2	150
Sole Wage Earner	14006	468	14.5	3.3	93	342	13.6	2.4	87	320	15.0	2.3	96	592	13.7	4.2	88
Not Employed	37237	1075	33.3	2.9	80	1174	46.8	3.2	113	702	32.9	1.9	79	1224	28.4	3.3	68
Professional	9642	501	15.5	5.2	144	*261	10.4	2.7	97	*392	18.4	4.1	171	715	16.6	7.4	154
Executive/Admin./Managerial	7128	*312	9.7	4.4	122	*171	6.8	2.4	86	*278	13.0	3.9	164	*418	9.7	5.9	122
Clerical/Sales/Technical	20870	850	26.3	4.1	113	448	17.9	2.1	77	428	20.0	2.0	86	1153	26.8	5.5	115
Precision/Crafts/Repair	1102	*11	0.4	1.0	29	*17	0.7	1.5	54	*17	0.8	1.6	66	*72	1.7	6.5	136
Other Employed	13810	479	14.8	3.5	96	*439	17.5	3.2	114	*320	15.0	2.3	97	727	16.9	5.3	110
H/D Income $75,000 or More	15443	701	21.7	4.5	126	*323	12.9	2.1	75	622	29.1	4.0	169	962	22.3	6.2	130
$60,000 - 74,999	8775	409	12.7	4.7	129	*265	10.6	3.0	108	*268	12.6	3.1	128	624	14.5	7.1	148
$50,000 - 59,999	7850	*397	12.3	5.1	141	*228	9.1	2.9	104	*314	14.7	4.0	168	581	13.5	7.4	154
$40,000 - 49,999	9648	*351	10.9	3.6	101	*103	4.1	1.1	38	*184	8.6	1.9	80	521	12.1	5.4	113
$30,000 - 39,999	11493	367	11.4	3.2	89	*436	17.4	3.8	136	*140	6.5	1.2	51	493	11.4	4.3	89
$20,000 - 29,999	12298	335	10.4	2.7	76	*302	12.0	2.5	88	*207	9.7	1.7	71	513	11.9	4.2	87
$10,000 - 19,999	14330	*508	15.7	3.5	99	578	23.0	4.0	144	*289	13.5	2.0	85	*385	8.9	2.7	56
Less than $10,000	9953	*162	5.0	1.6	45	*274	10.9	2.8	99	*113	5.3	1.1	48	*232	5.4	2.3	49
Census Region: North East	18074	415	12.9	2.3	64	405	16.1	2.2	80	424	19.8	2.3	98	788	18.3	4.4	91
North Central	20967	986	30.5	4.7	131	813	32.4	3.9	139	579	27.1	2.8	116	980	22.7	4.7	97
South	32182	761	23.6	2.4	66	706	28.1	2.2	78	*411	19.2	1.3	54	1110	25.8	3.4	72
West	18567	1067	33.0	5.7	160	585	23.3	3.2	113	724	33.9	3.9	164	1432	33.2	7.7	161
Marketing Reg.: New England	4705	*170	5.3	3.6	100	*134	5.3	2.9	102	*136	6.4	2.9	121	*246	5.7	5.2	109
Middle Atlantic	15444	*320	9.9	2.1	58	375	15.0	2.4	87	*347	16.2	2.2	94	599	13.9	3.9	81
East Central	11580	422	13.1	3.6	101	*449	17.9	3.9	139	*247	11.6	2.1	90	440	10.2	3.8	79
West Central	13616	688	21.3	5.1	141	473	18.8	3.5	124	440	20.6	3.2	136	857	19.9	6.3	131
South East	18271	*448	13.9	2.5	68	*351	14.0	1.9	69	*242	11.3	1.3	56	593	13.8	3.2	68
South West	10224	*236	7.3	2.3	64	*253	10.1	2.5	89	*106	4.9	1.0	43	*419	9.7	4.1	85
Pacific	15950	945	29.3	5.9	165	*474	18.9	3.0	106	619	28.9	3.9	163	1157	26.8	7.3	151
County Size A	35658	1462	45.3	4.1	114	1097	43.7	3.1	110	968	45.3	2.7	114	1875	43.5	5.3	110
County Size B	27101	939	29.1	3.5	96	760	30.3	2.8	100	709	33.2	2.6	110	1520	35.3	5.6	117
County Size C	13387	*369	11.4	2.8	77	*176	7.0	1.3	47	*249	11.7	1.9	78	*498	11.5	3.7	77
County Size D	13644	*460	14.2	3.4	94	*476	19.0	3.5	125	*211	9.9	1.5	65	*417	9.7	3.1	64
MSA Central City	29169	1028	31.8	3.5	98	876	34.9	3.0	108	665	31.1	2.3	96	1390	32.3	4.8	99
MSA Suburban	42524	1590	49.3	3.7	104	1120	44.6	2.6	94	1163	54.4	2.7	115	2335	54.2	5.5	114
Non-MSA	18096	*610	18.9	3.4	94	*513	20.4	2.8	101	*309	14.5	1.7	72	*585	13.6	3.2	67
Single	14479	584	18.1	4.0	112	*417	16.6	2.9	103	404	18.9	2.8	117	742	17.2	5.1	107
Married	51935	2169	67.2	4.2	116	1469	58.5	2.8	101	1277	59.8	2.5	103	2850	66.1	5.5	114
Other	23376	475	14.7	2.0	57	623	24.8	2.7	95	456	21.4	2.0	82	718	16.7	3.1	64
Parents	35881	1479	45.8	4.1	115	993	39.6	2.8	99	784	36.7	2.2	92	2464	57.2	6.9	143
Working Parents	24725	1086	33.6	4.4	122	648	25.8	2.6	94	652	30.5	2.6	111	1894	43.9	7.7	160
Household Size: 1 Person	15017	336	10.4	2.2	62	405	16.2	2.7	97	276	12.9	1.8	77	421	9.8	2.8	58
2 Persons	28950	1119	34.7	3.9	108	738	29.4	2.5	91	825	38.6	2.8	120	971	22.5	3.4	70
3 or More	45822	1774	54.9	3.9	108	1366	54.4	3.0	107	1036	48.5	2.3	95	2917	67.7	6.4	133
Any Child in Household	39070	1623	50.3	4.2	116	1187	47.3	3.0	109	893	41.8	2.3	96	2730	63.3	7.0	146
Under 2 Years	6763	*280	8.7	4.1	115	*209	8.3	3.1	111	*129	6.1	1.9	80	554	12.8	8.2	171
2-5 Years	14794	472	14.6	3.2	89	*474	18.9	3.2	115	*358	16.8	2.4	102	1251	29.0	8.5	176
6-11 Years	18719	588	18.2	3.1	87	551	22.0	2.9	105	*355	16.6	1.9	80	1121	26.0	6.0	125
12-17 Years	17576	958	29.7	5.5	152	593	23.6	3.4	121	*530	24.8	3.0	127	1058	24.6	6.0	125
White	75919	2888	89.4	3.8	106	1869	74.5	2.5	88	1841	86.1	2.4	102	3901	90.5	5.1	107
Black	10706	*239	7.4	2.2	62	*511	20.4	4.8	171	*225	10.5	2.1	88	*215	5.0	2.0	42
Spanish Speaking	8317	*273	8.5	3.3	91	*217	8.7	2.6	93	*132	6.2	1.6	67	519	12.0	6.2	130
Home Owned	60568	2236	69.2	3.7	103	1557	62.1	2.6	92	1658	77.6	2.7	115	3154	73.2	5.2	108

Spring 1998

BASE: FEMALE HOMEMAKERS	TOTAL U.S. '000	YOPLAIT CUSTARD STYLE A '000	B % DOWN	C % ACROSS	D INDEX	YOPLAIT LIGHT A '000	B % DOWN	C % ACROSS	D INDEX	STORE'S OWN BRAND A '000	B % DOWN	C % ACROSS	D INDEX
All Female Homemakers	89789	3128	100.0	3.5	100	2042	100.0	2.3	100	6961	100.0	7.8	100
Men	89789	3128	100.0	3.5	100	2042	100.0	2.3	100	6961	100.0	7.8	100
Women	39088	1149	36.7	2.9	84	833	40.8	2.1	94	2477	35.6	6.3	82
Household Heads	89789	3128	100.0	3.5	100	2042	100.0	2.3	100	6961	100.0	7.8	100
Homemakers	89789	3128	100.0	3.5	100	2042	100.0	2.3	100	6961	100.0	7.8	100
Graduated College	18398	834	26.7	4.5	130	687	33.7	3.7	164	1959	28.1	10.6	137
Attended College	24064	1211	38.7	5.0	144	747	36.6	3.1	137	2019	29.0	8.4	108
Graduated High School	31577	742	23.7	2.3	67	401	19.6	1.3	56	2076	29.8	6.6	85
Did not Graduate High School	15751	*341	10.9	2.2	62	*207	10.1	1.3	58	908	13.0	5.8	74
18-24	7780	*242	7.7	3.1	89	*123	6.0	1.6	69	*518	7.4	6.7	86
25-34	18631	724	23.1	3.9	111	*366	17.9	2.0	86	1523	21.9	8.2	105
35-44	20651	1015	32.5	4.9	141	571	28.0	2.8	122	2000	28.7	9.7	125
45-54	15603	674	21.6	4.3	124	537	26.3	3.4	151	1398	20.1	9.0	116
55-64	10181	*185	5.9	1.8	52	*232	11.3	2.3	100	596	10.0	6.8	88
65 or over	16943	*288	9.2	1.7	49	*213	10.4	1.3	55	825	11.9	4.9	63
18-34	26410	966	30.9	3.7	105	489	23.9	1.9	81	2041	29.3	7.7	100
18-49	55960	2344	74.9	4.2	120	1409	69.0	2.5	111	4816	69.2	8.6	111
25-54	54886	2413	77.1	4.4	126	1474	72.2	2.7	118	4921	70.7	9.0	116
Employed Full Time	41154	1627	52.0	4.0	113	1213	59.4	2.9	130	3489	50.1	8.5	109
Part-time	11398	588	18.8	5.2	148	*255	12.5	2.2	98	926	13.3	8.1	105
Sole Wage Earner	14006	430	13.8	3.1	88	309	15.1	2.2	97	882	12.7	6.3	81
Not Employed	37237	913	29.2	2.5	70	574	28.1	1.5	68	2546	36.6	6.8	88
Professional	9642	528	16.9	5.5	157	*385	18.8	4.0	175	969	13.9	10.1	130
Executive/Admin./Managerial	7128	*376	12.0	5.3	151	*258	12.6	3.6	159	*549	7.9	7.7	99
Clerical/Sales/Technical	20870	882	28.2	4.2	121	468	22.9	2.2	99	1841	26.5	8.8	114
Precision/Crafts/Repair	1102	*16	0.5	1.4	42	*33	1.6	3.0	130	*80	1.2	7.3	94
Other Employed	13810	*413	13.2	3.0	86	*324	15.9	2.3	103	975	14.0	7.1	91
H/D Income $75,000 or More	15443	798	25.5	5.2	148	475	23.3	3.1	135	1353	19.4	8.8	113
$60,000 - 74,999	8775	496	15.9	5.7	162	*379	18.6	4.3	190	835	12.0	9.5	123
$50,000 - 59,999	7850	388	12.4	4.9	142	*268	13.1	3.4	150	639	9.2	8.1	105
$40,000 - 49,999	9648	*250	8.0	2.6	74	*151	7.4	1.6	69	808	11.6	8.4	108
$30,000 - 39,999	11493	260	8.3	2.3	65	*274	13.4	2.4	105	1115	16.0	9.7	125
$20,000 - 29,999	12298	*372	11.9	3.0	87	*195	9.6	1.6	70	995	14.3	8.1	104
$10,000 - 19,999	14330	*468	15.0	3.3	94	*273	13.4	1.9	84	785	11.3	5.5	71
Less than $10,000	9953	*95	3.0	1.0	27	*25	1.2	0.3	11	*430	6.2	4.3	56
Census Region: North East	18074	734	23.5	4.1	117	*295	14.4	1.6	72	1023	14.7	5.7	73
North Central	20967	851	27.2	4.1	117	511	25.0	2.4	107	1071	15.4	5.1	66
South	32182	810	25.9	2.5	72	*362	17.7	1.1	49	2487	35.7	7.7	100
West	18567	733	23.4	3.9	113	874	42.8	4.7	207	2380	34.2	12.8	165
Marketing Reg.: New England	4705	*266	8.5	5.7	163	*94	4.6	2.0	88	333	4.8	7.1	91
Middle Atlantic	15444	508	16.2	3.3	94	*214	10.5	1.4	61	808	11.6	5.2	68
East Central	11580	471	15.0	4.1	117	*222	10.9	1.9	84	727	10.4	6.3	81
West Central	13616	563	18.0	4.1	119	*422	20.7	3.1	136	932	13.4	6.8	88
South East	18271	*520	16.6	2.8	82	*230	11.2	1.3	55	1388	19.9	7.6	98
South West	10224	*186	5.9	1.8	52	*120	5.9	1.2	51	835	12.0	8.2	105
Pacific	15950	614	19.6	3.9	111	741	36.3	4.6	204	1938	27.8	12.1	157
County Size A	35658	1280	40.9	3.6	103	948	46.4	2.7	117	2588	37.2	7.3	94
County Size B	27101	1027	32.8	3.8	109	638	31.2	2.4	103	2210	31.7	8.2	105
County Size C	13387	*376	12.0	2.8	81	*183	9.0	1.4	60	1122	16.1	8.4	108
County Size D	13644	*446	14.3	3.3	94	*273	13.4	2.0	88	1041	15.0	7.6	98
MSA Central City	29169	970	31.0	3.3	95	683	33.4	2.3	103	2281	32.8	7.8	101
MSA Suburban	42524	1631	52.1	3.8	110	981	48.0	2.3	101	3319	47.7	7.8	101
Non-MSA	18096	*527	16.8	2.9	84	*378	18.5	2.1	92	1361	19.6	7.5	97
Single	14479	438	14.0	3.0	87	*243	11.9	1.7	74	758	10.9	5.2	68
Married	51935	2199	70.3	4.2	122	1430	70.0	2.8	121	4764	68.4	9.2	118
Other	23376	492	15.7	2.1	60	369	18.1	1.6	69	1438	20.7	6.2	79
Parents	35881	1546	49.4	4.3	124	869	42.6	2.4	106	3564	51.2	9.9	128
Working Parents	24725	1168	37.3	4.7	136	639	31.3	2.6	114	2551	36.7	10.3	133
Household Size: 1 Person	15017	282	9.0	1.9	54	251	12.3	1.7	73	718	10.3	4.8	62
2 Persons	28950	743	23.7	2.6	74	776	38.0	2.7	118	2150	30.9	7.4	96
3 or More	45822	2104	67.3	4.6	132	1016	49.7	2.2	97	4093	58.8	8.9	115
Any Child in Household	39070	1723	55.1	4.4	127	976	47.8	2.5	110	3769	54.1	9.6	124
Under 2 Years	6763	*366	11.7	5.4	155	*212	10.4	3.1	138	671	9.6	9.9	128
2-5 Years	14794	855	27.3	5.8	166	*402	19.7	2.7	119	1337	19.2	9.0	117
6-11 Years	18719	823	26.3	4.4	126	*380	18.6	2.0	89	1704	24.5	9.1	117
12-17 Years	17576	656	21.0	3.7	107	*494	24.2	2.8	123	1824	26.2	10.4	134
White	75919	2799	89.5	3.7	106	1797	88.0	2.4	104	6203	89.1	8.2	105
Black	10706	*187	6.0	1.7	50	*131	6.4	1.2	54	*453	6.5	4.2	55
Spanish Speaking	8317	*366	11.7	4.4	126	*176	8.6	2.1	93	680	9.8	8.2	106
Home Owned	60568	2440	78.0	4.0	116	1559	76.4	2.6	113	5233	75.2	8.6	111

Spring 1998

Source: NCS Part 1 SPRING 1999 Wgt: POP
Table Base: TOTAL

Choices System
Simmons Market Research Bureau

Oct 1, 1999

Row	CELL	TOTAL	Eat Yogurt	Cups Eaten Last 30 Days - Heavy 6+	Breyers OR Breyers Blended Low Fat OR Breyers Mix'n Crunch Low Fat	Dannon
TOTAL	(000)	194341	89349	23171	26991	42514
	Resps	15718	7755	2154	2305	3900
	Vert%	100.0	100.0	100.0	100.0	100.0
	Horz%	100.0	45.98	11.92	13.89	21.88
	Index	100	100	100	100	100
Sex - Male	(000)	93172	31736	7532	8943	13910
	Resps	6793	2461	628	668	1148
	Vert%	47.94	35.52	32.51	33.13	32.72
	Horz%	100.0	34.06	8.08	9.6	14.93
	Index	100	74	68	69	68
Sex - Female	(000)	101169	57613	15639	18048	28604
	Resps	8925	5294	1526	1637	2752
	Vert%	52.06	64.48	67.49	66.87	67.28
	Horz%	100.0	56.95	15.46	17.84	28.27
	Index	100	124	130	128	129
Age - 18-24	(000)	24799	11089	2393	3524	5377
	Resps	1481	725	158	236	364
	Vert%	12.76	12.41	10.33	13.06	12.65
	Horz%	100.0	44.71	9.65	14.21	21.68
	Index	100	97	81	102	99
Age - 25-34	(000)	38805	18184	4351	5531	8316
	Resps	2591	1326	356	384	634
	Vert%	19.97	20.35	18.78	20.49	19.56
	Horz%	100.0	46.86	11.21	14.25	21.43
	Index	100	102	94	103	98
Age - 35-44	(000)	43798	20400	5484	6005	9458
	Resps	3722	1861	529	545	926
	Vert%	22.54	22.83	23.67	22.25	22.25
	Horz%	100.0	46.58	12.52	13.71	21.59
	Index	100	101	105	99	99
Age - 45-54	(000)	33496	15840	4662	5073	8022
	Resps	3194	1603	478	514	862
	Vert%	17.24	17.73	20.12	18.8	18.87
	Horz%	100.0	47.29	13.92	15.15	23.95
	Index	100	103	117	109	109
Age - 55-64	(000)	21893	10455	2921	3160	5268
	Resps	2143	1062	315	312	551
	Vert%	11.27	11.7	12.6	11.71	12.39
	Horz%	100.0	47.76	13.34	14.44	24.06
	Index	100	104	112	104	110
Age - 65+	(000)	31551	13382	3360	3697	6073
	Resps	2587	1178	318	314	563
	Vert%	16.23	14.98	14.5	13.7	14.28
	Horz%	100.0	42.41	10.65	11.72	19.25
	Index	100	92	89	84	88

*Projection relatively unstable because of sample base - use with caution.
**Number of cases too small for reliability - shown for consistency only.

Source: NCS Part 1 SPRING 1999 Wgt: POP
Table Base: TOTAL

Choices System
Simmons Market Research Bureau

Oct 1, 1999

Row	CELL	TOTAL	Eat Yogurt	Cups Eaten Last 30 Days - Heavy 6+	Breyers OR Breyers Blended Low Fat OR Breyers Mix'n Crunch Low Fat	Dannon
Race - White	(000)	162987	75114	20157	21501	36422
	Resps	14061	6927	1955	2025	3541
	Vert%	83.87	84.07	87.0	79.66	85.67
	Horz%	100.0	46.09	12.37	13.19	22.35
	Index	100	100	104	95	102
Race - Black	(000)	22997	9759	1771	4546	4153
	Resps	1023	478	104	197	207
	Vert%	11.83	10.92	7.64	16.84	9.77
	Horz%	100.0	42.44	7.7	19.77	18.06
	Index	100	92	65	142	83
Race - Asian	(000)	6837	3771	1091	*735	1663
	Resps	392	228	66	46	103
	Vert%	3.52	4.22	4.71	2.72	3.91
	Horz%	100.0	55.15	15.95	10.75	24.31
	Index	100	120	134	77	111
Race - Other	(000)	1520	705	**152	*209	*276
	Resps	242	122	29	37	49
	Vert%	0.78	0.79	0.66	0.77	0.65
	Horz%	100.0	46.37	10.0	13.75	18.19
	Index	100	101	84	99	83
Race - Not White Or Black	(000)	8357	4475	1243	944	1939
	Resps	634	350	95	83	152
	Vert%	4.3	5.01	5.36	3.5	4.56
	Horz%	100.0	53.55	14.87	11.29	23.2
	Index	100	116	125	81	106
Resp. Spanish/Hispanic Origin	(000)	19775	9444	1981	2557	4021
	Resps	1049	552	125	140	249
	Vert%	10.18	10.57	8.55	9.47	9.46
	Horz%	100.0	47.75	10.02	12.93	20.34
	Index	100	104	84	93	93
Highest Compl. Edu - Grade School - 8 Years Or Less	(000)	13259	4734	*937	*1581	1739
	Resps	482	171	40	55	66
	Vert%	6.82	5.3	4.04	5.86	4.09
	Horz%	100.0	35.71	7.07	11.92	13.12
	Index	100	78	59	86	60
Highest Compl. Edu - High School - 9-11 Years	(000)	18512	7070	1378	2905	3187
	Resps	1305	515	117	200	234
	Vert%	9.53	7.91	5.95	10.76	7.5
	Horz%	100.0	38.19	7.44	15.69	17.21
	Index	100	83	62	113	79
Highest Compl. Edu - High School - 12 Years (Graduated)	(000)	67904	27655	6693	8741	12603
	Resps	5023	2205	570	710	1050
	Vert%	34.94	30.95	28.88	32.39	29.64
	Horz%	100.0	40.73	9.86	12.87	18.56
	Index	100	89	83	93	85

*Projection relatively unstable because of sample base - use with caution.
**Number of cases too small for reliability - shown for consistency only.

Source: NCS Part 1 SPRING 1999 Wgt: POP
Table Base: TOTAL

Choices System
Simmons Market Research Bureau

Oct 1, 1999

Row	CELL	TOTAL	Eat Yogurt	Cups Eaten Last 30 Days - Heavy 6+	Breyers OR Breyers Blended Low Fat OR Breyers Mix'n Crunch Low Fat	Dannon
Highest Compl. Edu - College - Less Than 1 Year	(000)	12270	6163	1449	1628	3022
	Resps	1033	532	129	149	277
	Vert%	6.31	6.9	6.25	6.03	7.11
	Horz%	100.0	50.23	11.81	13.27	24.63
	Index	100	109	99	96	113
Highest Compl. Edu - College - 1 Year	(000)	12095	6284	1687	1896	3022
	Resps	1026	554	151	164	267
	Vert%	6.22	7.03	7.28	7.03	7.11
	Horz%	100.0	51.95	13.95	15.68	24.98
	Index	100	113	117	113	114
Highest Compl. Edu - College - 2 Years	(000)	18785	9230	2464	2534	4458
	Resps	1695	851	231	232	434
	Vert%	9.67	10.33	10.63	9.39	10.49
	Horz%	100.0	49.14	13.12	13.49	23.73
	Index	100	107	110	97	108
Highest Compl. Edu - College - 3 Years	(000)	8183	4264	1199	1227	2250
	Resps	719	392	115	113	217
	Vert%	4.21	4.77	5.18	4.55	5.29
	Horz%	100.0	52.11	14.66	14.99	27.5
	Index	100	113	123	108	126
Highest Compl. Edu - College - 4 Years (Graduate)	(000)	23927	13005	3925	3461	6033
	Resps	2397	1348	401	366	673
	Vert%	12.31	14.56	16.94	12.82	14.19
	Horz%	100.0	54.35	16.4	14.46	25.22
	Index	100	118	138	104	115
Highest Compl. Edu - Attended Graduate School - No Degree	(000)	5818	3349	1103	970	1855
	Resps	603	359	124	97	208
	Vert%	2.99	3.75	4.76	3.6	4.36
	Horz%	100.0	57.56	18.95	16.68	31.88
	Index	100	125	159	120	146
Highest Compl. Edu - Attended Graduate School - Degree	(000)	13588	7594	2337	2048	4345
	Resps	1435	828	276	219	474
	Vert%	6.99	8.5	10.08	7.59	10.22
	Horz%	100.0	55.89	17.2	15.07	31.98
	Index	100	122	144	109	146
Marital Status Resp. - Single (Never Married)	(000)	45936	20032	4557	6431	9703
	Resps	2567	1233	303	385	630
	Vert%	23.64	22.42	19.67	23.83	22.82
	Horz%	100.0	43.61	9.92	14.0	21.12
	Index	100	95	83	101	97
Marital Status Resp. - Married	(000)	111082	51858	13867	14923	24618
	Resps	10640	5266	1477	1527	2644
	Vert%	57.16	58.04	59.85	55.29	57.91
	Horz%	100.0	46.68	12.48	13.43	22.16
	Index	100	102	105	97	101

*Projection relatively unstable because of sample base - use with caution.
**Number of cases too small for reliability - shown for consistency only.

© Copyright Simmons 1999

Row	CELL	TOTAL	Eat Yogurt	Cups Eaten Last 30 Days - Heavy 6+	Breyers OR Breyers Blended Low Fat OR Breyers Mix'n Crunch Low Fat	Dannon
Marital Status Resp. - Separated	(000)	3810	1859	**400	*716	*825
	Resps	231	108	25	39	48
	Vert%	1.96	2.08	1.73	2.65	1.94
	Horz%	100.0	48.78	10.5	18.79	21.65
	Index	100	106	88	135	99
Marital Status Resp. - Widowed	(000)	13742	6249	1726	1958	3034
	Resps	922	459	145	144	232
	Vert%	7.07	6.99	7.45	7.26	7.14
	Horz%	100.0	45.47	12.56	14.25	22.08
	Index	100	99	105	103	101
Marital Status Resp. - Divorced	(000)	19771	9352	2621	2962	4334
	Resps	1358	689	204	210	346
	Vert%	10.17	10.47	11.31	10.97	10.2
	Horz%	100.0	47.3	13.26	14.98	21.92
	Index	100	103	111	108	100
Employed Full Time (30+ Hours)	(000)	103608	46489	12296	14382	22719
	Resps	8684	4139	1175	1266	2123
	Vert%	53.31	52.03	53.07	53.28	53.44
	Horz%	100.0	44.87	11.87	13.88	21.93
	Index	100	98	100	100	100
Employed Part Time (<30 Hours)	(000)	21925	11786	3049	3418	5474
	Resps	1903	1070	299	319	538
	Vert%	11.28	13.19	13.16	12.66	12.87
	Horz%	100.0	53.76	13.91	15.59	24.97
	Index	100	117	117	112	114
Employed Full Or Part Time	(000)	125533	58274	15345	17799	28193
	Resps	10587	5209	1474	1585	2661
	Vert%	64.59	65.22	66.23	65.95	66.31
	Horz%	100.0	46.42	12.22	14.18	22.46
	Index	100	101	103	102	103
Not Employed	(000)	68809	31075	7826	9192	14321
	Resps	5131	2546	680	720	1239
	Vert%	35.41	34.78	33.77	34.05	33.69
	Horz%	100.0	45.16	11.37	13.36	20.81
	Index	100	98	95	96	95
Retired	(000)	31349	13329	3349	3629	5983
	Resps	2541	1156	321	309	554
	Vert%	16.13	14.92	14.45	13.45	14.07
	Horz%	100.0	42.52	10.68	11.58	19.09
	Index	100	92	90	83	87
Temporarily Unemployed	(000)	8409	3334	*703	*921	1552
	Resps	479	221	50	56	106
	Vert%	4.33	3.73	3.03	3.41	3.65
	Horz%	100.0	39.64	8.36	10.95	18.45
	Index	100	86	70	79	84

© Copyright Simmons 1999

*Projection relatively unstable because of sample base - use with caution.
**Number of cases too small for reliability - shown for consistency only.

Source: NCS Part 1 SPRING 1999 Wgt: POP
Table Base: TOTAL

Choices System
Simmons Market Research Bureau

Oct 1, 1999

Row	CELL	TOTAL	Eat Yogurt	Cups Eaten Last 30 Days - Heavy 6+	Breyers OR Breyers Blended Low Fat OR Breyers Mix'n Crunch Low Fat	Dannon
Disabled	(000)	7692	2841	*839	*825	1197
	Resps	419	171	50	57	78
	Vert%	3.96	3.18	3.62	3.06	2.82
	Horz%	100.0	36.93	10.9	10.72	15.56
	Index	100	80	91	77	71
Full Time Student	(000)	4525	2263	*628	*809	1164
	Resps	250	135	43	42	71
	Vert%	2.33	2.53	2.71	3.0	2.74
	Horz%	100.0	50.02	13.88	17.87	25.71
	Index	100	109	116	129	118
Homemaker	(000)	14059	8198	2018	2604	3939
	Resps	1311	807	202	237	407
	Vert%	7.23	9.18	8.71	9.65	9.26
	Horz%	100.0	58.31	14.35	18.52	28.02
	Index	100	127	120	133	128
Never Worked	(000)	2775	*1110	**289	**404	**487
	Resps	131	56	14	19	23
	Vert%	1.43	1.24	1.25	1.5	1.15
	Horz%	100.0	40.0	10.42	14.58	17.55
	Index	100	87	87	105	80
Occupation - Professional	(000)	19785	10918	3507	3194	5547
	Resps	1916	1088	360	322	581
	Vert%	10.18	12.22	15.14	11.83	13.05
	Horz%	100.0	55.18	17.73	16.15	28.03
	Index	100	120	149	116	128
Occupation - Technicians & Related Support	(000)	4196	2294	789	861	1089
	Resps	590	311	103	105	159
	Vert%	2.16	2.57	3.4	3.19	2.56
	Horz%	100.0	54.66	18.8	20.52	25.96
	Index	100	119	158	148	119
Occupation - Managers/Administrators	(000)	18405	8927	2294	2206	4427
	Resps	1564	782	212	197	409
	Vert%	9.47	9.99	9.9	8.17	10.41
	Horz%	100.0	48.5	12.46	11.99	24.05
	Index	100	105	105	86	110
Occupation - Administrative Support/Clerical	(000)	18275	9727	2458	3067	5058
	Resps	2081	1101	297	340	581
	Vert%	9.4	10.89	10.61	11.36	11.9
	Horz%	100.0	53.23	13.45	16.78	27.68
	Index	100	116	113	121	127
Occupation - Sales	(000)	14743	6805	1877	1959	3232
	Resps	1065	522	148	153	261
	Vert%	7.59	7.62	8.1	7.26	7.6
	Horz%	100.0	46.16	12.73	13.28	21.92
	Index	100	100	107	96	100

*Projection relatively unstable because of sample base - use with caution.
**Number of cases too small for reliability - shown for consistency only.

Source: NCS Part 1 SPRING 1999 Wgt: POP
Table Base: TOTAL

Choices System
Simmons Market Research Bureau

Oct 1, 1999

Row	CELL	TOTAL	Eat Yogurt	Cups Eaten Last 30 Days - Heavy 6+	Breyers OR Breyers Blended Low Fat OR Breyers Mix'n Crunch Low Fat	Dannon
Occupation - Craft/Precision Production	(000)	13954	4259	*798	1185	1773
	Resps	772	260	56	80	122
	Vert%	7.18	4.77	3.44	4.39	4.17
	Horz%	100.0	30.52	5.72	8.49	12.7
	Index	100	66	48	61	58
Occupation - Operators/Fabricators	(000)	14129	5145	1460	1950	2344
	Resps	1006	370	108	136	170
	Vert%	7.27	5.76	6.3	7.22	5.51
	Horz%	100.0	36.42	10.33	13.8	16.59
	Index	100	79	87	99	76
Occupation - Farmers/Ranchers-Owners/Managers	(000)	*706	**146	**39	**31	**61
	Resps	52	15	4	4	7
	Vert%	0.36	0.16	0.17	0.11	0.14
	Horz%	100.0	20.62	5.5	4.34	8.7
	Index	100	45	46	31	40
Occupation - Service Workers	(000)	17220	8560	1853	2702	4074
	Resps	1280	662	164	204	324
	Vert%	8.86	9.58	8.0	10.01	9.58
	Horz%	100.0	49.71	10.76	15.69	23.66
	Index	100	108	90	113	108
Occupation - Farm Laborers	(000)	**235	**80	**23	**9	**38
	Resps	18	6	2	1	3
	Vert%	0.12	0.09	0.1	0.03	0.09
	Horz%	100.0	33.99	9.8	3.66	16.1
	Index	100	74	82	26	74
Occupation - Other Laborers	(000)	4086	1508	**301	*641	*546
	Resps	261	101	24	43	44
	Vert%	2.1	1.69	1.3	2.38	1.29
	Horz%	100.0	36.91	7.35	15.69	13.37
	Index	100	80	62	113	61
Occupation - Proprietors	(000)	1461	*466	**101	**145	**201
	Resps	114	47	10	15	22
	Vert%	0.75	0.52	0.44	0.54	0.47
	Horz%	100.0	31.9	6.92	9.91	13.74
	Index	100	69	58	71	63
Occupation - Professional/Managerial	(000)	38171	19826	5795	5382	9968
	Resps	3478	1868	571	517	989
	Vert%	19.64	22.19	25.01	19.94	23.45
	Horz%	100.0	51.94	15.18	14.1	26.11
	Index	100	113	127	102	119
Occupation - Professional/Technical	(000)	23981	13211	4296	4055	6636
	Resps	2506	1399	463	427	740
	Vert%	12.34	14.79	18.54	15.02	15.61
	Horz%	100.0	55.09	17.91	16.91	27.67
	Index	100	120	150	122	126

*Projection relatively unstable because of sample base - use with caution.
**Number of cases too small for reliability - shown for consistency only.

Source: NCS Part 1 SPRING 1999 Wgt: POP
Table Base: TOTAL

Choices System
Simmons Market Research Bureau

Oct 1, 1999

Row	CELL	TOTAL	Eat Yogurt	Cups Eaten Last 30 Days - Heavy 6+	Breyers OR Breyers Blended Low Fat OR Breyers Mix'n Crunch Low Fat	Dannon
Occupation - Technical/Clerical/Sales	(000)	37208	18826	5123	5887	9380
	Resps	3735	1934	548	598	1001
	Vert%	19.15	21.07	22.11	21.81	22.06
	Horz%	100.0	50.6	13.77	15.82	25.21
	Index	100	110	115	114	115
Occupation - Clerical/Sales	(000)	33012	16533	4334	5026	8290
	Resps	3145	1623	445	493	842
	Vert%	16.99	18.5	18.71	18.62	19.5
	Horz%	100.0	50.08	13.13	15.22	25.11
	Index	100	109	110	110	115
Occupation - Other Employed	(000)	36363	15429	3675	5332	7061
	Resps	2614	1152	302	388	547
	Vert%	18.71	17.27	15.86	19.75	16.61
	Horz%	100.0	42.43	10.11	14.66	19.42
	Index	100	92	85	106	89
No. in H/H - One	(000)	25941	12415	3361	3418	6250
	Resps	1644	851	236	225	453
	Vert%	13.35	13.89	14.51	12.67	14.7
	Horz%	100.0	47.86	12.96	13.18	24.09
	Index	100	104	109	95	110
No. in H/H - Two	(000)	66269	29812	8226	8284	14158
	Resps	5796	2816	833	785	1418
	Vert%	34.1	33.37	35.5	30.69	33.3
	Horz%	100.0	44.99	12.41	12.5	21.36
	Index	100	98	104	90	98
No. in H/H - Three	(000)	36686	16822	4108	5513	8210
	Resps	3021	1465	384	472	759
	Vert%	18.88	18.83	17.73	20.43	19.31
	Horz%	100.0	45.85	11.2	15.03	22.38
	Index	100	100	94	108	102
No. in H/H - Four	(000)	36875	16850	4304	5654	7470
	Resps	3104	1544	427	495	719
	Vert%	18.97	18.86	18.57	20.95	17.57
	Horz%	100.0	45.69	11.67	15.33	20.26
	Index	100	99	98	110	93
No. in H/H - Five	(000)	16091	7650	1997	2566	3877
	Resps	1279	643	177	210	343
	Vert%	8.28	8.56	8.62	9.51	9.12
	Horz%	100.0	47.54	12.41	15.95	24.09
	Index	100	103	104	115	110
No. in H/H - Six	(000)	7866	3686	801	904	1745
	Resps	565	286	66	79	142
	Vert%	4.05	4.13	3.46	3.35	4.1
	Horz%	100.0	46.86	10.18	11.49	22.18
	Index	100	102	85	83	101

*Projection relatively unstable because of sample base - use with caution.
**Number of cases too small for reliability - shown for consistency only.

Source: NCS Part 1 SPRING 1999 Wgt: POP
Table Base: TOTAL

Choices System
Simmons Market Research Bureau

Oct 1, 1999

Row	CELL	TOTAL	Eat Yogurt	Cups Eaten Last 30 Days - Heavy 6+	Breyers OR Breyers Blended Low Fat OR Breyers Mix'n Crunch Low Fat	Dannon
No. in H/H - Seven	(000)	2399	1098	**276	**387	*358
	Resps	173	85	21	28	35
	Vert%	1.23	1.23	1.19	1.44	0.84
	Horz%	100.0	45.77	11.51	16.15	14.91
	Index	100	100	97	116	68
No. in H/H - Eight Or More	(000)	2215	1018	**98	**264	*446
	Resps	136	65	10	11	31
	Vert%	1.14	1.14	0.42	0.98	1.05
	Horz%	100.0	45.96	4.42	11.9	20.13
	Index	100	100	37	86	92
H/H Inc. - Less Than $10,000	(000)	13055	5953	1412	1914	2551
	Resps	498	229	61	68	101
	Vert%	6.72	6.66	6.09	7.09	6.0
	Horz%	100.0	45.6	10.81	14.66	19.54
	Index	100	99	91	106	89
H/H Inc. - $10,000 - $14,999	(000)	11420	4878	1238	1256	2094
	Resps	565	267	73	67	126
	Vert%	5.88	5.46	5.34	4.65	4.93
	Horz%	100.0	42.72	10.84	11.0	18.34
	Index	100	93	91	79	84
H/H Inc. - $30,000 Or More	(000)	135770	64374	17188	19634	31389
	Resps	12650	6335	1785	1885	3230
	Vert%	69.86	72.05	74.18	72.74	73.83
	Horz%	100.0	47.41	12.66	14.46	23.12
	Index	100	103	106	104	106
H/H Inc. - $40,000 Or More	(000)	113680	54376	14692	16688	26729
	Resps	10880	5510	1562	1649	2831
	Vert%	58.5	60.86	63.41	61.83	62.87
	Horz%	100.0	47.83	12.92	14.68	23.51
	Index	100	104	108	106	107
H/H Inc. - $50,000 Or More	(000)	93417	45103	12537	13718	22584
	Resps	9129	4644	1341	1381	2419
	Vert%	48.07	50.48	54.11	50.82	53.12
	Horz%	100.0	48.28	13.42	14.68	24.18
	Index	100	105	113	106	111
H/H Inc. - $60,000 Or More	(000)	75146	36590	10034	11177	18529
	Resps	7512	3845	1098	1151	2025
	Vert%	38.67	40.95	43.3	41.41	43.58
	Horz%	100.0	48.69	13.35	14.87	24.66
	Index	100	106	112	107	113
H/H Inc. - $75,000 Or More	(000)	53149	25674	7119	7594	13135
	Resps	5528	2830	820	834	1498
	Vert%	27.35	28.73	30.72	28.14	30.9
	Horz%	100.0	48.31	13.39	14.29	24.71
	Index	100	105	112	103	113

*Projection relatively unstable because of sample base - use with caution.
**Number of cases too small for reliability - shown for consistency only.

Source: NCS Part 1 SPRING 1999 Wgt: POP
Table Base: TOTAL

Choices System
Simmons Market Research Bureau

Oct 1, 1999

Row	CELL	TOTAL	Eat Yogurt	Cups Eaten Last 30 Days - Heavy 6+	Breyers OR Breyers Blended Low Fat OR Breyers Mix'n Crunch Low Fat	Dannon
H/H Inc. - $100,000 Or More	(000)	30093	14647	3989	4301	7407
	Resps	3193	1648	465	466	886
	Vert%	15.48	16.39	17.22	15.94	17.42
	Horz%	100.0	48.67	13.26	14.29	24.61
	Index	100	106	111	103	113
No. of Children - One	(000)	29887	13868	3351	4707	6983
	Resps	2403	1188	318	402	627
	Vert%	15.38	15.52	14.46	17.44	16.43
	Horz%	100.0	46.4	11.21	15.75	23.37
	Index	100	101	94	113	107
No. of Children - Two	(000)	30257	14430	3943	4657	6726
	Resps	2516	1295	382	401	631
	Vert%	15.57	16.15	17.02	17.26	15.82
	Horz%	100.0	47.69	13.03	15.39	22.23
	Index	100	104	109	111	102
No. of Children - Three	(000)	10496	5005	1107	1586	2388
	Resps	865	431	102	126	222
	Vert%	5.4	5.6	4.78	5.88	5.62
	Horz%	100.0	47.68	10.55	15.11	22.75
	Index	100	104	88	109	104
No. of Children - Four	(000)	3436	1541	*424	**396	*587
	Resps	240	119	31	29	51
	Vert%	1.77	1.72	1.83	1.47	1.38
	Horz%	100.0	44.84	12.33	11.52	17.09
	Index	100	98	103	83	78
No. of Children - Five	(000)	1223	*560	**72	**149	**144
	Resps	70	35	6	6	13
	Vert%	0.63	0.63	0.31	0.55	0.34
	Horz%	100.0	45.76	5.85	12.19	11.75
	Index	100	100	49	88	54
No. of Children - Six	(000)	*525	**249	**63	**38	**123
	Resps	31	16	5	2	7
	Vert%	0.27	0.28	0.27	0.14	0.29
	Horz%	100.0	47.44	11.91	7.32	23.35
	Index	100	103	100	53	107
No. of Children - Seven	(000)	**77	**72	**0	**0	**40
	Resps	8	7	0	0	4
	Vert%	0.04	0.08	0.0	0.0	0.09
	Horz%	100.0	93.52	0.0	0.0	52.2
	Index	100	203	0.0	0.0	239
No. of Children - Eight	(000)	**37	**15	**0	**0	**15
	Resps	2	1	0	0	1
	Vert%	0.02	0.02	0.0	0.0	0.04
	Horz%	100.0	42.08	0.0	0.0	42.08
	Index	100	92	0.0	0.0	192

*Projection relatively unstable because of sample base - use with caution.
**Number of cases too small for reliability - shown for consistency only.

Source: NCS Part 1 SPRING 1999 Wgt: POP
Table Base: TOTAL

Choices System
Simmons Market Research Bureau

Oct 1, 1999

Row	CELL	TOTAL	Eat Yogurt	Cups Eaten Last 30 Days - Heavy 6+	Breyers OR Breyers Blended Low Fat OR Breyers Mix'n Crunch Low Fat	Dannon
No. of Children - Nine Or More	(000)	**90	**16	**0	**0	**16
	Resps	4	1	0	0	1
	Vert%	0.05	0.02	0.0	0.0	0.04
	Horz%	100.0	17.67	0.0	0.0	17.67
	Index	100	38	0.0	0.0	81
No Children	(000)	118315	53594	14211	15457	25492
	Resps	9579	4662	1310	1339	2343
	Vert%	60.88	59.98	61.33	57.27	59.96
	Horz%	100.0	45.3	12.01	13.06	21.55
	Index	100	99	101	94	98

*Projection relatively unstable because of sample base - use with caution.
**Number of cases too small for reliability - shown for consistency only.

Source: NCS Part 1 SPRING 1999 Wgt: POP
Table Base: TOTAL

Choices System
Simmons Market Research Bureau

Oct 1, 1999

Row	CELL	TOTAL	Eat Yogurt	Cups Eaten Last 30 Days - Heavy 6+	Breyers OR Breyers Blended Low Fat OR Breyers Mix'n Crunch Low Fat	Dannon
TOTAL	(000)	194341	89349	23171	26991	42514
	Resps	15718	7755	2154	2305	3900
	Vert%	100.0	100.0	100.0	100.0	100.0
	Horz%	100.0	45.98	11.92	13.89	21.88
	Index	100	100	100	100	100
Television - 3Rd Rock From the Sun	(000)	13163	6705	1991	2096	3474
	Resps	1118	604	193	188	322
	Vert%	6.77	7.5	8.59	7.77	8.17
	Horz%	100.0	50.94	15.13	15.92	26.39
	Index	100	111	127	115	121
Television - Chicago Hope	(000)	13896	7543	2063	2859	3948
	Resps	1205	678	194	245	363
	Vert%	7.15	8.44	8.9	10.59	9.29
	Horz%	100.0	54.28	14.84	20.58	28.41
	Index	100	118	124	148	130
Television - Everybody Loves Raymond	(000)	17579	8894	2539	2717	4726
	Resps	1544	811	255	241	436
	Vert%	9.05	9.95	10.96	10.07	11.12
	Horz%	100.0	50.59	14.44	15.46	26.88
	Index	100	110	121	111	123
Television - Just Shoot Me	(000)	14932	7808	2106	2413	4215
	Resps	1345	736	213	242	410
	Vert%	7.68	8.74	9.09	8.94	9.91
	Horz%	100.0	52.29	14.1	16.16	28.23
	Index	100	114	118	116	129
Television - King of Queens	(000)	8438	4233	1057	1505	2363
	Resps	714	372	102	124	216
	Vert%	4.34	4.74	4.56	5.58	5.56
	Horz%	100.0	50.17	12.53	17.84	28.0
	Index	100	109	105	128	128
Television - Law & Order	(000)	24151	11523	3083	3714	6224
	Resps	2092	1063	319	326	577
	Vert%	12.43	12.9	13.3	13.76	14.64
	Horz%	100.0	47.71	12.76	15.38	25.77
	Index	100	104	107	111	118
Television - Malcolm & Eddie	(000)	4844	2329	*515	*1277	*1061
	Resps	256	118	33	60	56
	Vert%	2.49	2.61	2.22	4.73	2.49
	Horz%	100.0	48.07	10.64	26.36	21.9
	Index	100	105	89	190	100
Television - Martha Stewart Living	(000)	8903	5719	1495	1935	3025
	Resps	802	515	145	162	278
	Vert%	4.58	6.4	6.45	7.17	7.12
	Horz%	100.0	64.23	16.79	21.73	33.98
	Index	100	140	141	156	155

*Projection relatively unstable because of sample base - use with caution.
**Number of cases too small for reliability - shown for consistency only.

Source: NCS Part 1 SPRING 1999 Wgt: POP
Table Base: TOTAL

Choices System
Simmons Market Research Bureau

Oct 1, 1999

Row	CELL	TOTAL	Eat Yogurt	Cups Eaten Last 30 Days - Heavy 6+	Breyers OR Breyers Blended Low Fat OR Breyers Mix'n Crunch Low Fat	Dannon
Television - Nash Bridges	(000)	15990	7607	1961	2558	3934
	Resps	1314	653	179	212	355
	Vert%	8.23	8.51	8.46	9.48	9.25
	Horz%	100.0	47.57	12.26	16.0	24.6
	Index	100	103	103	115	112
Television - Party of Five	(000)	11468	6095	1464	2073	3168
	Resps	905	497	137	152	264
	Vert%	5.9	6.82	6.32	7.68	7.45
	Horz%	100.0	53.14	12.77	18.08	27.62
	Index	100	116	107	130	126
Television - Promised Land	(000)	9999	5028	1246	1534	2508
	Resps	813	419	116	122	223
	Vert%	5.15	5.63	5.38	5.68	5.9
	Horz%	100.0	50.28	12.46	15.34	25.09
	Index	100	109	104	110	115
Television - Star Trek: Deep Space Nine	(000)	8035	4287	899	1451	2196
	Resps	631	340	81	104	165
	Vert%	4.13	4.8	3.88	5.38	5.17
	Horz%	100.0	53.35	11.18	18.06	27.33
	Index	100	116	94	130	125
Television - Touched By An Angel	(000)	30080	15349	4060	5140	8123
	Resps	2547	1359	381	433	748
	Vert%	15.48	17.18	17.52	19.04	19.11
	Horz%	100.0	51.03	13.5	17.09	27.0
	Index	100	111	113	123	123
Television - Walker, Texas Ranger	(000)	28852	12099	2717	3889	5689
	Resps	2184	982	254	300	490
	Vert%	14.85	13.54	11.73	14.41	13.38
	Horz%	100.0	41.93	9.42	13.48	19.72
	Index	100	91	79	97	90
Radio - Adult Contemporary	(000)	16509	8867	2715	2618	4834
	Resps	1452	829	266	254	455
	Vert%	8.49	9.92	11.72	9.7	11.37
	Horz%	100.0	53.71	16.44	15.86	29.28
	Index	100	117	138	114	134
Radio - All News	(000)	4173	2438	669	808	1437
	Resps	412	243	75	82	145
	Vert%	2.15	2.73	2.89	2.99	3.38
	Horz%	100.0	58.42	16.03	19.36	34.44
	Index	100	127	134	139	157
Radio - Classic Rock	(000)	10494	4988	1401	1194	2547
	Resps	897	458	127	116	247
	Vert%	5.4	5.58	6.05	4.42	5.99
	Horz%	100.0	47.53	13.35	11.37	24.27
	Index	100	103	112	82	111

*Projection relatively unstable because of sample base - use with caution.
**Number of cases too small for reliability - shown for consistency only.

Page 2

92

Source: NCS Part 1 SPRING 1999 Wgt: POP
Table Base: TOTAL

Choices System
Simmons Market Research Bureau

Oct 1, 1999

Row	CELL	TOTAL	Eat Yogurt	Cups Eaten Last 30 Days - Heavy 6+	Breyers OR Breyers Blended Low Fat OR Breyers Mix'n Crunch Low Fat	Dannon
Radio - Easy Listening	(000)	728	*354	**73	**122	**144
	Resps	70	37	10	14	16
	Vert%	0.37	0.4	0.32	0.45	0.34
	Horz%	100.0	48.67	10.04	16.78	19.8
	Index	100	106	84	121	91
Radio - Jazz	(000)	3982	2278	605	700	1179
	Resps	344	208	66	63	120
	Vert%	2.05	2.55	2.61	2.59	2.77
	Horz%	100.0	57.21	15.2	17.59	29.6
	Index	100	124	128	127	135
Radio - Modern Rock	(000)	4786	2629	*543	717	1303
	Resps	388	221	54	64	113
	Vert%	2.46	2.94	2.34	2.66	3.07
	Horz%	100.0	54.94	11.34	14.99	27.23
	Index	100	119	95	108	124
Radio - Spanish	(000)	2974	1588	**301	**488	*733
	Resps	173	91	22	25	46
	Vert%	1.53	1.78	1.3	1.81	1.72
	Horz%	100.0	53.4	10.12	16.41	24.63
	Index	100	116	85	118	113
Radio - Urban Contemporary	(000)	6374	2686	*507	1292	1420
	Resps	392	197	43	84	106
	Vert%	3.28	3.01	2.19	4.79	3.34
	Horz%	100.0	42.14	7.95	20.27	22.28
	Index	100	92	67	146	102
Interactive Comp Serv-Ever Use/Subscribe	(000)	80433	40912	11692	11796	21216
	Resps	7253	3891	1142	1106	2078
	Vert%	41.39	45.79	50.46	43.7	49.9
	Horz%	100.0	50.86	14.54	14.67	26.38
	Index	100	111	122	106	121

*Projection relatively unstable because of sample base - use with caution.
**Number of cases too small for reliability - shown for consistency only.

Source: NCS Part 1 SPRING 1999 Wgt: POP
Table Base: TOTAL

Choices System
Simmons Market Research Bureau

Sep 30, 1999

Row	CELL	TOTAL	Female	Female 18-24
TOTAL	(000)	194341	101169	12404
	Resps	15718	8925	859
	Vert%	100.0	100.0	100.0
	Horz%	100.0	52.06	6.38
	Index	100	100	100
Bridal Guide	(000)	1738	1310	435
	Resps	351	287	87
	Vert%	0.89	1.3	3.51
	Horz%	100.0	75.4	25.05
	Index	100	145	392
Cosmopolitan	(000)	8982	7659	2390
	Resps	1712	1457	339
	Vert%	4.62	7.57	19.26
	Horz%	100.0	85.27	26.6
	Index	100	164	417
Family Circle	(000)	15647	14411	685
	Resps	2886	2666	117
	Vert%	8.05	14.24	5.52
	Horz%	100.0	92.1	4.38
	Index	100	177	69
Glamour	(000)	6588	5991	1943
	Resps	1375	1258	290
	Vert%	3.39	5.92	15.66
	Horz%	100.0	90.93	29.49
	Index	100	175	462
Jet	(000)	8285	4539	704
	Resps	713	436	72
	Vert%	4.26	4.49	5.67
	Horz%	100.0	54.79	8.5
	Index	100	105	133
Ladies' Home Journal	(000)	10623	9780	309
	Resps	2018	1863	69
	Vert%	5.47	9.67	2.49
	Horz%	100.0	92.06	2.91
	Index	100	177	46
Life	(000)	10178	5756	752
	Resps	2207	1337	160
	Vert%	5.24	5.69	6.06
	Horz%	100.0	56.55	7.39
	Index	100	109	116
Mademoiselle	(000)	4084	3603	1410
	Resps	780	694	216
	Vert%	2.1	3.56	11.37
	Horz%	100.0	88.22	34.53
	Index	100	169	541

*Projection relatively unstable because of sample base - use with caution.
**Number of cases too small for reliability - shown for consistency only.

Source: NCS Part 1 SPRING 1999 Wgt: POP
Table Base: TOTAL

Choices System
Simmons Market Research Bureau

Sep 30, 1999

Row	CELL	TOTAL	Female	Female 18-24
National Geographic	*(000)*	17414	7784	724
	Resps	2919	1511	122
	Vert%	8.96	7.69	5.84
	Horz%	100.0	44.7	4.16
	Index	100	86	65
Parenting	*(000)*	4369	3527	669
	Resps	822	676	103
	Vert%	2.25	3.49	5.39
	Horz%	100.0	80.73	15.32
	Index	100	155	240
Reader's Digest	*(000)*	30441	19062	1129
	Resps	4500	2897	184
	Vert%	15.66	18.84	9.1
	Horz%	100.0	62.62	3.71
	Index	100	120	58
Shape	*(000)*	2976	2506	579
	Resps	603	519	96
	Vert%	1.53	2.48	4.67
	Horz%	100.0	84.22	19.46
	Index	100	162	305
Spin	*(000)*	1850	871	414
	Resps	370	196	76
	Vert%	0.95	0.86	3.34
	Horz%	100.0	47.07	22.37
	Index	100	90	351
TV Guide	*(000)*	30885	18396	2093
	Resps	3604	2235	253
	Vert%	15.89	18.18	16.87
	Horz%	100.0	59.56	6.78
	Index	100	114	106
Vanity Fair	*(000)*	3278	2292	408
	Resps	669	517	86
	Vert%	1.69	2.27	3.29
	Horz%	100.0	69.93	12.45
	Index	100	134	195

*Projection relatively unstable because of sample base - use with caution.
**Number of cases too small for reliability - shown for consistency only.

Information Sources

"To know the road ahead, ask those coming back."

—Chinese Proverb

Introduction.

F.Y.I.

There is a great deal of secondary information that is available to both the entrepreneur and the student.

In this section we will review LNA, SRDS, and the GPO with a little detail. Plus an important new information resource—the Net.

A. Competitive Media Reporting:

Competitive Expenditures.

Competitive Media Reporting (LNA/MediaWatch) is in the business of reporting competitive advertising expenditures. They do this in a variety of ways, but for our purposes the most valuable is class/company/brand information. Here is an example from 1997.

Look at page 99 and you will see that Dannon Light Yogurt spent $10,094.3M in calendar year 1997. This compares with $1,168.4M for Breyers Light (on page 100). Dannon had an increase. Breyers had a decrease.

Yogurt Competitive Expenditures ($M)

(Index versus year ago)

	1997	1996	Index
Dannon Lt.	$10,094.3	$1,385.9	(728)
Breyers Lt.	1,168.4	3,693.1	(32)

This information can be used to determine what media your key competitors are using. If their sales are strong, one factor could be their relative media weight; another factor is media selection.

B. Standard Rate and Data Service (SRDS):

Media Information.

SRDS provides rates and mechanical requirements for virtually all media. On page 101-2 you will find the listings for *Ladies Home Journal* and *Working Woman* from the SRDS Consumer Magazines book.

Spend some time looking at these pages. You will learn circulation (for CPM calculations), rates, and who knows, you may want to write to Barbara Litrell for a job when the class is over.

C. Government Printing Office (GPO):

Interesting Information About the Category.

The GPO is one of the most overlooked sources of information for marketing. The United States government researches and writes many publications each year.

These are free—or very inexpensive. The key is whether anything has been written about the category in which you do business.

To get a listing of all that is available, just write to the GPO:

Superintendent of Documents
Government Printing Office
Washington, DC 20402-9325

D. Surf the Net:

"The Web" Another Great Resource.

The Internet is also a great source of information. Use search engines to find information on brands and categories. Check trade organizations and every source reviewed earlier in the library.

Read competitive advertising. Many advertisers include Web site addresses in their regular consumer advertising.

Be sure to check every possible link. Here are a few:

• A.C. Nielsen Company   http://www.nielsen.com
• Standard Rate and Data Service http://www.srds.com/index.html
• Simmons Market Research Bureau http://www.smrb.com
• Competitive Media Reporting   http://www.cmr.com

Following pages used by permission of Competitive Media Reporting (LNA/MediaWatch) and SRDS.

CLASS/BRAND $

QUARTERLY AND YEAR-TO-DATE ADVERTISING DOLLARS (000)

CLASS/COMPANY/BRAND	CLASS CODE	Period	10-MEDIA TOTAL	MAGAZINES	SUNDAY MAGAZINES	NEWSPAPERS	OUTDOOR	NETWORK TELEVISION	SPOT TELEVISION	SYNDICATED TELEVISION	CABLE TV NETWORKS	NETWORK RADIO	NATIONAL SPOT RADIO
F139 COMB COPY & MISC DAIRY PRODUCTS---							*CONTINUED*						
DAIRY MKT INC (CONTINUED)													
UNITED DAIRY ASSN	F139-9	96 YTD	54.0	--	--	--	26.1	--		--	--	--	27.9
UNITED DAIRY DAIRY PDTS	F139	Q1	3.2	--	--	--	3.2	--	--	--	--	--	--
		Q2	11.2	--	--	--	11.2	--	--	--	--	--	--
		Q3	9.6	--	--	--	9.6	--	--	--	--	--	--
		Q4	24.0	--	--	--	24.0	--	--	--	--	--	--
		97 YTD	64.0	--	--	--	64.0	--	--	--	--	--	--
		96 YTD	--	--	--	--	--	--	--	--	--	--	--
WESTERN DAIRY FRMRS ASSN	F139-9	Q1	7.6	--	--	--	7.6	--	--	--	--	--	--
		Q2	7.5	--	--	--	7.5	--	--	--	--	--	--
		Q3	12.5	--	--	--	11.4	--	--	--	--	--	1.1
		Q4	25.4	--	--	--	11.4	--	--	--	--	--	14.0
		97 YTD	53.1	--	--	--	38.0	--	--	--	--	--	15.1
COMPANY TOTAL		Q1	804.2	--	7.0	701.8	93.6	--	1.8	--	--	--	--
		Q2	257.6	--	17.5	--	234.5	--	5.6	--	--	--	--
		Q3	326.4	--	26.1	0.4	221.3	--	77.5	--	--	--	1.1
		Q4	278.9	--	55.6	178.0	29.4	--	0.4	--	--	--	15.5
		97 YTD	1,667.1	--	106.2	880.2	578.8	--	85.3	--	--	--	16.6
		96 YTD	3,469.1	--	116.6	86.1	1,578.2	--	32.6	--	--	--	1,655.6
DAISY BRAND OF TX INC													
DAISY LIGHT SOUR CREAM	F139	Q2	0.1	--	--	--	--	--	0.1	--	--	--	--
		Q3	7.9	--	--	--	--	--	7.9	--	--	--	--
		97 YTD	8.0	--	--	--	--	--	8.0	--	--	--	--
		96 YTD	160.0	157.7	--	--	--	--	2.3	--	--	--	--
DAISY REG & LIGHT SOUR CREAM	F139	Q2	1.3	--	--	--	--	--	1.3	--	--	--	--
		97 YTD	28.1	--	--	--	--	--	28.1	--	--	--	--
		96 YTD	29.4	--	--	--	--	--	29.4	--	--	--	--
DAISY SOUR CREAM	F139	Q1	151.2	--	--	14.0	--	--	137.2	--	--	--	--
		Q2	207.9	--	--	--	--	--	207.9	--	--	--	--
		Q3	327.4	--	--	21.4	--	--	255.6	--	--	--	50.4
		Q4	136.5	--	--	--	--	--	108.3	--	--	--	28.2
		97 YTD	823.0	--	--	35.4	--	--	709.0	--	--	--	78.6
		96 YTD	835.8	147.0	--	--	--	--	688.8	--	--	--	--
COMPANY TOTAL		Q1	151.2	--	--	14.0	--	--	137.2	--	--	--	--
		Q2	209.3	--	--	--	--	--	209.3	--	--	--	--
		Q3	363.4	--	--	21.4	--	--	291.6	--	--	--	50.4
		Q4	136.5	--	--	--	--	--	108.3	--	--	--	28.2
		97 YTD	860.4	--	--	35.4	--	--	746.6	--	--	--	78.6
		96 YTD	995.8	304.7	--	--	--	--	691.1	--	--	--	--
DANONE GROUPE SA													
DANNON CHUNKY FRUIT FAT FREE YOGURT	F139	Q1	143.8	143.8	--	--	--	--	--	--	--	--	--
		Q2	1,139.6	1,139.6	--	--	--	--	--	--	--	--	--
		Q3	703.6	703.6	--	--	--	--	--	--	--	--	--
		97 YTD	1,987.0	1,987.0	--	--	--	--	--	--	--	--	--
DANNON CHUNKY FRUIT YOGURT	F139	Q1	705.9	--	--	--	--	--	705.9	--	--	--	--
		Q2	1,436.2	--	--	--	--	--	1,061.3	--	--	--	374.9
		Q3	421.9	--	--	--	--	--	303.1	--	--	--	118.8
		97 YTD	2,564.0	--	--	--	--	--	2,070.3	--	--	--	493.7
		96 YTD	3,332.5	--	--	--	--	--	3,332.5	--	--	--	--
DANNON CO SPORTING EVENT	F139-8	Q1	66.0	66.0	--	--	--	--	--	--	--	--	--
		97 YTD	66.0	66.0	--	--	--	--	--	--	--	--	--
		96 YTD	90.3	90.3	--	--	--	--	--	--	--	--	--
DANNON DANNIMALS YOGURT	F139	Q3	53.2	--	--	--	--	--	--	--	--	--	53.2
		97 YTD	53.2	--	--	--	--	--	--	--	--	--	53.2
---- CONTINUED ----													

2842

CLASS/BRAND $

LNA/MEDIAWATCH MULTI-MEDIA SERVICE
January - December 1997

QUARTERLY AND YEAR-TO-DATE ADVERTISING DOLLARS (000)

CLASS/COMPANY/BRAND	CLASS CODE	Period	10-MEDIA TOTAL	MAGAZINES	SUNDAY MAGAZINES	NEWSPAPERS	OUTDOOR	NETWORK TELEVISION	SPOT TELEVISION	SYNDICATED TELEVISION	CABLE TV NETWORKS	NETWORK RADIO	NATIONAL SPOT RADIO
F139 COMB COPY & MISC DAIRY PRODUCTS --							CONTINUED						
DANNON GROUPE SA (CONTINUED)													
DANNON DOUBLE DELIGHTS RED FAT YGRT	F139	Q3	291.3	291.3									
		97 YTD	291.3	291.3									
DANNON DOUBLE DELIGHTS YOGURT	F139	Q1	3,280.1					2,522.0	0.5		757.6		
		Q2	1,293.3						975.5		317.8		
		Q3	2,940.0	1,136.1				1,113.6	8.1	352.6	315.4		14.2
		Q4	162.0	157.6							5.0		
		97 YTD	7,676.0	1,283.7				3,635.6	984.1	352.6	1,395.8		14.2
		96 YTD	9,895.8	3,193.7				5,422.1	12.9		1,267.1		
DANNON LIGHT DUETS FAT FREE YOGURT	F139	Q1	824.0	824.0									
		Q2	994.4	994.4									
		97 YTD	1,818.4	1,818.4									
		96 YTD	2,010.5	2,010.5									
DANNON LIGHT YOGURT	F139	Q2	217.0										217.0
		Q3	5,688.4					1,333.7	734.1	2,512.0	1,108.6		
		Q4	4,188.9					1,232.5	607.6	1,585.8	763.0		
		97 YTD	10,094.3					2,566.2	1,341.7	4,097.8	1,871.6		217.0
		96 YTD	1,385.9	1,069.7					14.6		1.9		299.7
DANNON SOCCER FESTIVAL	F139-8	Q3	10.7										10.7
		97 YTD	10.7										10.7
DANNON SPRINKLINS LOW FAT YOGURT	F139	Q4	74.8	74.8									
		97 YTD	74.8	74.8									
		96 YTD	821.8	98.0				210.7					
DANNON SPRINKLINS MSC CRST YOGURT	F139	Q1	16.4	16.4									
		Q4	42.0	42.0					1.6				
		97 YTD	58.4	58.4									
		96 YTD	100.5	100.5						46.0	465.5		
DANNON WINTERFEST	F139-8	Q4	66.0	66.0									
		97 YTD	66.0	66.0									
DANNON YOGURT	F139	Q2	0.4			0.4							
		Q3	443.1			430.0				13.1			
		Q4	19.8										19.8
		97 YTD	463.3			430.4				13.1			19.8
COMPANY TOTAL		Q1	5,253.2	1,050.2				2,522.0	706.4		757.6		217.0
		Q2	4,863.9	2,134.0		0.4			2,036.8		317.8		374.9
		Q3	10,552.2	2,131.4		430.0		2,447.3	1,045.3	2,877.7	1,424.0		196.9
		Q4	4,554.2	340.4				1,232.5	607.6	1,585.8	768.0		19.8
		97 YTD	25,223.4	5,655.6		430.4		6,201.8	4,396.1	4,463.5	3,267.4		808.6
		96 YTD	21,344.8	6,562.7				8,284.5	3,363.4	46.0	2,768.5		299.7
DARIGOLD FARMS													
DARIGOLD DAIRY POTS	F139	Q1	9.4										9.4
		Q3	44.0				44.0						
		97 YTD	53.4				44.0						9.4
		96 YTD	180.9	6.9			54.2						119.8
DARIGOLD YOGURT	F139	Q2	0.1						0.1				
		97 YTD	0.1						0.1				
		96 YTD	0.2						0.2				
----- CONTINUED -----													

2843

LNA/MEDIAWATCH MULTI-MEDIA SERVICE
January - December 1997

CLASS/BRAND $

QUARTERLY AND YEAR-TO-DATE ADVERTISING DOLLARS (000)

CLASS/COMPANY/BRAND	Period	CLASS CODE	10-MEDIA TOTAL	MAGAZINES	SUNDAY MAGAZINES	NEWSPAPERS	OUTDOOR	NETWORK TELEVISION	SPOT TELEVISION	SYNDICATED TELEVISION	CABLE TV NETWORKS	NETWORK RADIO	NATIONAL SPOT RADIO
F139 COMB COPY & MISC DAIRY PRODUCTS--						CONTINUED							
UNILEVER													
BREYERS LIGHT YOGURT	Q1	F139	1,166.2	238.0	--	--	--	--	653.0	--	275.2	--	--
	Q2		1.2	--	--	--	--	--	1.2	--	--	--	--
	Q3		1.0	--	--	--	--	--	1.0	--	--	--	--
	Q4		--	--	--	--	--	--	--	--	--	--	--
	97 YTD		1,168.4	238.0	--	--	--	--	655.2	--	275.2	--	--
	96 YTD		3,693.1	1,570.1	--	--	--	--	1,606.9	--	516.1	--	--
KNUDSEN DAIRY PDTS	Q1	F139	5.2	--	--	5.2	--	--	--	--	--	--	--
	Q2		66.1	--	--	66.1	--	--	--	--	--	--	--
	Q3		66.1	--	--	66.1	--	--	--	--	--	--	--
	Q4		--	--	--	--	--	--	--	--	--	--	--
	97 YTD		137.4	--	--	137.4	--	--	--	--	--	--	--
	96 YTD		57.1	7.9	--	49.2	--	--	--	--	--	--	--
COMPANY TOTAL	Q1		1,171.4	238.0	--	5.2	--	--	653.0	--	275.2	--	--
	Q2		67.3	--	--	66.1	--	--	1.2	--	--	--	--
	Q3		67.1	--	--	66.1	--	--	1.0	--	--	--	--
	Q4		--	--	--	--	--	--	--	--	--	--	--
	97 YTD		1,305.8	238.0	--	137.4	--	--	655.2	--	275.2	--	--
	96 YTD		3,750.2	1,578.0	--	49.2	--	--	1,606.9	--	516.1	--	--
V&V FOOD PDTS INC — V&V SUPREMO CREAM	Q1	F139	10.5	--	--	--	--	--	10.5	--	--	--	--
	Q2		3.1	--	--	--	--	--	3.1	--	--	--	--
	Q3		13.5	--	--	--	--	--	13.5	--	--	--	--
	Q4		24.9	--	--	--	--	--	24.9	--	--	--	--
	97 YTD		52.0	--	--	--	--	--	52.0	--	--	--	--
WELLS DAIRY CO — WELLS BLUE BUNNY DAIRY PDTS	Q2	F139	10.5	--	--	--	--	--	10.5	--	--	--	--
	97 YTD		10.5	--	--	--	--	--	10.5	--	--	--	--
WILCOX DAIRY — WILCOX DAIRY PDTS	Q1	F139	7.1	--	--	--	--	--	7.1	--	--	--	--
	Q2		9.1	--	--	--	--	--	9.1	--	--	--	--
	Q3		14.9	--	--	--	--	--	14.9	--	--	--	--
	Q4		6.7	--	--	--	--	--	6.7	--	--	--	--
	97 YTD		37.8	--	--	--	--	--	37.8	--	--	--	--
	96 YTD		27.5	--	--	--	--	--	27.5	--	--	--	--
WILD ORCHID — WILD ORCHID DAIRY PDTS	Q2	F139	47.7	--	--	--	47.7	--	--	--	--	--	--
	97 YTD		47.7	--	--	--	47.7	--	--	--	--	--	--
CLASS TOTAL	Q1		16,804.0	3,299.1	7.0	752.2	352.9	4,121.8	4,937.1	1,067.0	1,851.4	--	415.5
	Q2		13,127.9	2,536.8	17.5	215.6	793.0	1,357.8	6,126.9	436.1	1,149.3	--	494.9
	Q3		27,014.2	4,758.2	353.4	545.3	599.7	4,848.7	9,354.6	4,180.9	2,149.8	--	270.4
	Q4		15,942.5	2,007.9	55.7	348.1	293.4	1,897.5	7,609.8	2,143.0	1,056.7	--	173.7
	97 YTD		72,888.6	12,602.0	433.6	1,861.2	2,039.0	12,225.8	28,028.4	7,827.0	6,507.2	--	1,354.5
	96 YTD		78,854.2	19,420.5	293.2	479.4	2,597.7	20,392.8	20,933.1	2,884.0	8,628.2	--	3,225.3
F141 CITRUS FRUITS--													
DOLE FOOD CO INC — DOLE CANNED PINEAPPLE	Q1		442.8	442.8	--	--	--	--	--	--	--	--	--
	Q2		701.9	701.9	--	--	--	--	--	--	--	--	--
	Q3		316.0	316.0	--	--	--	--	--	--	--	--	--
	Q4		137.0	137.0	--	--	--	--	--	--	--	--	--
	97 YTD		1,598.5	1,598.5	--	--	--	--	--	--	--	--	--
	96 YTD		38.7	--	--	38.7	--	--	--	--	--	--	--
DOLE CANNED PINEAPPLE&TS JC	Q1	F141	310.5	310.5	--	--	--	--	--	--	--	--	--
	Q2		220.0	220.0	--	--	--	--	--	--	--	--	--
	Q3		382.0	382.0	--	--	--	--	--	--	--	--	--
	Q4		137.0	137.0	--	--	--	--	--	--	--	--	--
	97 YTD		1,050.3	1,050.3	--	--	--	--	--	--	--	--	--
---- CONTINUED ----													

LADIES' HOME

JOURNAL

A Meredith Corporation Publication

Location ID: 8 MLST 49 **Mid 001254-000**
Published monthly by Meredith Corporation, 125 Park Ave., 19th Fl., New York, NY 10017. Phone 212-557-6600.
E-Mail jseilheimer@mdp.com

For shipping info., see Print Media Production Source.

PUBLISHER'S EDITORIAL PROFILE

LADIES' HOME JOURNAL is for active, empowered women who are evolving in new directions. It addresses informational needs with highly focused features and articles on a variety of topics including beauty and fashion, food and nutrition, health and medicine, home decorating and design, parenting and self-help, personalities and current events. Rec'd 5/20/94.

1. PERSONNEL

Pub—Michael Brownstein.
Adv Dir—Kristine Welker.
Mktg Dir—Susan Parkes.
Research Dir—David Forier.

2. REPRESENTATIVES and/or BRANCH OFFICES

Chicago, IL 60611—Christi Neill, Mgr, 333 N. Michigan Ave, Ste. 1101. Phone 312-580-7757.
San Francisco, CA 94111—Janet Davy, Mgr. 100 Pine St., Ste. 2850. Phone 415-421-9650.
Los Angeles, CA 90025—Kuuipo Cashman, Mgr, 11766 Wilshire Blvd., Ste. 260. Phone 310-479-4663. Fax 310-479-6663.
Royal Oak, MI 48067—Albaum Maiorana & Associates, Inc., 418 West 5th St., Ste. C. Phone 810-546-2222. Fax 810-546-0019.
New York, NY 10017—Peter Mason, Travel Mgr, 125 Park Ave. Phone 212-551-7051.
New York, NY 10017—Edwin Kabakow, Pres., 212-297-0022; Louis George Pepe, Exec VP, Media People, Inc., 317 Madison Ave. Fax 212-972-0144.

3. COMMISSION AND CASH DISCOUNT

15% to recognized agencies. Bills rendered the 15th of month preceding issue date.

4. GENERAL RATE POLICY

Announcement of any change in rates will be made 30 days prior to the closing date of the first issue to be affected by the new rates. All orders will be accepted at the prevailing rate of the issue in which space is ordered.

ADVERTISING RATES
Effective January 1, 1999.
Rates received September 15, 1998.

5. BLACK/WHITE RATES

1 page (420 lines)	139,900.
2/3 page (286 lines)	100,300.
1/2 page, Digest or Checkerboard	85,200.
1/3 page (143 lines)	53,900.
1/6 page	28,900.

DEALER AND STORE LISTINGS

Details regarding retail programs are available upon request.

CUSTOM MARKETING

Individually customized combinations of other Meredith publications can be combined with LHJ to maximize effective advertising exposures. For additional details see your account manager.

6. COLOR RATES

2-Color:	
1 page	143,800.
2/3 page	100,500.
1/2 page, Digest or Checkerboard	83,600.
1/3 page	53,100.
4-Color:	
1 page	147,900.
2/3 page	112,100.
1/2 page, Digest or Checkerboard	87,500.
1/3 page	60,700.

7. COVERS

4-Color:

2nd cover	178,200.	4th cover	210,300.
3rd cover	163,100.		

Non-cancellable 2 months prior to national closing date.

8. INSERTS

Available.

9. BLEED

No charge.

11. CLASSIFIED/MAIL ORDER/SPECIALTY RATES

NATIONAL TRAVEL RATES

BLACK AND WHITE RATES:

	1 ti	2 ti	3 ti
Spread	198,400.	188,480.	178,560.
1 page	99,200.	94,240.	89,280.
2/3 page	70,980.	67,430.	63,880.
1/2 page	60,230.	57,220.	54,200.
1/3 page	38,070.	36,170.	34,270.
1/6 page	20,390.	19,375.	18,350.

COLOR RATES:

	1 ti	2 ti	3 ti
2-Color:			
Spread	229,000.	217,555.	206,110.
1 page	114,500.	108,778.	103,055.
2/3 page	80,000.	76,010.	72,000.
1/2 page	63,675.	60,490.	57,300.
1/3 page	42,300.	40,175.	38,060.
4-Color:			
Spread	235,900.	224,100.	212,350.
1 page	117,950.	112,050.	106,175.
2/3 page	89,275.	84,810.	80,350.
1/2 page	69,670.	66,200.	62,700.
1/3 page	48,370.	45,950.	43,525.

12. SPLIT-RUN

Geographic split runs are available in offset only along regional lines. Premiums do not earn any discounts and are not subject to 15% agency commission. Splits along regional lines will include subscription copies. Spot market splits within any regions will run in subscriber copies only. Geographic and spot market splits are available in every issue, subject to mechanical capacity.

13a. GEOGRAPHIC and/or DEMOGRAPHIC EDITIONS

Region:	Circulation (000's)
NewEngland	195
Mid-Atlantic	691
EastNorth Central	713
WestNorth Central	378
Southeast	615
EastSouth Central	282
WestSouth Central	388
Mountain	242
Pacific	462

REGIONAL RATES PER THOUSAND

All Regional ads are eligible for Multiple Impression Discounts. Regional edition insertions also contribute to Multiple Impression Discount levels.

BLACK AND WHITE RATES:

	1 pg	2/3 pg	(*)	1/3 pg
Under 250,000 circulation	57.94	57.94	57.94	57.94
250 to 599,999	49.31	34.98	29.70	21.55
600,000 to 1,399,999	46.94	33.24	28.10	20.57
1,400,000 to 1,999,999	44.47	31.45	26.65	19.51
2,000,000 to 2,999,999	42.03	29.74	25.18	18.47
3,000,000 to 3,999,999	39.55	27.96	23.73	17.36
4,000,000 and over	37.08	26.24	22.16	16.28

COLOR RATES:

	1 pg	2/3 pg	(*)	1/3 pg
2-Color:				
Under 250,000 circulation	57.94	57.94	57.94	57.94
250,000 to 5999,999	53.03	36.75	30.64	21.92
600,000 to 1,399,999	50.39	34.84	29.16	20,72
1,400,000 to 1,999,999	47.75	32.97	27.65	19.64
2,000,000 to 2,999,999	45.10	31.17	26.11	18.55
3,000,000 to 3,999,999	42.44	29.39	24.50	17.45
4,000,000 and over	39.81	27.51	23.03	16.43

	1 pg	2/3 pg	(*)	1/3 pg
4-Color:				
Under 250,000 circulation	57.94	57.94	57.94	57.94
250,000 to 5999,999	54.64	41.38	32.25	24.66
600,000 to 1,399,999	51.94	39.37	30.67	23.46
to,400,000 to 1,999,999	49.07	37.30	29.03	22.19
2,000,000 to 2,999,999	46.30	35.26	27.44	20.91
3,000,000 to 3,999,999	43.71	33.17	25.79.	19.73.
4,000,000 and over	41.10	31.08	24.23	18.48

(*) 1/2 page, Checkerboard & Digest.

REGIONAL ROLL OUT PROGRAM

This program allows partial regional rebate to advertisers geographically testing a product prior to running national space. See your Account Manager for details.

SPOT (TEST) MARKETS

Rates are for full-page units only regardless of size or coloration at a 53.65 CPM. Minimum charge is 4900.00. Testing capabilities through Behaviorscan test markets are available at a rate of 4900.00 per page for geographic area.
Full latitude is necessary on all advertisements to meet mechanical and make-up considerations.

STANDARD SPOT MARKETS

Market:	Circ
Portland/Bangor	20,000
Burlington/Concord	20,000
Boston/Springfield	87,000
Providence	30,000
Hartford	38,000
New York Metro	225,000
Albany/Schenectady	20,000
Buffalo	25,000
Rochester	19,000
Syracuse/Binghampton	35,000
Philadelphia	136,000
Harrisburg/York/Scranton	51,000
Pittsburgh/Erie	76,000
Baltimore	37,000
Washington DC	67,000
Toledo	22,000
Columbus	44,000
Dayton	20,000
Cincinnati	37,000
Cleveland	68,000
Indianapolis	72,000
South Bend/Fort Wayne	22,000
Effingham/ S. Illinois Bal.	12,000
Chicago	112,000
Peoria/Springfield	50,000
Detroit	77,000
Grand Rapids	52,000
Saginaw	20,000
Marquette/Eau Claire	30,000
Green Bay	19,000
Madison	19,000
Milwaukee	37,000
Minneapolis	93,000
Des Moines/Cedar Rapids	49,000
St. Louis	46,000
Springfield/Hannibal	38,000
North & South Dakota	40,000
Nebraska	38,000
Kansas City	38,000
Topeka/Wichita	36,000
Richmond/Norfolk/Roanoke	77,000
Charleston/Wheeling	41,000
Greensboro/Raleigh	87,000
Charlotte/Greenville/Spartanburg	85,000
Charleston	32,000
Atlanta	68,000
Savannah/Augusta	40,000
Miami	48,000
Tampa/st Petersburg	91,000
Jacksonville	46,000
Louisville/Lexington	55,000
Memphis	32,000
Nashville	37,000
Knoxville/Chattanooga	52,000
Birmingham/Mobile	79,000
Jackson	27,000
Arkansas	43,000
New Orleans/Shreveport	59,000
Oklahoma City/Tulsa	55,000
Dallas/Fort Worth	90,000
San Antonio	47,000
Houston/Beaumont	63,000
Armarillo/Lubbock/El Paso	31,000
Montana	15,000
Boise	15,000
Wyoming	10,000
Denver/Colorado Springs	57,000
New Mexico	25,000
Phoenix/Tucson	65,000
Utah	30,000
Nevada	25,000
Alaska	8,000
Seattle	51,000
Spokane	25,000
Portland/Eugene	52,000
San Francisco	71,000
Sacramento/Eureka	47,000
Los Angeles/Bakers/Fresno	165,000
San Diego	28,000
Hawaii	15,000

REGIONAL TRAVEL EDITIONS

BLACK AND WHITE RATES:

	1 ti	2 ti	3 ti
Spread	63,115.	59,960.	56,800.
1 page	31,560.	29,990.	28,400.
2/3 page	22,350.	21,250.	20,120.
1/2 page	18,900.	17,960.	17,010.
1/3 page	13,800.	13,140.	12,450.
56 lines	4,020.	3,820.	3,620.

COLOR RATES:

	1 ti	2 ti	3 ti
2-Color:			
Spread	68,020.	64,630.	61,220.
1 page	34,500.	32,320.	30,600.
2/3 page	23,525.	22,345.	21,170.
1/2 page	19,690.	18,700.	17,725.
1/3 page	12,920.	13,300.	12,600.
4-Color:			
Spread	70,130.	66,630.	63,100.
1 page	35,060.	33,300.	31,570.
2/3 page	26,200.	25,260.	23,900.
1/2 page	20,720.	19,680.	18,650.
1/3 page	15,850.	15,050.	14,270.
56 lines	7,210.	6,860.	6,500.

METRO SELECT

BLACK AND WHITE RATES:

1 page	56,915.	1/2 page	34,550.
2/3 page	40,750.	1/3 page	21,060.

COLOR RATES:

2-Color:	
1 page	60,000.
2/3 page	41,940.
1/2 page	34,930.
1/3 page	22,140.
4-Color:	
1 page	61,775.
2/3 page	46,775.
1/2 page	36,515.
1/3 page	25,335.

CIRCULATION:
Publisher states: "Effective with January 1999 issue, rates based on a circulation average of 1,500,000."

HJ SELECT

BLACK AND WHITE RATES:

1 page	48,225.	1/2 page	29,350.
2/3 page	34,575.	1/3 page	18,650.

COLOR RATES:

2-Color:			
1 page	50,850.	1/2 apge	29,515.
2/3 page	35,640.	1/3 page	18,900.
4-Color:			
1 page	52,275.	1/2 page	31,000.
2/3 page	39,690.	1/3 page	21,500.

CIRCULATION:
Publisher states: "Effective with January 1999 issue, rates based on a circulation average of 900,000."

PD SELECT

BLACK AND WHITE RATES:

1 page	22,635.	1/2 page	13,780.
2/3 page	16,275.	1/3 page	8,675.

COLOR RATES:

2-Color:			
1 page	23,880.	1/2 page	13,900.
2/3 page	16,700.	1/3 page	8,860.
4-Color:			
1 page	24,650.	1/2 page	14,495.
2/3 page	18,600.	1/3 page	10,160.

CIRCULATION:
Publisher states: "Effective with January 1999 issue, rates based on a circulation average of 500,000."

REGIONAL SPLIT RUNS

BLACK AND WHITE RATES:

	Spread	Page
1st copy change	4000.	3500.
Each additional	3500.	3000.

COLOR RATES:

4-Color:		
1st copy change	5500.	4500.
Each additional	4500.	3500.

ISSUE AND CLOSING DATES:
Includes all Regional, Select Editions and Split Runs.

Issue:	Closing	Issue:	Closing
Feb/99	11/6	Aug/99	5/7
Mar/99	12/8	Sep/99	6/8
Apr/99	1/8	Oct/99	7/8
May/99	2/8	Nov/99	8/6
Jun/99	3/8	Dec/99	9/8
Jul/99	4/8		

14. CONTRACT AND COPY REGULATIONS

See Contents page for location—items 1, 2, 3, 7, 8, 10, 21 24, 25 30, 35, 36, 37.

15. GENERAL REQUIREMENTS

Also see SRDS Print Media Production Source.
Printing Process: Rotogravure National (Full Run) GAA/SWOP Standards.
Printing Process: Rotogravure Full Run; Offset Regional, Cover.
Trim Size: 7-7/8 x 10-1/2; No./Cols. 3.
Binding Method: Perfect.
Colors Available: Black and white; Black and one color; 4-color process; GAA/SWOP; 5th cylinder-offset.
Covers: Black and white; Black and one color; 4-color process.

NON-BLEED
AD PAGE DIMENSIONS

1 pg	7	x	10	1/3 v	2-1/4	x	10
2/3 v-	4-5/8	x	10	1/3 sq	4-5/8	x	4-7/8
2/3 h	7	x	6-3/4	1/6 v	2-1/4	x	4-7/8
1/2 v	3-3/8	x	10	Checkerbrd	3-1/2	x	4-7/8
1/2 h	7	x	4-7/8	Digest	4-5/8	x	6-1/2

16. ISSUE AND CLOSING DATES

Published monthly.

Issue:	On sale	Closing	Issue:	On sale	Closing
Dec/99	11/9	9/15	Feb/00	1/11	11/15
Jan/00	12/14	10/15	Mar/00	2/13	12/15

WORKING WOMAN

A MacDonald Communications, Inc. Publication

 ABC

M P A

Location ID: 8 MLST 8　　　　　**Mid 001289-000**
Published 10 times a year by MacDonald Communications, Inc., 135 W. 50th St., 16th flr., New York, NY 10020. Phone 212-445-6100. Fax 212-586-7449.
E-Mail leslibrody@aol.com
For shipping info., see Print Media Production Source.

PUBLISHER'S EDITORIAL PROFILE
WORKING WOMAN reports on news, trends, information, people and ideas as they impact women in business. Professional/managerial women turn to Working Woman as their key resource for managing the complexities of business today, from small business to the new corporate structure. Rec'd 3/25/96.

1. PERSONNEL
Pres—Barbara J. Litrell.
Pub—Phyllis Sparrow.
Dir Manufacturing—Edward Abrams.

2. REPRESENTATIVES and/or BRANCH OFFICES
Lake Bluff, IL 60044—Chip Wood, 12847 Sanctuary Lane. Phone 847-295-9780. Fax 847-295-9758.
Los Angeles 90048—Thecla Glueck, 6380 Wilshire Blvd., Ste. 1207. Phone 323-655-7426. Fax 323-655-1828.
Arden, NC 28704—The Robinson Agency, Inc., Brenda Robinson, P.O. Box 304. Phone 704-684-0064. Fax 704-684-0234. (Classified)
San Francisco 94111—Thecla Glueck, 500 Sansome St., Ste. 101. Phone 415-986-7762. Fax 415-986-7860.
Troy (Detroit), MI 48084—Laine Meyers, 3645 Crooks Rd. Phone 810-643-8447. Fax 810-643-0861.
Newport, RI 02840—The Victoria Group, 42 Thames Street. Phone 401-846-9880. Fax 401-846-5990. (Franchise & Business Opportunities)
Port Washington, NY 11050—M&G Communications, Inc., 9 Longview Rd. Phone 515-944-4412. Fax 516-767-3364. Fax 516-767-3364 (Direct Response/Mail Order)
Dallas, TX 75219—Carol Orr, 3500 Maple Ave. Ste. 1060. Phone 214-521-6116. Fax 214-521-6176.

continued
251

continued
251

WORKING WOMAN—cont
Alpharetta, GA 30202—Scott Rickles, 560 Jacaranda Court. Phone 770-664-4567. Fax 770-740-1399.

3. COMMISSION AND CASH DISCOUNT
15% to recognized agencies. Net 20 days.

ADVERTISING RATES
Effective February 1, 1999 (Issue/Card 31)
Rates received November 16, 1998.

5. BLACK/WHITE RATES
Spread	78,140.	1/2 page & digest	26,570.
1 page	39,095.	1/3 page	15,985.
2/3 page	29,540.	1/6 page	10,150.

VOLUME DISCOUNTS
3 pages	5%	18 pages	15%
6 pages	8%	24 pages	18%
12 pages	10%		

5a. COMBINATION RATES
Additional discounts beyond category or volume offered by Working Woman can be achieved in combination with other MacDonald Communications titles. See listing for MacDonald Communications Group Marketing & Sales in Cl. 22A.

6. COLOR RATES
2-Color:
Spread	89,695.	1/2 page & digest	30,565.
1 page	44,820.	1/3 page	51,135.
2/3 page	34,075.	1/3 page	18,470.

4-Color:
Spread	102,060.	1/2 page & digest..	34,670.
1 page	51,085.	1/3 page	58,185.
2/3 page	38,825.	1/3 page	21,060.

7. COVERS
2nd cover	56,160.	4th cover	64,045.
3rd cover	53,785.		

8. INSERTS
BUSINESS REPLY CARD:
Printed by publisher	31,105.
Supplied by advertiser	20,305.
Must be supported by a minimum of one full page advertisement. Other insert sizes, gatefolds and scent strips available.

9. BLEED
No charge.

11. CLASSIFIED/MAIL ORDER/SPECIALTY RATES
CATEGORY DISCOUNTS
Mail order	15%	Retail	15%

12. SPLIT-RUN
An A/B split is available at a national space cost plus additional production costs:
Black/white	3900.
2-color	4200.
4-color	4500.
Supplied insert/bin-in card	2500.

13. SPECIAL ISSUE RATES AND DATA
ISSUE & CLOSING DATES
	On sale	Closing	(**)
Tech/99		10/4	9/27
(**) Fractional ad.

13a. GEOGRAPHIC and/or DEMOGRAPHIC EDITIONS
Regional advertising is available. It can be broken down by either state or DMA.
Regional space cost is calculated at 65% of the national rate for up to 65% of the national circulation. Minimum print order is 50,000. There is an additional flat 2,000.00 net production charge for all regional run-of-book and BRC advertising.

14. CONTRACT AND COPY REGULATIONS
See Contents page for location—items 1, 2, 3, 7, 8, 10, 12, 14, 15, 21, 22, 24, 28, 30, 32, 34, 35, 36, 38, 39, 42.

15. GENERAL REQUIREMENTS
Also see SRDS Print Media Production Source.
Printing Process: Web Offset Full Run.
Trim Size: 8 x 10-1/2; No./Cols. 3.
Binding Method: Perfect.
Colors Available: 4-color process; Matched.
Covers: 4-color process.

NON-BLEED
AD PAGE DIMENSIONS
Sprd	14	x	10	1/2 h	7	x	4-3/4
1 pg	7	x	10	1/3 v	2-1/4	x	10
2/3 v	4-5/8	x	10	1/3 sq	4-5/8	x	4-3/4
1/2 v	3-1/2	x	10	Digest	4-5/8	x	6-7/8

16. ISSUE AND CLOSING DATES
Published 10 times a year.
Issue:	On sale	Closing	(**)
Feb/99	1/12	11/23	11/16
Mar/99	2/16	1/4	12/28
Apr/99	3/16	2/1	1/25
May/99	4/13	3/1	2/22
Jun/99	5/11	3/29	3/22
Jul-Aug/99	6/22	5/10	5/3
Sep/99	8/10	6/28	6/21
Oct/99	9/14	8/2	7/26
Nov/99	10/19	9/7	8/30
Dec-Jan/00.	10/25	11/1	12/14
(**) Fractional ad
Regional issues, inserts and gatefolds close 2 weeks prior to the national closing date.

17. SPECIAL SERVICES
Reader Service Cards.

18. CIRCULATION
Established 1978.
Summary data—for detail see Publisher's Statement.
A.B.C. 6-30-99 (6 mos. aver.—Magazine Form)
Tot. Pd	(Subs)	(Single)	(Assoc)
628,184	502,347	9,465	116,372
Average Non-Analyzed Non-Paid Circulation (not incl. above):
Total 9,853
TERRITORIAL DISTRIBUTION 4/99—629,240
N.Eng.	Mid.Atl.	E.N.Cen.	W.N.Cen.	S.Atl.	E.S.Cen
34,916	126,456	101,863	37,803	115,360	28,605
W.S.Cen.	Mtn. St.	Pac St.	Canada	Foreign	Other
51,760	36,372	91,060	2,447	635	1,963
Advertising rate base: 625,000.
% above/below rate base: 0.5.

252

From the October 1999 edition of *Consumer Magazine and Agri Media Rates and Data* published by SRDS (Standard Rate and Data Service)

Research

"The fewer the facts, the stronger the opinion."
—Arnold Glasow

Introduction.

Finding Out What You Don't Know.

The purpose for the Research section of the marketing planning document is to outline the information you've learned that will contribute to marketing the Brand.

In the Situation Analysis you learned what you know. Now you are smart enough to figure out what you don't know.

Research will give you that information. Usually this is information you've gathered just prior to the writing of the marketing document.

Changing Technology.

Technology is advancing so quickly in the marketing and advertising disciplines that the availability of resources and information is increasing at an incredible rate.

The whole idea of tracking sales from specific advertising through single-source data was judged to be prohibitive only a few years ago. This technology has changed our thinking from "we can't do that" to "we can't do that, yet."

Computers are part of the reason for that change. Computers are not just a better way to prepare documents and presentations, they have become a method of acquiring information.

This book, and your planning document, should be considered works-in-process because the technology and available resources are advancing quickly and because the learning is continual and never-ending. Professionals, however, rarely define it this way.

Two Research Sections:

There are two sections in the Marketing Plan that pertain to research—Summary and Evaluation.

1. Summary:

The first is a summary of the information that's currently on hand—this was probably developed in the research conducted during the last fiscal year.

This summary is used as a base of knowledge to write the marketing document or plan.

2. Evaluation:

The second research section falls under the label "Evaluation," and is an outline of research you intend to do during the coming year as part of the plan, and an evaluation of that plan, which will be revealed later (See Chapter Eleven).

The Evaluation portion of the plan will help determine methods to improve the plan for the following year.

Our Primary Concern—What Will We Communicate?

This first research is primarily concerned with what will be communicated to current and potential buyers and users of the Brand.

We tend, therefore, to think of this as creative research.

In reality, this research relates to the strategic positioning of the entire Brand as evidenced throughout the marketing plan.

Know Your Customer.

Advertising works when you know your customer.

Many people can and do bear testimony to this fact.

The better we know who will buy, recommend, or use the Brand, the better directed the advertising can be.

Three Pieces of Information.

We need to know three pieces of information in order to write advertising strategy. They are:

1. The Target Audience:

Who is going to buy the Brand? Whether it's a product or service, this is the first piece of information needed for the marketing plan—who is the target audience?

2. Factors that Motivate Purchase Behavior:

The second category of information needed is—what are the criteria the target audience use to make a purchase decision?

3. Unique Characteristics of the Brand:

The third is—what are the unique characteristics of the Brand or business, i.e., the point-of-difference.

When these questions have been answered, the writing of the marketing plan can begin.

We'll take the time to understand these three important points because this is what we are looking for in the research. After we analyze what we are looking for, we'll discuss how to find it.

Target Audience.

Who Will be Interested in the Brand?

The first question, then, addresses who is going to be interested in the Brand. These people are called your Target Audience and are the group to whom the advertising is written.

They can be buyers, users, or influencers of those who buy or use the Brand (or those you want to buy the brand).

Demographics.

This Target Audience, or target group, is usually described in terms of the physical population characteristics (demographics) of gender and age. For example, a judgment might be made to advertise to women 18 to 49. Public relations people refer to this group as a "public."

These basic demographics can be expanded to include income, education, geographic dispersion (where they live), professional status, home ownership, race, family size, etc. But, both secondary and primary research will be needed to acquire this kind of information.

There are syndicated services, such as SMRB and MRI that can provide some general research on Target Audience (see Note A at the end of Chapter One). Their usefulness depends on the type of product or service for which the plan is being written. They do not provide information that covers all businesses.

Psychographics.

The psychological or lifestyle and personal characteristics (psychographics) of your target audience can also be valuable.

Every brand has to make a decision if it is worth the time and money to psychologically describe the potential customer.

This is often described as lifestyle information, and VALS II is the most well-known supplier of this information.

This psychographic information is harder to acquire, and can be very expensive. However, it can be valuable to the creative product.

For example, when marketing a performing arts center, the motivations for buying tickets to see the "Nutcracker Suite" has little to do with the quality of the performance.

Parents, or just as likely grandparents, buy tickets for children to see the "Nutcracker" for the holiday season because they want to share the experience of visiting the theatre with the child.

Consequently, it is more important to market the performance to "Belongers," with an emotional appeal than it is to address the factors that motivate purchase behavior (see subsection below).

Usage.
Occasionally, a manufacturer will find it useful to classify the target group by how they use the product. For example, the way kids use Oreos is quite different from the way Grandma and Grandpa enjoy an oatmeal cookie like Archway.

Heavy Users.
Some good advertising agencies and some marketers find interviewing heavy users to be an especially fruitful method of gaining information.

After all, these people use the Brand more than the average user. They know more about it and know why they like it.

They understand its advantages and also understand how the Brand could be improved.

They are able to articulate precisely (and often at some length) why they buy the Brand (these are the factors that motivate purchase behavior), and they can tell you which factors are most important to them. This may not be the whole answer, but it will certainly be a good start.

Good account planning often begins with one-on-one interviews with heavy users.

Factors that Motivate Purchase Behavior.

Motivation and Rank Order.
The next issue addresses the factors that motivate purchase behavior. This information is defined first as the isolation of those parameters or factors the target group uses to decide between brands or companies

in a given category; and second, the rank order of those criteria used by the target group for brand selection.

These can be different for subgroups within the target audience.

This is the challenge of Integrated Marketing Communications (IMC). There can be so many different target groups for each product (with different factors motivating purchase behavior) that different research may be required for each target audience.

Example: Yogurt.

If we consider the yogurt example in the situation analysis, the factors a young woman between the ages of 18 and 34 uses to decide first, whether she will buy yogurt, and second, the criteria she uses to decide which brand of yogurt to buy, are quite different than the criteria a 60-year-old woman might use.

Both women are likely to be interested in good taste, but the younger woman probably wants low calories, while the older woman is also very interested in the calcium content.

Formal research may be necessary in order to isolate these factors, but simple observation can get you started.

Example: Office Supplies.

Here's an example of those motivating factors in the office supply business. Business people buy yellow pads from one retailer because that retailer makes sales calls to determine what its customers need, delivers the supplies, and then follows up after delivery with a call to assure customer satisfaction.

This is service. Their customers, and consequently their target audience, are those perfectly willing to pay a few cents extra for a yellow pad because it's cheaper than sending someone to a discount place to buy what the office needs. They know they can count on the people at the office supply store to take care of their needs.

At the other end of the spectrum is an office with tight controls on costs. To this target audience, it's important to save a few cents on every box of pencils.

Service versus price is one consideration, but there can be many more nuances in the decision-making process.

One office supply company may stock Write Bros. pens instead of BIC. Another office supply store may be closer to the buyer's office. Another may send a catalog. And another may have a Web site.

Clearly, businesses buy office supplies from one store because that store has what they need, but there is probably more to the decision than availability.

There are four potential factors that motivate purchase behavior in the office supplies business. They are price, service, availability, and convenience. Some people will judge price to be the most important factor, while to others convenience will outweigh the price factor.

Rank Order—The Importance of What is Most Important.

Consumers simply consider the factors that are important to them in rank order. This assumes that some considerations are more important than others.

It's the challenge of the researcher to find a way to provide this weight or importance consideration to the team—then you will know the rank order.

Knowledge of how target groups rank the factors they use to make decisions is mandatory for the development of strategic direction.

In order to be successful, the marketing plan (and advertising) must address the purchase criteria consumers use to buy the Brand. And that marketing plan and advertising ought to give more consideration to the factor or parameter at the top of the list.

There are a variety of ways to get this information.

Additional Examples.

Another example is the pork sausage business. People who eat pork sausage make their purchase decisions based on leanness and taste. Nothing else matters very much. (Of course, cost is a consideration in virtually every purchase decision, but a strategy based on cost will likely attract customers who will not be loyal in the long run. Most price brands are unadvertised.)

When Hunt first started selling their tomato "Catsup," the Brand was sold for a few cents less than Heinz "Ketchup."

The advertising for Hunt's Catsup, however, only featured quality and taste. Hunt wanted customers to look for and buy Hunt's for the quality, then they would be pleasantly surprised at the low price.

Back to the pork sausage. People simply do not care if the sausage was made yesterday or last week.

Certainly, if it was made too long ago, people will not buy it. But freshness is usually assumed to be acceptable. Freshness is not an important factor when it comes to purchase motivation.

It only makes sense to address those factors in the marketing plan, and the resulting advertising, with which the target group is concerned.

There is a little interest in whether the package has a sell-by date, when it was processed, the delivery method, whether the whole hog was used or if it is just trimmings sausage, but mostly people want to know if it tastes good and is lean.

The advertising will probably tell the potential users that the sausage is good, lean sausage that tastes good. The Bob Evans Farms Sausage advertising shown on the next two pages does just that.

The headlines in these print advertisements address the factors the target group uses to make up their minds which brand of pork sausage they will buy. This is not subtle advertising.

A Simple But Important Point.

The point is simple.

The more precise the listing and rank ordering of the reasons the target group uses for purchase selection, the more powerful the advertising.

This is the single most important piece of information needed to market the Brand or business.

It is the backbone of the marketing plan, and as we have seen, it just may be the headline in the advertising.

It is the responsibility of the account planner to determine this information. The account planner's obligation is to learn everything there is to know about current and potential users of the Brand, including the criteria used to make decisions in the marketplace.

"IF YOU'RE NOT BUYING BOB EVANS SAUSAGE, YOU MIGHT BE GETTING JUST LEFTOVERS."

Some sausage makers don't put the best cuts of pork into their sausage like we do at Bob Evans Farms.

They take the hams, and sell them as ham. They take the loins, and sell them as pork chops. Then they make sausage with what's left over – the pork trimmings.

Well at Bob Evans Farms, we don't settle for just leftovers. In fact, we include all the choice fresh hams and tenderloins in every pound of sausage we make.

That's why Bob Evans Sausage is tastier than a lot of other sausage. And why it cooks up plump and tender every time.

So try Bob Evans Farms Sausage. It's so meaty and delicious, you'll never have leftovers again.

Bob Evans FARMS®
WE DO IT RIGHT.
OR WE DON'T DO IT.™

© 1980 Bob Evans Farms, Inc.

"SOME COMPANIES LIMIT THE MEAT IN THEIR SAUSAGE. WE LIMIT THE FAT."

There's a good reason why Bob Evans Farms Sausage won't cook away in your frying pan like some other sausage does.

You see, at Bob Evans Farms, we limit the amount of fat in every ounce of sausage we make. So there's just enough to bring out the farm fresh taste.

That's why Bob Evans Sausage always cooks up so tender and delicious. Not greasy. And why it won't shrink to nothing in your frying pan.

And while some companies don't put the best cuts of pork in their sausage, we include all the choice fresh hams and tenderloins. Not just the trimmings.

So try Bob Evans Sausage. Because while we always limit the fat in our sausage, there's no limit on the taste.

Bob Evans
FARMS®
WE DO IT RIGHT.
OR WE DON'T DO IT.°

© 1980 Bob Evans Farms, Inc.

Unique Characteristics of the Brand.

The Importance of Differentiation.

This last issue is the Brand's point-of-difference.

In order to understand what differentiates the Brand or business in the minds of customers, there must be a solid understanding of the competition.

If the office supply store is, in reality, no store at all but a delivery service run from a small room and a warehouse, then your point-of-difference has to be service.

If you have chosen to differentiate pork sausage by positioning it as the Brand with little waste because it is lean, then the Brand had better be able to deliver on that claim because it's the major criterion for making a purchase decision.

Ideally, your point-of-difference is also a motivating factor for making a purchase decision.

In the example of the office supply retailer, you don't want good delivery to set you apart from your competition if your customers judge a large selection of brands to be the primary reason for store selection and judge delivery to be of minor importance.

The USP.

Rosser Reeves, the Ted Bates advertising legend who developed the USP (Unique Selling Proposition), related the story of a couple of guys who came into his office one day to convince him to handle their advertising. They sold chocolate for a living. He asked if there was something unusual or different about their particular chocolate candy. They said no.

He probed a little, and finally they mentioned that their chocolate had a little candy coating.

He, of course, wanted to know what that did. One said that it prevented the chocolate from melting in your hands.

Rosser Reeves recognized immediately that this was a unique selling proposition; a method of differentiating this candy in the marketplace. M&Ms has used the line ever since.

Most often, the unique characteristics of the Brand work in concert with the factors that motivate purchase behavior. However, sometimes a brand is so unusual that the strategy is simply to communicate that it's different.

V-8 juice is a natural illustration of this point. The product was invented to differentiate the tomato juice category.

Preparing The Research Plan.

Initial Information and Hypothesis.

If the information on these three pieces of information is complete, your hypothesis should be clear.

The only need remaining to substantiate is the hypothesis, which you'll update from time to time.

Quite often, the knowledge of what isn't known is needed before it can be determined what is needed. For example, you may need to know the percentage of office supply purchasers who consider service important and what price differential they will pay for good service.

If the information is incomplete or not substantiated, you'll need to conduct the research necessary to completely answer the three categories of information—target audience, factors that motivate purchase behavior, and unique characteristics of your brand—before you will be able to write strategy.

If the advertising always addresses these three points in its strategic direction, the Brand will be more likely to have advertising that will effectively position the Brand in the marketplace.

Write down your target audience, factors that motivate purchase behavior, and unique characteristics of it.

Do it before you conduct your research to determine how much you know. Write it in the Worksheet space.

Worksheet for Strategy.

Target Audience:

_____

_____

Factors That Motivate Purchase Behavior:

_____

_____

Unique Characteristics of the Brand:

_____

_____

Questionnaire Design.

The next step is to design a questionnaire that will allow you to acquire the information you need. See Note B at the end of this chapter for more information on writing a questionnaire.

Here is how to prepare the Research Plan itself.

A. Objectives:

What We Want to Do.

The objectives of the research are synonymous with objectives in general. They tell us what we want to do.

For example:

To gather information relating to how consumers make purchase decisions in the yogurt category.

To isolate those characteristics of the Brand that are judged to be the most compelling when switching brands.

Research objectives can also be used to simply reinforce the overall marketing objectives:

To gain information that will aid the Brand to achieve the marketing objective.

These objectives are less specific, and as a result, less desirable.

The more specific the research objectives can be, the easier it will be to implement the research and learn what you need to know.

B. Strategies:

Definitions.

Research Strategy defines how you will acquire the information. That means specifically the kind of research you'll need to fulfill the objective—but not how it's constructed (that is Methodology).

Talk to Your Target.

In order to determine how consumers make purchase decisions in the yogurt category, it might be necessary to first talk with them in a focused discussion group environment (these are also known as group sessions or "focus groups"), but the same basic information can be gained in one-on-one interviews.

Both of these methodologies are qualitative in nature.

> *To gain initial input via two focused group sessions among key purchasing agents of yogurt.*

or…

> *To gain initial information through one-on-one interviews with the Target Audience.This information will be used to provide background knowledge for a quantitative study.*

In situations where little historical research is available, a good way to start is to get a solid grasp of the way consumers think about the Brand and the category in some type of qualitative research, then substantiate your hypotheses through quantitative research.

The key to good qualitative research is the people to whom you talk.

Group Sessions vs. One-on-One.

Small businesses and college students in Campaigns classes will probably find the group sessions too expensive. But this is not necessarily a bad thing.

If you want to find out how women think about yogurt, hang out in the dairy aisle of the grocery store.

When someone picks up a package of Dannon Fruit-on-the-Bottom Yogurt, ask why. They might be taken aback, but you'll get the information you want. After you've talked to eight or ten people you'll start to get an idea of the criteria motivating purchase behavior in the yogurt category.

Be sure to talk to people who buy Yoplait and store brands, so you start to develop a complete understanding of the category. It's virtually certain the information you glean in this research will not be as sacrosanct as that from a focused group session. It will, however, be less expensive.

Quantitative and Qualitative.

The quantitative research will include questions to allow you to understand the factors motivating purchase behavior, usage patterns and attitudes of both the category and the Brand, and their respective advertising, along with a host of other information.

The qualitative research will give you positive reinforcement that what you intend to do is correct. It's a way to gain additional insight into problems without total knowledge of the questions that should be asked.

It's a method of gaining consumer input into the problem or question facing the Brand. This may include understanding the target audience, the factors that motivate purchase behavior, and the isolation of the unique characteristics of the Brand. The results of the qualitative research most often should then be put into a quantitative study.

This quantitative research will be the primary information gathering vehicle and will probably provide the basis or rationale for the marketing strategic direction.

C. Methodology:

How, Where, When, How Many.
Research methodology will be described in this section outlining how, where, when, sample size, and any unusual conditions.

Most often, this will be fairly straightforward. Methodology is the "nuts and bolts" of doing it.

It's important to point out anything that's not normally accepted. For example, a typical Methodology section might read:

> *The research was conducted using face-to-face interviews with respondents who were found using the intercept technique in shopping malls and business districts. The research was conducted during the first two weekends in October.*

> *A total of 532 interviews were completed. The research was verified using a random sample of respondents from the telephone book, using a table of random numbers to first determine the page number and a second table of random numbers to identify the phone number and find the respondent. Fifty interviews were conducted in this fashion in order to verify the intercepts.*

This allows the reader to make a judgment concerning the validity of the study.

D. Summary of Findings:

Show the Most Significant Learning First.
The results of the research are shown here. The information should be rank ordered to show the most significant learning first.

Quite often, these findings are numbered with the most important of the findings or results being number one.

It is important that you go beyond a basic tabulation of the questions. Findings should exhibit key learning. If you were doing a survey on computer usage and one of the questions related to how respondents use their computers, the tabulations could show that 47% of respondents use their computers for personal usage. A bigger finding might be:

Over half of all respondents use personal computers at home for business.

Inexperienced researchers are often guilty of not recognizing the key findings. They overlook something that may appear obvious to them, but has not been substantiated in the past.

Additional Information.
The questionnaire is attached as an exhibit or an appendix, usually with the number of responses filled in the blank spaces.

This exhibit is to be used only if the reader (management) wants more information. The most important information is shown here in the written portion of the document. (See Note B for more information.)

For more information, please also read:

1. **Hitting The Sweet Spot**
   Fortini-Campbell, Lisa
   The Copy Workshop, Chicago, IL 1991.

   Chapters Ten, Eleven, and Twelve will prove useful to you as you write the research segment of this planning document.

2. **Positioning: The Battle for Your Mind**
   Ries, Al and Trout, Jack
   McGraw-Hill, New York, 1986.

   The first nine chapters relate to this discussion on research.

3. **Strategic Advertising Campaigns**
   Schultz, Don E., and Barnes, Beth E.
   NTC Business Books, Chicago, IL 1994. Fourth Edition.

   Chapter Four relates to this chapter on research.

4. **Truth, Lies & Advertising.**
   The Art of Account Planning
   Steel, Jon
   AdWeek Books, 1998.

5. **Successful Advertising Research Methods**
   Haskins, Jack and Kendrick, Alice
   NTC Business Books, Chicago, 1994.

Interviewing

"First you have to learn to think like a consumer."
—Lisa Fortini-Campbell, Ph.D.

Introduction.

The Benefit to You.

Asking questions directly of potential users or buyers of your Brand is a luxury most professionals ignore.

If you choose to do interviewing yourself, you will benefit greatly from the experience.

You will learn more than if you simply read the summary of the results from research someone else conducted. And you will gain new respect for those people who are hired to do the interviewing.

Finally, you will generate useful results for your campaign that will become the foundation of your marketing strategic direction.

Interviewing is an integral part of the research process. It is vitally important that you do it well.

The Importance of Good Interviewing.

Poor interviewing can destroy all the careful work that has been completed to this point.

Care was taken to make judgments concerning the factors that motivate purchase behavior among a difficult target group, and that judgment was used to write a questionnaire. You pre-tested the questionnaire and found it to be solid, and it seemed to get the information you wanted from the research.

Gaining Insight.

This is the time to gain significant insight into your target audience. To do that you can't just stop some passerby and ask him or her to complete a questionnaire. Interview the respondent.

That means that you need to use some judgment as you are working your way through the questions.

If a respondent gives you a reason why they buy that Brand, probe to learn more. Ask them if there are any other reasons. Then ask it again. Keep asking until the respondent has no more answers. Then go to the next question—ask why.

Keep probing until you have a total understanding of what each person uses to make up his or her mind about the category and the Brand.

Be Thorough.

You must interview the respondents thoroughly to get the information. Go beyond what is on the questionnaire. Learn. Put yourself in their place and ask questions until you understand how they think.

Probe.

When the interviewers fail to probe sufficiently, or are careless in stratifying the sample, or are lazy and skip questions when it's difficult to get the information—the quality of the research goes down.

Control.

Never let your respondents fill out the questionnaires by themselves unsupervised. You will dramatically decrease the utility of the information.

Do the interviewing yourself.

Advice for Student Groups.

Everyone Should Do Some Interviewing.

If you are a student group, make certain that every member of your group completes some interviewing.

You will learn as much from looking people in the eye and reading their body language as you will from what they say.

Be sure to write notes on the back of each questionnaire about that interview. Then type out a few paragraphs (or pages if you want) about what you learned from the respondents at the end of each interviewing session.

These notes and information will help you learn to think like the consumer.

Advice for Entrepeneurs.

Don't Just Sell—Learn.

If you're an enterepeneur, you can learn a great deal by talking with your customers—or potential customers.

Learn from them. Don't just try to sell to them. Try to get to know them, and understand how your product or service fits into their lives.

Harry was a client of mine many years ago. He once told me that focus groups were a lazy man's way to get information.

He told me this as we were trying to introduce Ortega's line of Taco products. He explained that if we would just stop by the grocery store on our way home from work every day and talk with people who were buying or about to buy Mexican food, we would learn a great deal.

The women we talked with might have thought we were a little strange, but after a short period we knew a great deal about why people bought tacos, who they were, how they were different from other consumers, as well as virtually anything else we wanted to know.

This same concept can work for you.

Get Out of Your Office.

Get out of your office and away from your side of the desk or the counter. Really get to know the people who just might make your business prosper.

And, if you sell a food product for a living, "learn to hang out in grocery stores." Thanks, Harry.

The Questionnaire

"Inquiring minds want to know."
—National Enquirer

How To Get The Most Out of Yours.

The Face-to-Face Advantage.

As an entrepreneur or a student in an Advertising Campaigns class you have the luxury of being able to conduct your interviewing face-to-face.

You may not judge this to be that much of a benefit, but there's a great advantage in being able to see your respondents' faces. You'll learn as much from what you see as you will from what they say.

Once your business grows, you'll start hiring more people to work for you. After you graduate, the market researchers do most of the work—you'll only see reports. It's not as good.

You'll have to rely on the numbers to tell you what people think. That's okay, and you should learn to understand what the numbers tell you, but you learn something different when you look into peoples' faces.

Learn to read body language. Pay attention to what they're saying between the questions.

Learn to understand what they're not saying.

What you learn from the way people talk is quite often just as important as what they say.

All this listening and watching will help you understand the users, both current and potential, of the category and Brand.

The One-Page Advantage.

The questionnaire itself should be short and to the point.

Get the questionnaire onto one piece of paper. Get it on one side of that piece of paper, if you can.

Each time you write a question, ask yourself, "what will I do with this information?" If you don't know the answer, there's a good chance you should cut the question.

Direct Questions. Direct Answers.
Don't be afraid to ask what criteria people use to make a decision in the category.

The single mistake most often made by students is that they don't learn the most important reason why people choose a brand. They try to ask the question in a convoluted way that doesn't get the information.

Don't be reluctant to just ask the question in a straightforward manner. "How do you decide which brand you'll buy in this category?"

Do-It-Yourself.
The next mistake most often made is that students want to have respondents fill out the questionnaire by themselves. Wrong. Wrong. Wrong. And wrong. Never allow respondents to do that.

Sometimes there is no choice, but as the previous note indicated, this can often dramatically decrease the utility of the information you collect.

Imagine every possible way a question can be answered and then decide if you will get the information you want from that question. Then...

Pre-Test.
Be sure to pre-test your questionnaire.

Go to six or eight respondents and administer the questionnaire.

Make sure it flows well.

Make sure you are getting the answers you need.

Ask the Right People.
Finally, when you actually start interviewing people, make sure they are members of the target group or the user base.

One semester I taught advertising campaigns, and Nutri-System, the weight-loss centers, was the client.

Students were not getting the kind of answers that seemed correct.

I finally discovered they were interviewing other students—skinny ones, at that. The research was a waste because those people didn't understand what it's like to want to lose weight.

Have Some Fun.

I would expect every entrepreneur and every member of a student team to interview at least fifty members of the user base.

This will take more than an hour or two, so I hope you make it fun.

I've found that business people who truly like their customers tend to do better and enjoy their jobs more.

I've also found that students who enjoy their work get better grades.

Problems & Opportunities

*"If you think the problem's bad now,
just wait till it's been solved."*

—Epstein's Law

Introduction.

A Result of Knowledge Gained...

This section of the marketing document is a summation of the problems and the opportunities. These will come out of the knowledge gained from the Situation Analysis and from the research that has been conducted.

Problems and Opportunities should be written to give direction to the marketing objectives.

An Example.

When my son was born, my sister called to ask if I knew the objective for raising children. I said I had not really thought about it, but she pointed out that there are some significant problems with raising children.

In the beginning you have to do everything for them. After that, they are messy, noisy, and generally out of control. She pointed out that, as a business person, I understood Odiorne's Management by Objectives, and that clearly raising children would be easier to accomplish if I have a solid grasp of the objectives.

Finally, she explained that the objective in the first two years is to teach them to walk and talk, and for the next sixteen years the objective is to teach them to sit down and shut up.

This objective could never have been established if the problem had not been determined in advance.

My sister could not have come up with this objective if she had not first completed the Situation Analysis, completed the research, and then defined the problems and opportunities.

Understanding Problems.

Problems are derived from situations of weakness.

It is insufficient to tell the reader of the planning document that sales are weak so there is an opportunity for advertising.

You need to dig deeper.

There may be a great deal of research completed in order to determine precisely what the problems are.

Examples: Duds and Suds.

When Milk Duds did their research, according to Reis & Trout, they found that a significant problem in the candy bar category was that candy bars did not last very long. This certainly was not true of Milk Duds. They found a category problem that the Brand could easily address.

The opportunity related to this problem was to take advantage of the desire for longer-lasting candy by advertising the fact that Milk Duds last a long time. In fact, it is impossible to eat Milk Duds quickly.

In the early 1970s, Ivory had been losing sales for a long time. To simply say the problem was that Ivory was losing sales is not only sophomoric, but it doesn't get to the heart of the problem.

Determining that Ivory washes quite well in soft water but rinses poorly in hard water identifies at least one of the problems. But it's not the only problem.

Another problem, which might not have appeared to be a problem until examined, was that Ivory was perceived as either a complexion soap or a soap for babies. The volume opportunity is not with babies'-bottoms positioning.

The volume opportunity is in the shower—not only because people use more soap in the shower, but because the water is continually beating down on the bar of soap melting it away.

Identifying Opportunities.

Once the problem has been identified, then the opportunities can be thought through.

Opportunity: Ivory Soap.

The account person who wrote the recommendation to show Ivory Bar Soap in the shower in their advertising, deserves a raise. This is where the volume opportunity is in the bar soap business.

For years, Ivory was showing ladies' faces and babies' bottoms. But some account-type recognized a significant opportunity for Ivory, probably through a detailed business analysis, to determine how the category was used.

A Common Mistake.

The most common error people make at this stage is writing problems and opportunities that can be solved by the advertising creative strategy they want to recommend.

This is kind of like telling Dad you want to borrow the car because you can drive by the hardware store and get the nails he needs while you are really trying to impress your friends.

This description of a problem is usually not well thought out and only serves to illustrate what the writers really wanted to do before they did any homework.

You need to work to determine the real problems in the category or with the Brand. Then you need to write them in such a way that the reader understands that you really know the business.

This section of your Marketing Plan is one that can be used to convince the reader that you have invested considerable work in it and that you really do know what is going on and what will work.

Getting to the Heart of the Issue.

Writing the problems and their matching opportunities is, at best, difficult. It requires a mind that wants to get to the heart of the issue.

The "Onion Theory" of problem-solving requires us to peel back all the layers of useless information. To do this and to identify what will really push the business ahead is an incredible challenge.

Doing it successfully is at the heart of a successful marketing plan.

Your business analysis must include analyses of shipment and sales, media spending, competitive strategy, promotion dollars, promotion events, public opinion, attitudes, awareness, usage behavior, and on and on and on.

The purpose for this is to remind you to recognize all the external factors that might normally be glossed over.

For example: Ivory sells more in soft water areas, Midas sells better in areas that use salt on the highways, and pork sausage does not sell well in predominantly Jewish neighborhoods.

All these things must come out of your Situation Analysis and your study of the category through secondary and then primary research.

Archway Cookies sell better to grandpas than to moms and dads. More bath oil is sold for therapeutic reasons than for hygienic reasons. People don't want credit cards for credit; convenience is the primary reason to get plastic for your wallet.

Translate the information into problems and opportunities that are real and can be implemented.

An A-1 Example.

The problem with A-1 Steak Sauce was not one of taste. The problem was simply that people could not remember to put it on the table.

Almost every household had a bottle . . . somewhere. Usually, it was in the back of the cupboard on the top shelf.

So the problem was simple—get the bottle out where people would see it on a regular basis, and they will use it. And, eventually they'll have to buy another bottle.

The related opportunity—write the word "Refrigerate" on the package.

That put the bottle where it was easily accessible, probably on the door of the refrigerator, and everyone in the family saw it on a regular basis.

Sales went up—what a surprise!

The Problems and Opportunities segment of the Heublein Grocery Products marketing plan for A-1 probably looked something like the following:

> *Problem: In-home inventory is strong; home usage is sporadic.*

> *Opportunity: Motivate current users to use more A-1 Steak Sauce by finding a way for the user to have visual contact with the bottle immediately prior to key usage times.*

The problem and related opportunity became a lead or advance statement for the marketing objectives—which include advertising, promotion, public relations, and merchandising objectives.

Additional Examples.

The marketing pro who convinced the American Dental Association to agree to the copy on the side of the Crest package really understood what would motivate consumers in the toothpaste category.

> Problem: Since dentists rarely endorse specific brands, concerned consumers have little basis for brand selection.

> Opportunity: A form of flouride that can be used in toothpaste and has been proven to reduce cavities in children.

> Opportunity: Secure an endorsement, however qualified, from the American Dental Association (ADA).

The flouride formula used by Crest was indeed proven to be helpful in building up stronger tooth enamel, which was thus more resistant to decay, and the ADA was willing to acknowledge this.

By the way, one of the key people on this project was John Smale, who went on to become chairman of P&G, and then GM.

So it pays to solve problems.

Competitive Response.

It is important that problems go beyond simply being set-ups for what you want to do in the advertising.

Try to think about what your competition will do when you isolate, analyze, and finally solve a significant marketing problem. Instead of solving the problem, you could end up getting your teeth kicked in.

Anticipating Response.

When Hunt did all that research to find out what the significant problems were in the prepared tomato sauce (ketchup) business, what do you think they discovered? Right, the stuff doesn't come out of the bottle fast enough—especially when it is a new bottle.

So, some good marketing professional at Hunt-Wesson decided the best thing to do was to make bottles with bigger openings.

> Problem: Consumers prefer a thick product, but this thickness makes it difficult to remove the product from the bottle.

> Opportunity: Increase the size of the bottle's opening so the sauce will come out faster.

Hunt's Catsup soon had wide mouth bottles, and their advertising showed how quickly it came out and how convenient it was.

3. Problems and Opportunities

Within a few weeks, Heinz had contracted for the use of the Carly Simon song "Anticipation" and used it as the audio track in television advertising that showed people sitting around waiting for the great taste of Heinz.

They communicated that you could not have good taste if it came out of the bottle too fast. This is just one of those things you have to put up with in life. If you want great-tasting ketchup, you are just going to have to wait for it. When was the last time you saw a wide mouth ketchup bottle?

Preferred Format

When it comes to format, I favor having at least one (maybe more) opportunity for each problem.

List them as separate events rather than as many opportunities that will aid us to solve a plethora of problems.

For more information, please also read:

1. **Positioning: The Battle for Your Mind**
   Ries, Al and Trout, Jack
   McGraw-Hill, New York, 1986.

   Reread this timeless classic for a clear understanding of what you hope to do with this segment of the plan.

2. **How to Write a Successful Marketing Plan**
   Roman Hiebing & Scott Cooper
   NTC Business Books, Lincolnwood, IL, 1997

   Chapter Three discusses this topic.

3. **Management Decisions by Objectives**
   Odiorne, George S.
   Prentice-Hall, Englewood Cliffs, NJ, 1969.

   Odiorne's discussion on the purpose for setting objectives will help you write the Problems and Opportunities segment.

Marketing Objective

"If you don't know where you are going, any road will get you there."
—The Koran

Introduction.

A Marketing Objective Is Most Often a Sales Number.

A marketing objective is quantifiable. Most of the time that means it is a sales number. Sometimes it doesn't have to be just a sales number, it could also be a quantifiable objective that addresses awareness, usage, attitudes, etc. But these are not common.

There are some cases when the marketing objective is not a number, but only when the people involved don't have the "chutzpah" to do what they know is right. To pick a number and live with it and try to achieve it throughout the year is a difficult taskmaster. But the work will be better for it. "Just do it."

The marketing objective is most often a sales number.

It is a gauge against which progress will be measured.

If you were the Brand Manager on Johnson & Johnson Baby Shampoo in the early 1970s, when they were running their adult campaign, you would have been seeing regular increases of 25% to 30% a year.

This is not common for a mature brand like Johnson & Johnson Baby Shampoo, but they'd recently started to run a campaign that told consumers to try it on their own hair, instead of just using it on their baby's hair.

After all, if it was mild enough for a baby, it certainly wouldn't hurt an adult's hair, either. So establishing a marketing objective that required sales increases of +25% was not only reasonable, it may have been too easy to get the objective.

Fulfilling the objective with very little effort is sometimes called "skating," where you can move ahead without working hard.

The purpose for this segment of the marketing planning document is to determine the volume commitment for next year.

This will require the combined talents of an economist, a marketing sage, and a prophet.

But, assuming your crystal ball is at the shop, we will track you through the process.

A. Number:

A Marketing Objective Should Be Measurable.
Remember, the marketing objective is a number.

This is because there must be a method by which you can determine if you have achieved that objective at the end of the year.

If not, then a change in strategy may be in order for the following year.

"SMAC"
Procter & Gamble uses the an acronym SMAC to describe objectives. They should be Specific, Measurable, Achievable, and Compatible (with everything else going on with the Brand at that time).

Examples of good marketing objectives might be:

- *To ship 329,500 units in Fiscal Year 1999.*

- *To increase share of market by +1.9%, from 8.2% to 10.1%.*

- *To increase top-of-mind awareness by +10%, from 73% to 83%, as evidenced by the 1999 tracking study.*

B. Rationale:

Defend Your Objective.
This segment of the marketing plan is used to defend your quantifiable objectives.

These number objectives should be substantiated with more numbers in the Rationale section.

The goal is to make the numbers go beyond believable to the point where the reader believes that you really do have a crystal ball.

For example, in the case of Johnson & Johnson Baby Shampoo, to substantiate an increase in sales of +28% the rationale could include the following:

1. **Sales History:**
   If sales have exceeded 20% for the past three years, show the specific numbers and outline why there has been such a dramatic increase in the past three years.

2. **Attitudinal Changes:**
   Show the numbers indicating that more consumers now think the Brand is good for their own hair.

3. **Marketing Effort:**
   If there is a significant change in the marketing plan for this year, then it should be discussed here.

   For example, if the new strategy is rolling into another third of the country, if the strategy will finally be available for network television, or if a new flag has been prepared for the packaging, then there is a rationale that the increase in sales will be spread over a broader audience.

Defend Your Projections.

It is absolutely essential that numbers be used to defend your market projections.

Some students make the mistake of believing that if they write something down it will instantly become believable—if they read something in the newspaper, it must be true, because they read it in the newspaper. Wrong.

It must be made believable, and the best way to make it so is to substantiate it with numbers.

As a classroom teacher, I have become such a fanatic about making sure that students support what they write, that a group of students bought me a rubber stamp with SUPPORT written in 36-point type.

I use it every semester. Thanks.

For more information, please also read:

1. **Strategic Advertising Campaigns**
   Schultz, Don E., and Barnes, Beth E.
   NTC Business Books, Chicago, 1994. Fourth Edition.

   Chapters Four and Six relate to this chapter.

2. **Management Decisions by Objectives**
   Odiorne, George S.
   Prentice-Hall, Englewood Cliffs, NJ, 1969.

   Odiorne's discussion of objectives and their purpose in marketing will prove valuable to the entire planning document, but will be especially useful here.

3. **Advertising Management**
   Batra, Rajeeve, Myers, John G., and Aaker, David A.
   Prentice Hall, Upper Saddle River, NJ, 1996. Fifth Edition.

Marketing Flow Chart

"A picture is worth a thousand words."
—Chinese Proverb

Introduction.

Now that you've established your objective, you know what needs to be accomplished during the coming year—or the planning period under consideration.

But the question keeps coming up about what we are really doing here. A flow chart can help.

Understanding the Process.

Putting it in Perspective.

A schematic flow chart may aid you in understanding the process and putting it in perspective.

Page 137 of this text shows an example of a marketing flow chart.

It diagrams the process you will go through in order to market a product or to fulfill a marketing plan.

The "Marketing Molecule."

As I was making the original of this schematic, I had a secretary who was certain it had something to do with chemistry. She insisted on calling it the marketing molecule—I still use that name.

The marketing flow chart you see here is one that was made for a new food product, so it includes the actual development of the product. Your flow chart will probably be different.

Decision Points.

The schematic diagram simply shows the decision-making points and the sources of information needed to make those decisions.

You will notice that the flow chart is like a recipe—it calls for specific things to take place at specific points in time.

For example:

> You can tell that pricing decisions need to be made before a budget can be established for the media plan.

> You need to establish a creative strategy before you can write advertising copy.

> You need to determine how the category is viewed before you can set marketplace positioning for the Brand.

Some Decisions Have Been Made.

In many cases, some of these decisions have already been made. Issues like pricing and distribution are most often not taken on by the advertising agency.

A great advertising agency does everything it can to get into every aspect of their clients' businesses, but this is not common. Don't shy away from these, but they aren't the first issues for advertising people to tackle.

The Importance of Margins.

A good, solid business analysis may reveal a category where margins have eroded to the point where a little more margin may allow a significant increase in the advertising.

This will lead to an increase in the share of voice for the Brand. This may increase preference and volume.

On the other hand, you may find a category where the margins are high, leaving a niche large enough to drive a powerful price Brand.

Make a molecule fit what you want it to do.

Make Your Own Flow Chart.

The Process the Marketing Document Will Describe.

Study the chart. It will help you understand the process the marketing document will describe.

You may want to make your own marketing flow chart—one that meets the needs of the Brand you are about to market.

Some Approaches.

This schematic was done in a drawing program.

There are also scheduling programs, such as MacProject that can help you add another level of organization to this critical process.

You may want to start with chalk and a blackboard or pencil and paper.

If you have a wall or bulletin board, yarn and some 3" x 5" cards can help you develop a "marketing molecule" of your own.

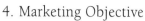

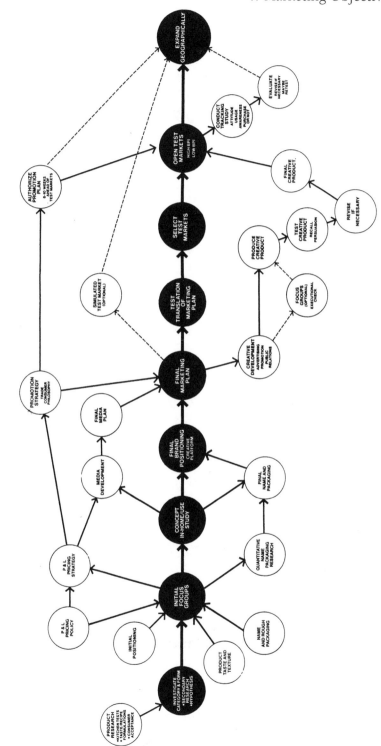

Marketing Flow Chart:

Budget

"The budget is the power to choose."
—John F. Kennedy

Introduction.

Purpose.

The purpose for the Budget segment of the marketing planning document is two-fold:

1. To provide substantiation for the quantity of money that will be spent during the coming year

2. To outline where the money will be spent

Format Variations.

Some plan outlines call for the Budget to be in the Situation Analysis or in the Marketing Strategy.

We will give more importance to the elements within the budget, however, by placing the budget in its own section or chapter.

Because of that importance, we make it easier for the reader to find the budget segment and to understand how and why marketing monies will be allocated.

Occasionally, a marketing plan will have the budget at the end of the plan near evaluation, but here in Chapter Five between the Marketing Objective and the Marketing Strategy seems ideal.

We know what we want to do in the objective, and the budget provides the resources for how we will do it as outlined in the strategy.

Be Prepared to Defend Your Budget.

The budget should be defended in as many ways as possible.

If you're developing a substantiation for the budget in a case study for an Advertising Campaigns class or for a contest like the American Advertising Federation's NSAC, one point of substantiation might be the budget that is given in the case, or you might find substantiation through your secondary research. But that is just not good enough.

You must be as certain that the quantity of dollars recommended to the client is as correct as is possible.

While we will suggest a method to support what you are recommending, there is really only one way to be certain that the quantity of dollars is right, and that is through testing (see Chapter Eleven for more detail).

At a major packaged goods company like General Mills or P&G, preparing for a budget meeting is a rite of passage for young advertising people. Successfully defending your budget will be a critical factor in your success or failure.

Rights, Responsibilities, and Risks.

The key management of your client has the right to know how and why you developed the number you did. They will want to know the support for what you want to spend.

They have a right to expect a reasonable rate of return on their investment, and you have the responsibility to present a sound, logical plan to deliver on that return.

In an advertising class or an AAF/NSAC contest, the penalty is a bad grade or losing at the regional level.

In the real world, the penalty is much more severe because the risk is much greater. Don't let anyone tell you that gambling in Las Vegas is a greater risk than what you'll be doing for the next quarter of a century—or more.

Getting It Right.

First, you need to generate the numbers so you can use good judgment to determine the right budget.

Then you have to defend those numbers.

Normally, if you can convince a client or boss that your rationale for the initial numbers is correct, they'll buy the whole line of thinking.

The real test, of course, comes when you actually spend the money.

The Need for Test Markets.

Since most clients make the mistake of underspending, it is usually a good idea to recommend a test market to measure the impact of increasing advertising weight by 50% or so.

This should be done in one or two markets—representing at least 1% of the U.S. population.

More detail on this testing can be found in Chapter Twelve, Testing.

It is likely that we will not have the results of that test market when this section is being written, yet we still have to substantiate the budget.

The Straight Line Method.

For a brand that has been around for a few years, I recommend the straight line method. It is easy to understand for those who have not worked with forecasting before.

Quite simply, you will project two numbers and then multiply them together.

First, project the number of units you believe the brand will sell during the period under consideration—probably next year.

Then, project the advertising to sales ratio (or the case rate, if it is a packaged goods brand).

Next, multiply the number of cases to be sold (as defined by the marketing objective) by the newly discovered projected advertising to sales ratio.

Here's how to do it, step-by-step:

First, Project Units Sold:

To project the number of units you expect the Brand to sell during the year under consideration, you need to have a record of sales for the past three to five years.

One clear way to make the projection is to plot the information on graph paper, with one axis showing sales and the other axis representing time.

Then you can plot sales over time, and it is a simple matter to see where you think sales will go.

Remember that it is likely you have created an outstanding marketing plan for this brand, while a lukewarm or mediocre plan may have been used in the past.

This would indicate that it is likely you will surpass a straight line method of sales projection.

Unit Sales Over Time

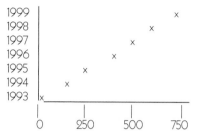

It is clear that sales are not exactly in a straight line.

In 1993 sales were only 15 units while in 1994, 180 units were sold.

In 1995—250 units, in 1997—500 units.

On this basis, we should assume that sales in 1999 would be 750 units because we can show a straight line to project sales in the future.

If we feel that the Marketing Plan we are recommending is significantly better than anything that has been used in the past, we might be able to substantiate 775 units or even 800 units to be sold in 2000.

Determine the Advertising to Sales Ratio:

History and Inertia.
This will likely remain unchanged.

If the brand spent 5.25% on advertising last year, and the same percentage in the year before that, you will have a hard time defending an Advertising to Sales Ratio (A to S Ratio) of anything other than 5.25%.

The same is true for packaged goods products. If the Brand has been spending $1.00 a case on advertising in each of the past five years, it is pretty likely that it will spend $1.00 on advertising for each case sold next year.

If the rate has been changing in recent years, plot the rates on graph paper showing time on one axis and advertising as a percent of sales (or case rate) on the other axis.

After you have a visual representation of the rates over time, you will be able to project the following year.

This may be as simple as continuing a straight line into the future (as we did for the volume projection), but more likely it will require clustering or judgment to forecast the following year's rate.

New Products.

If it is a new product, the forecasting is a little more difficult.

It may be that you will have to find information that has been written by professionals and published.

For example, when the AAF case study was Saturn, there were a variety of articles published in *Automotive Week, AdWeek,* and *Advertising Age* that addressed volume expectations for Saturn.

Allocate Elements of the Budget.

The Great Allocation Debate.

There has been very little written on the subject of how much to allocate to advertising and how much for promotion or public relations.

For example, when Bud Frankel, of the sale promotion agency Frankel & Co. wrote his book on sales promotion, he spent many pages pointing out how and why dollars allocated to sales promotion will yield great and immediate sales.

On the other hand, a book written by David Ogilvy, of the ad agency Ogilvy & Mather, maintained that advertising would not only yield greater sales in the long run, but that the use of sales promotion was generally in poor taste—kind of like being a bait fisherman in the movie *A River Runs Through It.* (See the quote at the beginning of Chapter Nine.)

Both these books were written by authors with a vested interest in the allocation of marketing dollars.

As you review the chapters on media planning and sales promotion, you'll gain additional understanding of what these tools are intended to do.

Quantity and Category.

The marketing budget must break out the quantity of money that will be needed for advertising and for sales promotion. A dollar amount will be needed for each of the following:

1. **Advertising**
    a. Media
    b. Production

2. **Sales Promotion**
   a. Event
   b. Production

3. **Public Relations**
   a. Legislative action
   b. Publicity
   c. Production

4. **Direct Marketing**
   a. Mail
   b. Telemarketing
   c. Miscellaneous Media
   d. Production

5. **Event Marketing**
   a. Event
   b. Production

6. **Miscellaneous...**

The Debate Continues...

The issue becomes: how much do you give to advertising and how much to sales promotion. There's no right answer that works in every case.

If you're working on a Brand that's used advertising and sales promotion in the past, look at what's been used and what's been successful.

Generally speaking, I think too much is spent on sales promotion. By giving your customers, whether they're current or potential, additional value, you're training them to buy only when value is present.

Think about it. If you're a student at a university, how often do you go to Pizza Hut when you've got a coupon versus how often you go to a competitor when there's a coupon? Or how often do you go to Pizza Hut when you don't have a coupon?

Most packaged goods companies allocate about a third to a half of their budget to sales promotion with the remainder going to advertising.

If you need people to act immediately, you may need to give them a better value, but the cost of motivation may be quite high.

If you can wait a little longer, the cost is lower, and if the decision is made based on the product rather than the incentive, they'll probably end up being more loyal customers.

Adding the Details.

Clearly, there will be detail given in each element of the marketing plan for each of these entries.

For example, your Media Budget will have specific numbers for each medium, and it will be outlined by quarter, half, and total year. (See Chapter Eight for more detail on what a media budget will entail.)

The Production Budget for each element should contain information for print or commercial production, including: talent, prints, shipping, printing, photography, editing, etc. This will be included in the creative segment of the document.

These don't have to be complete working estimates, but the writer of the marketing document should recognize the need for the various elements of the budget and provide a budget number that includes all the required monies.

For more information, please also read:

1. **Strategic Advertising Campaigns**
   Schultz, Don E., and Barnes, Beth E.
   NTC Business Books, Chicago, 1994. Fourth Edition.

   Chapters Four and Eight relate to this chapter.

2. **Advertising Media Planning**
   Sissors, Jack Z., and Bumba, Lincoln
   NTC Business Books, Chicago, 1992, Fourth Edition.

   Chapter Sixteen will provide more insight into the budgeting process as outlined in this chapter.

3. **Advertising Management**
   Aaker, David A., Batra, Rajeev, Myers, John G.
   Fourth Edition, Prentice Hall, Englewood Cliffs, NJ, 1992.

   Chapter Sixteen provides some additional information that will supplement Schultz's discussion of budget setting.

4. **How Much is Enough?/When Ads Work**
   John Phillip Jones
   Lexington Books (1992/1995)

   In these two books, this respected professor, a former JWT/London advertising executive, addresses, among other things, the relative performance of advertising and sales promotion.

Marketing Strategy

"Don't gamble.
Take all your savings and buy
some good stock and hold it
'til it goes up, then sell it.
If it don't go up, don't buy it."

—Will Rogers

Introduction.

How You Intend to Achieve the Objective.

The marketing strategy is how you intend to achieve, or deliver, the marketing objective. This section is dedicated to marketing strategy.

Remember, the marketing objective is a number. An objective is what you want to do; a strategy is how you're going to do it.

So the marketing strategy is how the Brand will sell enough cases to finally deliver the objective.

Account Management.

Developing and executing marketing strategy is the essence of an account manager's career—the same as it is for someone in brand management on the client side.

Sometimes students and professionals in smaller markets have the idea that an account executive is the liaison with the client—that means they take work developed by other people at the agency and deliver it to the client. That's not the account executive's reason for being. That's the job of guys on bicycles who risk their lives in midtown traffic.

Account people are responsible for strategy development. The account manager should be excited about this part of the plan.

Account Planning.

In the last few years, we've seen the emergence of the account planner. An account planner is half researcher and half account manager.

It's the account planner's responsibility to represent the consumer in any and all conversations concerning the development of marketing strategy. Lisa Fortini-Campbell's book, *Hitting the Sweet Spot,* is a great source of information on this subject.

It is the goal of the account planner to understand how the consumer uses and thinks about the product.

When Goodby & Silverstein developed a campaign for Sega, the planner spent weeks playing video games with kids ten to fifteen years old.

He spent time in their homes, in video arcades, at shopping malls, and anywhere else these kids would talk with him, so he could get a better grasp of their thought processes when it came to video games.

The popular "Got Milk" campaign came from asking consumers to go without milk for a week. The account planner then talked to these deprived milk users and developed deeper insight into the importance of milk to the average consumer.

The result was a "deprivation strategy" and breakthrough advertising.

If your group does not have an account planner, consider changing things around so that you have someone whose job is account planning—understanding the consumer.

Second best is to make someone pull double duty in order to fill this position. If not, the job will fall squarely on the shoulders of the account manager, copywriter, and researcher.

The goal is to create a stronger marketing strategy—marketing strategy that will be strong enough to deliver the marketing objective.

The Five Ps.

The marketing strategy is many strategies. It should be divided into a section for each of the five Ps—promotion, product, price, place (distribution), and people.

The first of these will receive the most attention because it addresses the marketing plan. Promotion (with a capital "P") includes advertising, sales promotion, merchandising, public relations, and any other form of marketing communications appropriate for your particular needs.

In most cases, for student work, product, price, and place can be handled briefly. Entrepeneurs will labor for years on these elements.

Strategy as Objective.

A marketing strategy is a specific discipline objective. That means the precise language found in Chapter Seven for a creative objective will be found in this section as a marketing strategy. For example, the marketing strategy might be:

> *To establish Simplicity Patterns as the quick and easy way for the target audience to obtain the clothes they want.*

Now, turn to the example in Note A following Chapter Seven, on page 181 and compare the creative objective that is listed there with this marketing strategy.

The Creative Objective is:

> *To establish Simplicity Patterns as the quick and easy way for the target audience to obtain the clothes they want.*

You see precisely the same language is used in both cases.

The Marketing Strategy for Creative is the Creative Objective.

There is a reason for this. Remember: an objective is what you want to do, and a strategy is how you will do it.

The marketing objective is a number. The marketing strategy is how you will fulfill that number.

But on the next level, the marketing strategy becomes the objective— what you want to accomplish in creative or media or any other specific marketing discipline. Take a look at the diagram below.

Then the creative strategy, which you will develop, will tell management how you plan to accomplish the creative objective. The creative strategy becomes a subset of marketing strategy—same with media.

147

One More Example.

This time, suppose that we have been asked to market Levi's Dockers. We may write our marketing strategy, under promotion, as follows:

> *To deliver a target audience of men 35 and older with special attention given to those with higher income and education.*

Turn this time to the objectives in Chapter Eight on Media, where you will find the objectives for a media plan (page 191).

Look at the first example. It uses exactly the same language as does this marketing strategy. The media strategy then becomes a subset of the marketing strategy.

Here is how to prepare this segment of the Marketing Planning document.

A. Promotion:

This is Promotion with a capital "P," not to be confused with sales promotion.

At Least Two Segments—Probably More.

The promotion part of the marketing strategy will be divided into at least two major segments—advertising and sales promotion, but it is far more likely in this era of increased costs and reduced efficiency to have multiple segments.

We will discuss five here and give suggestions for more.

Here is a quick summary of these segments:

  • **Advertising** is intended to work over the long run. Advertising provides an intangible, logical, or emotional reason to buy without the immediate discount or reward—other than the benefits offered by the brand itself.

  • **Sales promotion** uses a tangible motivation to buy in the near future—a bribe if you will, though *incentive* is a more commonly used word.

  • **Public relations** seeks to build positive relations with specific groups of people, most of whom will be stakeholders of the brand—employees, consumers, stockholders, legislators, etc. Media relations are also important.

• **Direct marketing** attempts to build a relationship with the consumer by communicating directly with him or her instead of going through a retailer. If you already have a customer base, and you have their names and addresses, or you have a very narrow target audience, some sort of direct-marketing program will probably be appropriate.

• **Event marketing** involves relationships with customers based on a specific event, usually sporting or cultural in nature. Students are often the target of this type of marketing, from Orientation Week and sporting events all the way to Spring Break.

• **Miscellaneous.** We will also cover a few other areas that may have application for a student project. They are: personal selling, packaging, merchandising, and promotional products.

"IMC"

These initials stand for "Integrated Marketing Communications," when all the elements of reaching the end consumer are pulled together in a synergistic process.

MarCom stands for Marketing Communications, and often companies have MarCom departments and managers. Students with degrees in advertising not only look to advertising agencies for careers, but to MarCom departments of major advertisers.

MarCom is the same as IMC, except that IMC recognizes the integration part. Certainly any good MarCom manager will understand the importance of synergism, so you may find me referring to IMC as MarCom, or MarCom as IMC from time to time. You'll be able to figure it out.

There can be a synergism that takes place when everything uses the same advertising campaign line, but integrated marketing communications is really more than that. It is marketing planning with the consumer as the focus.

Account Planning/Personal Media Network.
Account Planning and other concepts such as the "personal media network" are IMC concepts applied to advertising.

Consumer Insight/Brand Contact Points.
"Consumer insight" and "brand contact points" are similar concepts applied to IMC.

Both are really trying to get the consumer's perception and a more effective consumer connection into the work.

IMC is interested in getting a response, not to the advertising, but to the Brand. And advertising is just one of the channels.

But, for most brands, it is the most important channel—and one of the biggest parts of the marketing budget.

So the next part of our document will begin with advertising.

1. Advertising:

This advertising portion of the plan will be subdivided into creative, media, and production.

It's common to include an overall advertising strategy statement before the specifics of a creative or media strategy are stated.

a. Creative:

The marketing strategy that addresses creative is an objective in the Creative segment of the planning document. It depends on the level in the plan as to where it is placed.

This, then, is how the advertising creative product will contribute to the fulfillment of the overall marketing objective, but also it is what you want the advertising creative product to accomplish.

When you begin this statement with the words "To establish," whether it is at the Marketing Strategy or Creative Objective level, it is easier to understand the purpose of the statement. It will also force the thinking to be about what the Brand will become as a result of the advertising.

The complete marketing creative strategy should be as follows:

To establish (the Brand name) as _____.

Here is a specific example:

To establish Simplicity Patterns as the quick and easy way for the Target Audience to obtain the clothes they want.

Here is another example:

To establish Nestle as having superior quality chocolate within the solid milk chocolate segment of the total candy line.

Usually, there is only one marketing strategy written for the creative function, as there is usually only one creative objective.

b. Media:

The marketing strategies that address media are also media objectives and help fulfill the overall marketing objective.

Again, these strategies state specifically what the media plan is intended to accomplish.

In media, however, it is common to have more than one objective, since media marketing strategies contain statements that address the target audience, geography, seasonality, continuity or flighting, creative constraints, and reach versus frequency.

The language used here will be identical to the language used in the objective section of the media portion of the plan.

Examples of a media marketing strategy are:

Target Audience:
To deliver advertising to women 18 to 34 primarily, with secondary importance given to men of the same age.

Geography:
To advertise throughout the United States with additional support in those areas with greatest sales potential.

Seasonality, target audience media habits, and other factors may also play a part. Additional information and detail can be found in Chapter Eight.

c. Production:

The marketing strategy that addresses production will explain how production helps achieve the marketing objectives.

Each separate advertising medium will require production. It is common to explain production in the section to which the production pertains: Production of advertising elements will go in the Creative segment, production of sales promotion pieces will go in Sales Promotion.

Television production is obviously quite different from newspaper production. Both have an opportunity to spend more money to achieve more quality, or to have a little less quality for a little less money.

The Unattainable Triad: Price, Quality, Time.
The Law of the Unattainable Triad was developed for production people. The three elements of this triangle are: price, quality, and time.

You can generally have two of the three at the cost of the third. That is, you can have it fast and in the best possible quality, but you will pay through the nose for it.

151

It is impossible to have high quality, low prices, and fast turnaround time simultaneously

A decision must be made which of these will impact generally in the plan.

2. Sales Promotion:

Sales promotion is an attempt by the manufacturer to stimulate behavior in the marketplace The primary approach is to change the perception of the basic value (or price) of the product by either reducing cost or increasing what the consumer receives.

Value to the consumer (or the trade) increases either way.

This can be through direct decreased cost, as is done with a cents-off coupon, or more indirectly by providing more product for the same price, as is done with a "bonus pack" (i.e., 16 oz. for the price of 12 oz., often in a package that shows the extra size graphically).

Sales Promotion is usually considered more expensive than advertising. Sales increases that are solely a function of temporary price reductions are very expensive to the Brand—particularly if they do not last.

Sales promotion can only be considered successful if the consumer is converted to become a loyal user.

Two Segments: Consumer and Trade.

In planning, sales promotion can also be broken into two segments—consumer and trade.

If the plan shows synergism between these two promotion strategies, then an overall marketing strategy addressing sales promotion should be listed first. This will set the stage for the specific strategy that addresses consumer and trade promotion. If this takes places, we are said to be thinking in an integrated fashion.

a. Consumer Promotion:

Coupons, rebates, bonus packs, sweepstakes, and contests are some of the commonly used sales promotion events.

The marketing strategy statement written in this part of the marketing plan should be an overall statement that indicates how consumer sales promotion will contribute to achieving the marketing objective.

Individual events should be listed in Section Nine. (See Chapter Nine, Sales Promotion, for more detail.)

Consumer promotion can be used:
- to build trial;
- to "load" the consumer (build in-home inventory);
- to reinforce current usage; or
- to be competitive.

b. Trade Promotion:

The marketing strategy statement for trade promotion addresses how trade promotion will augment the marketing objective.

The most common trade promotion events in packaged goods are display allowances and advertising allowances.

3. Public Relations:

When public relations is built into the marketing plan, its strategy goes in this spot in the planning document.

Today, most public relations is divided into two major segments, marketing public relations (MPR) and corporate public relations (CPR).

Corporate public relations has to do with employee relations, stockholder and investor relations, legislative action, and crisis management. If you work on Tylenol and someone tampers with your capsules, that is crisis management—not marketing.

There are other needs and functions of public relations, but those are beyond the scope of this book.

Marketing public relations is the segment that is valuable in the marketing plan. Key elements of MPR are: press releases, press conferences, new product announcements, media relations, and consumer relations.

There are two key target groups for MPR: the media and the consumer. Public relations professionals refer to these target audiences as "publics."

Again, the marketing strategy for public relations will be identical to the objective in the public relations part of the document.

An example of a public relations objective is (See Chapter Ten):

To enhance public opinion of Nuprin as a quality source for sporting pain relief.

For the milk "Mustache" campaign, the advertising and public relations objectives were exactly the same:

To reposition milk as a contemporary adult beverage.

In many areas of marketing, particularly with high-tech and business–to–business, public relations are an important factor in the overall marketing operation.

4. Direct Marketing:

The goal of direct marketing is to convince the customer to order directly from the marketer. In the case of Solo-Flex, this is the manufacturer, while in the case of Land's End, it is a direct retailer (or direct merchant).

a. Direct Response Media:

Direct marketing can include direct mail, such as the Land's End catalogue, and direct response advertising on television or in radio, magazines, or newspapers. The Internet has made some aspects of direct marketing much easier and much less costly. It is, however, just as hard to find the right customers.

Relationship Marketing.

A related form of direct marketing is relationship marketing.

Once someone becomes a customer, relationship marketing focuses on enhancing the lifetime value of that customer. Sometimes this involves selling more goods and services.

Other times it involves merely building the relationship in whatever way is appropriate for the brand and category.

b. Telemarketing:

Telemarketing also has two segments.

Inbound telemarketing is from the consumer inbound to the advertiser. Usually, the customer calls to place an order or to ask a question. Land's End makes sure that everyting they publish has their 800 number on it. This allows customers to call with an order from the catalogue or to call and ask the attendant to look up the number from the shirt ordered six months ago.

Inbound telemarketing may be part of direct response marketing or relationship marketing—usually both.

Outbound telemarketing is from the company to the consumer. Many companies rely on the telephone as a sales tool.

A telemarketing strategy might be:

To reach the target audience at least once in each six-month period.

5. Event Marketing:

Event marketing (and sponsorship) is to consumers what public relations is to the media. Some consider event marketing a type of sales promotion.

But since it is different than most other forms, it is broken out into a different segment. There are consumer events and trade events.

a. **Consumer Events:**

If you have a student target, which is quite common in NSAC competitions, you may well have some sort of event marketing as part of your marketing plan.

You may also have advertising that supports the event and public relations that publicize the event.

Event marketing can be a sports-related, like Winston sponsoring a NASCAR race or Reebok sponsoring an Olympic team. Golf and tennis are attractive to marketers with an upscale target audience.

British Petroleum sometimes sponsors art exhibits or symphonies, and Phillip Morris supports cultural events. This is also event marketing. (Tobacco marketers have been active participants in events, as there were limits on where they could put their marketing dollars. Now, however, they can pay for lawsuits.)

b. **Trade Events:**

Trade shows are probably the greatest events. But this time, the target audience is the trade, not the consumer. The National Restaurant Show or the Sporting Goods Show at McCormick Place in Chicago are significant trade show events.

Comdex is a key event for the computer industry.

Small groups with specialized suppliers, such as the Direct Marketing Association, also have events that are critical for bringing key groups in specialized industries together.

Some of these events, such as MacWorld, attract both the consumer and the trade.

6. Miscellaneous:

Marketing strategy often addresses other elements than those listed above. The decision is a function of the objectives and budget available to the brand. As you can see, there is wide range of marketing tools available and a wide range of possible marketing decisions and priorities.

While there are many options, we have one name for it—the "marketing mix." The marketing mix chosen can also address such things as personal selling, packaging, merchandising, and promotional products.

a. **Personal Selling** requires someone to make sales calls that go directly to customers. For large packaged goods companies there is often a sales department whose job it is to check the grocery shelves, make recommendations to retail buyers, and establish and maintain good relations with "the trade."

b. **Packaging** can be a key element in the marketing mix. Sometimes, this can be the key communication vehicle for a brand. (Have you ever read all that copy on the back of a Bisquick package? The information includes: recipes, nutrition, fat content, ingredients, a Web address, and an 800 number. The package is a key marketing communications tool.)

c. **Merchandising** takes place at the store level. In fact, it's the promoting of the advertising or sales promotion of the Brand at the trade level.

   Merchandising is a term most often used for retail or generic clients. Occasionally, companies will call it merchandising when they have to sell the advertising or sales promotion to their own sales force or to the trade.

   When the California Washington Oregon Pear Bureau puts up point-of-purchase advertising over the Anjou pears in a Kroger store in Cincinnati, they refer to it as merchandising.

   According to the American Marketing Association, merchandising is *"The planning involved in marketing the right merchandise or service at the right place, at the right time, in the right quantities, and at the right price."*

d. **Promotional products** can range from that pen you picked up at the bank, and a good percentage of the T-shirts in your Free T-Shirt collection, to more expensive items adorned with logos and other messages.

   The Promotional Products Association's advertising theme is "Advertising that remains to be seen." And that is exactly what it is. It can be a very strong advertising or marketing tool.

   It is not uncommon for a marketing planning document to have no reference to merchandising or public relations.

The most common elements of Promotion are Advertising and Sales Promotion, and they should almost always be addressed in the Marketing Strategy section of your Planning Document.

B. Product:

In most marketing plans, the product segment of the marketing strategy will be short. It might simply be:

There will be no change in the product.

Product Improvements and New Products.

If, however, there is a product improvement, or if the marketing plan is for a new product introduction, this part of the strategy will explain how this new product will contribute to achieving the marketing objective.

Example: Bisquick.

For example, if you're working on Bisquick for General Mills, and the new research shows that Jiffy is both equal to and perceived to be equal in quality to Bisquick, then a product improvement may be in order. The strategy might be:

To provide product superiority over all competition as evidenced by consumer reaction.

This would require that the product not just be superior in a test-kitchen environment, but would have an improvement consumers could see in their own kitchens.

This is just one example of how Bisquick might strengthen its total marketing mix. This product improvement may work in concert with an increase in advertising spending, a new sales promotion plan, or even a change in price.

The Need to Define New Products.

Generally, a new product introduction will require more definition, including how the brand will address consumer demand in terms of how this product will fulfill consumers' criteria for making purchase decisions, and how it will be unique in the marketplace.

C. Pricing:

When there is a small amount of inflation, this segment will usually be short. A statement indicating no change in price is all that is needed.

The brand will maintain current pricing.

The strategy statement might also be short if the price needs to be increased only to cover a modest increase in production cost.

Only when the price will change dramatically up or down as a change of intent—how pricing will impact on demand—will this part of the plan be more than a sentence or two.

In that case, it will address why the change will contribute to the fulfillment of the marketing objective.

D. Distribution (Place):

Again, this part might be short if there is no change in how the product is distributed. This section should show how the distribution plan contributes to the volume opportunity expressed in the marketing objective.

This is true whether the plan dictates the use of company salespeople to sell the brand to wholesalers who warehouse and sell the brand to retailers who store the brand and sell it to the end user, or if it is a multi-level distribution system such as Amway or Nu-Skin.

The marketing strategy addressing distribution needs to communicate how this distribution system helps complete the marketing objective.

Areas of Opportunity.
Make certain all possible areas of opportunity are explored and found.

Example: Nestle.
Nestle discovered that they could significantly increase volume when they sought distribution in video stores.

They learned that each video store produced about the same volume as a convenience store.

They also learned they could double the volume of an average grocery store by placing a rack with chocolate bars in the dairy case.

Since retailers did not like the idea of multiple locations for candy bars in the supermarket, this tested distribution idea was only recommended for sales promotions events limited in time.

E. People:

A Relatively New Idea.
The inclusion of a "people" segment in the marketing strategy is a relatively new idea. It makes a great deal of sense because most successful new products are based on what consumers want.

The entire marketing plan is based on consumer wants and needs. And the business itself cannot succeed without the ongoing approval of people who buy the brand.

A "Consumer First" Focus.

In fact, a major thrust of IMC planning is working from a "Consumer First" focus. This is the primary focus of the account planner—as we discussed earlier.

The intent of this segment of the marketing strategy is to describe, in detail, who will buy, use, or influence buyers or users of the Brand. This will take a detailed analysis.

Target Audience Analysis.

Target Audience Analysis will identify the target audience and explain why it will buy enough of the brand to meet the marketing objective.

The Target Audience should be described in terms of demographics, psychographics, and any other information, including consumer wants and needs, that will impact the volume of the Brand.

The value of the account planner is easily recognized when writing this important section.

The Target Trade.

Sometimes the people are the trade. When you allocate more trade promotion dollars than consumer promotion dollars, you are making a decision that the people who buy the brand as middlemen are more important to the success of the brand than are the end users.

F. Rationale:

Defend Your Decisions.

Everything that has been written in the marketing strategy section must be defended. There should be quantifiable substantiation for each and every strategy.

The substantiation should show that the marketing strategy will provide the Brand with the impetus to achieve the marketing objective.

The specific execution of the marketing strategy will be listed or clarified within the specific disciplines of the planning document.

Example.

There will be a defense for why the marketing strategy for advertising creative will contribute to fulfilling the volume specified in the marketing objective.

It should be stated in a clear and quantifiable fashion in this portion of the document.

How that marketing strategy is put into action via a copy platform can be found in the seventh section of the plan (Chapter Seven, Advertising Creative), as will the substantiation, support, rationale, or defense for that segment of the plan.

Where to Find Support.

This information can come from secondary resource materials such as:
- Mediamark Research, Inc. (MRI)
- Simmons Market Research Bureau (SMRB)
- Leading National Advertisers (LNA)
- SRI International (VALS II)

(See Notes A and B in Chapter One for a more complete list.) This can also come from the primary research discussed in Chapter Two.

For more information, please also read:

1. **Strategic Advertising Campaigns**
   Schultz, Don E., and Barnes, Beth E.
   NTC Business Books, Chicago, 1994. Fourth Edition.

   Chapter Nine provides an overview of strategy development.

2. **Positioning: The Battle for Your Mind**
   Reis, Al and Trout, Jack
   McGraw-Hill, New York, 1981.

   The first nine chapters set the stage for strategy development.

3. **Marketing Warfare**
   Reis, Al and Trout, Jack
   McGraw-Hill, New York, 1986.

   Chapters Six through Ten will help with strategy development.

4. **Advertising & The Business of Brands**
   Bendinger, Altman, Avery, et al
   The Copy Workshop, Chicago 1999

   Chapters Seven and Eight of this introductory book provide useful overviews of Marketing Services and Strategy Development.

6. **How to Write a Successful Marketing Plan**
   Hiebing, Roman and Cooper, Scott
   NTC Business Books, Chicago/Lincolnwood, IL, 1997

   An excellent and comprehensive book, primarily written for
   Marketing Directors.

7. **Essentials of Advertising Strategy**
   Schultz, Don E., and Tannenbaum, Stanley
   NTC Business Books, Chicago/Lincolnwood, IL, 1991

   Chapters Five and Six are useful.

MarCom & Idea-Driven IMC

"We don't know who discovered water,
but we're pretty sure it wasn't a fish."

—Howard Gossage

Introduction.

Creativity and Creation.

Howard Gossage, the 1960s San Francisco firehouse adman, started his discussion about creativity this way...

"Creativity is quite different from creation, which happened a long time ago. One seventeenth century educator, the Reverend John Lightfoot, even fixed the exact moment. He said, 'Heaven and Earth, center and circumference, were made in the same instant of time ... the twenty-sixth of October, 4004 B.C. at nine o'clock in the morning.' At 9:30 the account executives came in and started talking about creativity."

This is exactly what has happened to "IMC."

IMC = Better MarCom

MarCom, short for marketing communications, has been around for years, particularly with marketers who used a relatively high proportion of public relations.

Integrated Marketing Communications (IMC) is a relatively new idea, but it's simply a better way to implement MarCom.

The premise was to make all elements of the marketing communications package work together, particularly with marketers who used a relatively high proportion of advertising and sales promotion.

It's kind of a synergistic thing.

Somebody said, let's make sure all elements of our marketing communications are integrated . . . and IMC was born.

Much of marketing is about budgets. So, in the haste to expand and learn how integration works, it's not surprising that it has become the bailiwick of the business and numbers people, who want to minimize risk and maximize returns on investment.

But in reality, at the heart of the most effective IMC for the biggest brands, is creativity.

For big brands, the creative concept is one that integrates.

Example: Apple.
"Think Different" helps integrate Apple Computer's communications across a wide range of disciplines.

It communicates. It differentiates. And it integrates.

Example: Nike.
"Just do it" has a similar effect. Nike is able to speak to a wide range of athletes, with very dissimilar "factors that motivate purchase behavior."

Example: Buddy Lee.
Lee Jeans, with a simple visual icon—Buddy Lee, a sales promotion gimmick from early in the brand's history—has given the brand a humorous contemporary feel to their advertising that integrates all the way through the point of sale.

That's an example from Mark Goldstein's agency, Fallon.

Getting Started.

First you have to allow your thinking to be integrated. You can think about which shirt, pants, and shoes you will wear, how they will look together, and how you will feel. So, if you can dress yourself, you are on your way to learning to thinking about how things integrate.

Example: Ford.
When Ford spent $10 million in advertising on November 1, 1999, they also sent a press release to virtually every newspaper, radio, and television station in the country.

Then they communicated this to their dealer network and told them this is the first time there has every been a "global road block."

The two-minute commercial featured all seven Ford nameplates on 38 networks. This was a new idea. This had both consumer and trade, as well as advertising and public relations, components.

This is an example of thinking integrated.

First, Get Their Attention.

Integration is about understanding your target audience and learning to think about what else you can do to get their attention.

Here are a few reasons why this is even more important:

1. **Ratings are down:**
    Remember that television viewership has been steadily declining since the early eighties. At the same time cost per point has been going up. This has forced advertisers to think about new ways to reach their target group.

2. **There are more media vehicles:**
    There are now over ten thousand consumer magazines in this country alone. Each one of them seeks a specific target audience, some are broad and some are narrow.

    Some of the newer, smaller magazines would never had survived in the era of high television ratings.

    There would have been no reason for advertisers to try to seek out smaller market segments.

    You can now buy advertising on the front of shopping carts, on the back of public bathroom stalls, on the sides of downtown trash cans, on bus benches, and on virtually any kind of clothing. (It is a novelty to see a T-shirt without a silk-screened message.)

    This growth in the number of media vehicles has dispersed the audience. This makes them more expensive to reach.

3. **The growth of cable:**
    Cable television is now available in almost 80% of America. This means there are more channels available, which means each channel has fewer people watching.

    This means the advertiser has to buy more networks or stations or programs then ever before.

    Ford bought 38 networks. Wow. Just a few years ago we only had four, and just a few years before that we only had three.

4. **People spend less time with the media:**
   With the increased use of video recorders and computers, people spend less time with traditional TV and other media vehicles. People are also more active than they have ever been.

   That leaves less time to spend with consumer media vehicles.

   Marry this with the increased number of vehicles and you can quickly see why it is important for advertisers to work harder to reach the same number of people they did in the past.

5. **Sales promotion is expected:**
   More consumers are buying when the Brand is on special. Midas runs a special on shock absorbers every spring. Many customers wait, even when their shock absorbers are worn out, to take advantage of the sale.

   This is common. Many shop the newspaper coupon ads to determine where they will go out to dinner on Friday night.

   Customers are less loyal, and the battle to keep your customers from going over to the competition takes place every day.

6. **The quantity of advertising is increasing:**
   Some studies indicate that the average American now sees 1,500 advertising messages a day—some say 3,000.

   Viewers can only remember eight or ten of those, and often they remember the storyline and not the advertiser.

   So the marketplace is a highly competitive environment that forces every marketer, every advertiser, every MarCom manager to be more creative and demand more productivity for every marketing communications investment.

   "More bang for the buck" will be more important in this new millennium than it has ever been.

   Advertisers have to find new ways to deliver the target group without breaking the bank.

Synergy-Synergy.

Little Ceasar's runs television advertising to communicate Pizza-Pizza. Then they use newspaper inserts to back up Pizza-Pizza with coupons to increase the value-price relationship.

Then they back it up again with direct mail to recent buyers to reinforce usage.

Example: Nuprin.

Nuprin identified a hole is the analgesic market. Their identified niche positioning was to convince sports enthusiasts that Nuprin would relieve the pain incurred during sporting accidents.

Advertising ran that showed grand slalom and downhill racers taking big-time tumbles. It was not only humorous, but reinforced the sports pain relief positioning.

Sports personalities said of pain that they would "Nupe it."

Nuprin sponsored downhill races at major ski resorts and gave away yellow buttons that read "Nupe it."

They gave away prizes to spectators with "Nupe it" buttons. They gave a special trade displace allowance during the promotion to get yellow in-store "Nupe it" signs.

The media was involved with special viewing locations to report on the races with "Nupe it" signs.

This is a great example of integrated thinking.

All of these Nuprin elements worked together:
1. Advertising
   a. Television
   b. Newspaper
   c. Radio
   d. Signage
2. Sales promotion
   a. Consumer
      - contest
      - coupons
   b. Trade
      - display allowance for POP
3. Public relations
   a. Press releases
   b. Press relations
4. Merchandising

This is an idea that takes advantage of creativity. Everything works together in a synergistic fashion so it is integrated.

But before it could work together, there had to be an idea.

Someone had to do the work to find the hole in the competitive analgesic positioning. Someone had to have the idea for the sports positioning, and someone had to recognize the idea was viable.

166

Mark Goldstein, director of account management at Fallon in Minneapolis, said: *"Integration isn't about charts and spreadsheets and datamining. Integration is about ideas ... ideas big enough to unify a brand and motivate consumers and employees and Wall Street..."*

Big Ideas Make Everything Bigger.

Integrated Marketing Communication is a new set of words for advertising campaigns that are bigger than just advertising.

All of the marketing communication elements work with the advertising and become part of the entire advertising campaign.

Advertising has always been about ideas—it's an idea business. And now those ideas have to drive the brand communication beyond advertising. And when the idea is right, everything works better.

The importance of those ideas will continue to grow as time goes on. As people watch less television and ratings decrease, as media options increase, and consumers become less loyal, advertisers will have to work harder to find ways to get their message in front of customers.

And ideas have the power to unify a brand's messages across all forms of marketing communications.

The Need for More Reach.
Michael Naples did a significant study in the early seventies and learned that advertisers need to increase frequency in order to have an impact on the viewers.

His study, and one by MacDonald, in England, taught us to think in terms of three-plus reach.

If those studies were done today, we might be thinking in terms of five-plus reach or six-plus reach. But most advertisers can't afford five-plus reach or even three-plus reach.

They can, however, use their creativity to find new ways to deliver that same target audience. And ideas have the power to drive the integration of the message.

Advertising Is an Idea Business.
As it grows into new forms of brand communications, it's still ideas that connect with consumers that will make the difference.

Advertising Creative

*"We believe imagination
is one of the last remaining
legal means you have to gain
an unfair advantage
over your competition."*

—Tom McElligott

Introduction.

The Importance of Creative Advertising.

Even in this day of Integrated Marketing Communications, the advertising creative product is most often the single element of the marketing plan that can provide the greatest impact on sales.

In a world where we work long and hard to gain a few more percentage points of efficiency, the difference between an effective and ineffective creative presentation can be significant.

For this reason, more time is spent on the development of advertising's creative product and more energy is consumed trying to make advertising stand out from all the other advertising that exists, than on any other element of marketing.

The Power of the Creative Message.

Never underestimate the power of the creative message.

When I was working on the introduction of Ortega Tacos, we had two potential messages.

The first described a taco and how to make and eat them. Our identified target audience was mostly uneducated about Mexican food.

The second simply told the target that Ortega Tacos are "Fun to Make. Fun to Eat." The target was the same.

The second commercial was many times more effective, memorable, and persuasive than the first. The strategy was essentially the same. The target was the same. But the creative staging of the message allowed more people to relate easily to the product.

Look at Nissan's Altima. It was a disappointment in Japan, yet sales went through the roof in this country. The car books panned it early on, yet consumers love it. Why? Brilliant advertising.

They took the Lexus positioning and made it available for $30,000 less. The advertising made the difference.

What about Federal Express? How successful would they be without *"When it absolutely positively has to be there overnight."* Or even McDonald's without *"You deserve a break today."*

These are examples of advertising that has made a significant difference in the success of a Brand in a highly competitive marketing environment.

A Definition of Creative Advertising.

My definition of creative advertising is advertising that is different from other advertising.

Many advertising art directors and copywriters will not even consider an advertisement that is similar to other ads.

Creative advertising is innovative and fresh. It is usually an application of something that is common in an uncommon way.

There are three primary reasons why so much time is spent on the creative side of advertising:

1. Sales Generator:

Advertising that is different attracts attention. In order to sell something to your target group, you must first have their attention. Then, and only then, will you be able to present an effective sales message.

While the numbers vary depending on who you talk with, most advertising professionals agree that the average American sees thousands of advertising messages a day, but can only remember about nine.

Of those nine, the average person incorrectly remembers the brand name for about half, so only four or five advertising messages a day are really doing what they need to be doing.

Now this is tempered somewhat, because different people remember different messages, but the point remains that little advertising is really memorable.

There is a high probability that the ones that are remembered are the ones that are different in some way from common advertising. If it's different, many people would judge it to be creative.

However, advertising is not judged to be creative just because it is different; it must also address a business reason for being. This business reason is most often called strategy.

If the advertising communicates the points in the creative strategy it is said to be "on strategy."

Benton & Bowles (a predecessor of DMB&B) used to say, "It isn't creative unless it sells." Now we all know that this isn't exactly true. Some very creative things might not sell, and some fairly uncreative things, like FREE, may sell very well.

But there is a higher probability of your advertising delivering that selling message effectively if it is "creative."

2. Career Advancement:

Copywriters and art directors progress in their careers by winning awards. They win awards by being creative.

At the same time, they must be on strategy in order to sell the advertising to their account management groups and to their clients. But their clear motivation is to win awards.

One of the best award competitions is the "Effies," which measure sales effectiveness as well as creativity.

Creative people gain prestige among their peers when they win awards. They also get raises based on winning awards. One midcareer copywriter in Los Angeles told me, "If I win a Belding it's worth a five thousand dollar raise." (A Belding is an award from the Los Angeles Advertising Club.)

3. It Is Fun:

Clients spend more time with the advertising creative product because it is one of the best ways to increase sales.

Clients get raises and promotions based on increasing sales for their brands. This is the story they tell; however, the truth is that it is just a lot more fun to work on advertising than a promotion allowance for a grocery chain in Ft. Wayne.

While the actual creation of the advertising is the responsibility of the copy and art members of the group (called the creative people), the creative process is the heart of advertising and is probably the most fun you will have working in business—advertising or any other business, for that matter.

Creative Development.

The Development Sequence.

It is important that you understand where creative development fits into the scheme of advertising development.

Some of this we've already covered, and in great detail, but we'll repeat it here so that you can recognize the chronology of the stages of creative development. In general, the process is as follows:

1. Understand Your Target Audience:
Know your audience—where they live, when they buy, demographics, psychographics, purchase cycle (how often they buy), and all the other information we discussed back in Chapter One when we discussed the Situation Analysis.

2. Understand Their Motivation:
Isolate the factors that motivate purchase behavior, and what is unique about your Brand.

The relationship between these two pieces of information will likely be the basis for your strategic direction.

3. Differentiate Your Brand:
This differentiation can take place either strategically or executionally.

4. Write a Creative Platform:
We will get to that in just a few paragraphs. Be patient.

5. Concept Development:
Here is where you will develop your selling premise. Quite often this selling premise will contain a campaign line.

Often that unique combination of motivating factors and brand uniqueness can be combined into a proposition. P&G often uses slogans that are propositions. Examples are:

> *Dirt can't hide from intensified Tide.*
> *Choosy Mothers Choose Jif.*
> *Bounty is the Quicker Picker-Upper.*

Bruce Bendinger presents this information in *The Copy Workshop Workbook*. His description of the process is *"Strategy + Structure + Style."* He thinks you should look for the "Selling Idea," since many very creative ideas don't actually sell.

As you spend more time in advertising, you will begin to recognize that there are many accepted labels for stages of the process, strategies, concepts, ideas, selling ideas, propositions, and even the elements of the advertising itself. So, you may run across some of this with other labels.

6. Advertising Execution:

This is the advertising itself. Tactics.

In the case of an Advertising Campaigns class, this will likely take the form of copy and layout, storyboards and scripts.

As computer sophistication and skills become more readily available, the finished quality of student work has become more polished. In fact, it has improved dramatically.

There is now even an entire magazine, *CMYK*, devoted to examples of outstanding student advertising. Find a copy and look at it.

Copy Platform. Creative Platform.

The purpose for this segment of the planning document is to present what was once called "The Copy Platform" and which we will refer to as the "Creative Platform."

Again, there are a variety of names and a variety of formats.

Y&R calls it "The Creative Work Plan." Many call it simply, "The Advertising Strategy" or "Communication Strategy."

Those who use Account Planners often use a "Creative Brief," which combines Strategy with other background materials to "brief" the creatives.

There is an example of a good, commonly used Creative Platform in Note A of this chapter. The remainder of this chapter will outline the purpose for each segment of the Creative Platform and how to write it.

A. Target Audience:

The Most Likely Candidate.

This is an outline of who is the most likely candidate to be motivated to do something as a result of the advertising.

Most often, it is stated in demographic terms, but psychographics and usage-related descriptions are also appropriate.

MRI or Simmons are good sources of information for the user-base, which can translate into the target audience referred to earlier. If psychographics are used, SRI International's VALS II can be used. This information will come from the Situation Analysis in Chapter One.

Marketing Strategy/People.

The language used in the People part of the Marketing Strategy should be represented here as you describe your Target Audience.

It need not be identical wording, but care should be taken to make certain that the same group of people is being addressed.

If you choose to describe the people who will use, buy, or influence buying behavior in a more extensive fashion, this is the place in your Marketing Plan to do so.

B. Objective:

"To Establish..."

This is what you want the advertising to do.

Usually this starts with the words *"To establish . . . "*

As you gain more experience you can use other phrasing to start a creative objective, but *"To establish . . . "* will start you off in the right direction, because it will force you to write what you want the advertising to accomplish.

Remember, this language should be exactly the same as the language found in the marketing strategy for advertising creative.

C. Strategy:

"To Convince..."

This is how you want the advertising specifically to accomplish the objective above. There are many formats, but the one I prefer is:

To convince: _____.

To buy: _____.

Instead of: _____.

Because: _____.

Of the many creative strategy formats that are in use by advertisers and advertising agencies, this one, developed by Wells Rich Greene, is good because it forces the writer to address competition.

Virtually every brand sold in the world today must compete with something. As Procter & Gamble says, "*A copy strategy is a document which identifies the basis upon which we expect our customers to purchase our brand in preference to competition.*"

That's why P&G believes in strong propositions.

D. Support:

A Reason to Believe...

Support is the reason to believe the strategy.

It can be either research that supports the strategy or an advertising "reason why."

In the case where a Brand's primary reason for purchase motivation is emotional, this segment will be a "reason why" the Brand should be purchased.

Some companies call this a "permission to believe."

The substantiation for this part of the Plan will most likely come from Section Two—Research. Specifically, it will be in answer to the questions asked in the primary research that address the criteria for purchase motivation.

In the case of Dannon Yogurt advertising to older women, the Brand might consider a Health Strategy. The Support might be:

> *One serving of Dannon Yogurt provides 30% of the daily recommended calcium requirement for adults. See package for details.*

Source Credibility.

Your Support should give the target group a reason to believe. A helpful concept for developing support is "Source Credibility."

The credibility of the advertising is not just who is delivering the message—as in public relation's view of "source credibility"—but it may encompass why the consumer will believe the advertising.

Certs added "Retsin" to their candy. Retsin gave permission for the consumer to believe that Certs were "two mints in one." It didn't matter what Retsin really was; it was a "reason why" Certs could be both a candy mint and a breath mint.

As you examine the use of celebrities in advertising, you will notice that some are more credible than others. Those who succeed have found their own way of adding source credibility to the message.

Best of all, some advertisers have become credible. NIKE, Apple Computer, and, years ago, Volkswagen each created their own "source credibility."

Public Relations and Source Credibility.

This is another reason why public relations has become a part of more and more marketing programs. The source credibility of third-party mentions, such as a news feature, can make the advertising more credible.

Entertainment brands, such as movies and rock musicians, work very hard to combine PR with advertising in their marketing.

E. Considerations:

This is where you would put other things that you would like to have built into the advertising, if space or time allowed.

Usually, this is not really pertinent to why people buy the Brand, but would be nice to include.

Also Known as "Mandatories."

This section of the creative platform sometimes will include all the client dictates. Some companies and their advertising agencies refer to these as "Mandatories," which can also include legal requirements.

F. Tone:

The Way That You Say It.

This is the philosophy of the advertising in tone form.

It may be a statement or just a couple of words about the best way to speak to the Target Audience.

It can also be a complete "Brand Character Statement," which marketers like P&G use to describe the "enduring values" of the Brand.

However, the shorter format of a couple of words or so is preferable.

Advertising should get to the point. So should your Tone Statement.

G. Rationale:

Reinforce Your Recommendation.

This is the section where you explain the decision-making process, including the defense for what you have chosen to recommend.

Remember, there are no right or wrong answers in this market planning document. The only thing that matters is how well you have supported what you want to do.

In Chapter Two you conducted research to determine:
1. Who is the Target Audience?
2. What are the factors that motivate purchase behavior?
3. What are the unique characteristics of the Brand?

Cite that information here as substantiation that the Creative Platform you are recommending will build the business better than any other strategic direction.

The account planner's "Consumer First" focus can be tremendously helpful at this stage—framing the recommendation in terms of insights into the Target Audience.

Your Goal.

Your goal in writing this Rationale segment of Chapter Seven is to prove that the Creative Platform you are recommending is a clear delineation of the Creative Objective, which is the Marketing Strategy.

This Marketing Strategy will, in turn, allow the fulfillment of the Marketing Objectives.

The substantiation in this segment should be quantified whenever possible, and it should be conclusive.

Three Reasons.

When I was working on Procter & Gamble business at Compton (now Saatchi & Saatchi), my boss told me that there are always three reasons to do something, and three reasons why something is right.

He said that if you only have two reasons you don't have enough evidence to do what you are recommending, and if you have four—then three are more important than one, and the least important reason should be eliminated. (There is a psychological superstition about threes, so you might as well use it to your benefit.)

There is a relationship that can be drawn between factors that motivate purchase behavior and the unique characteristics of the Brand.

This relationship forms the foundation of your Creative Strategy.

Example: Ivory.

Let's say, for example, you knew the following were all true:

1. More doctors recommend Ivory than any other cleaning bar.

2. Ivory is $99^{44}/_{100}\%$ pure—so obviously it is good for the baby's bath.

3. Ivory is inexpensive, so it is a good soap to keep by the back door when people come in from working outside.

4. Ivory is good in the bathtub because it floats (so when the kids are covered in dirt, you can still find the soap).

5. Ivory is good for washing dishes because it doesn't have any artificial creams or deodorants to get on the dishes.

6. Ivory is mild, so it is good as a woman's complexion soap.

You could sell Ivory Bar Soap with a strategy based on any of the reasons. You should select only one in order to keep the strategic direction tight.

Strategy development is the process of deciding which will build the most volume (or occasionally the correct volume).

The one you should select is the one that consumers use as criteria to make up their minds which brand of bar soap they will buy—the factor that motivates purchase behavior.

Niche Marketing Factors.

There are some exceptions to this rule—the most notable of which is when you are involved in niche marketing.

You still need to base your strategy on what your Target Audience uses to make decisions in the category. But when you are trying to find a small hole in the marketplace, the numbers may not indicate your criteria base for the niche, or what Reis and Trout call a "creneaux,"as being a major concern to those people who will buy the Brand.

Example: Rover.

For example, the primary reason why people buy a four-wheel drive utility vehicle is to provide safety. They believe that they will be in a situation when they will be on slick roads or off the road where they will need additional traction.

This is not the selling premise for Rover's four-by-four.

Rover maintains the elitist niche for four-wheel drive vehicles, and does quite well within that niche. At more than twice the price of most American or Japanese-made four-wheel drives, they couldn't survive on the base premise of off-road or slick road safety.

Look for Visual Opportunities.

The Rationale segment of the Creative section can be a great place to use a visual device.

Example: Levi's Stretch Jeans.

For example, during a project for Levi's stretch jeans we found that our target audience wanted jeans that were not really a fashion jean, but not a basic jean either.

They liked the idea of an American pair of jeans, but wanted to feel like it was a little European. But they didn't really want the expense of an imported product.

The strategy of where the Brand would fit in the marketplace was starting to get complicated, and we felt a visual representation would make things clearer.

A visual device made it much easier to communicate the strategic direction, or positioning, for this new Brand from Levis. We used the following visual device:

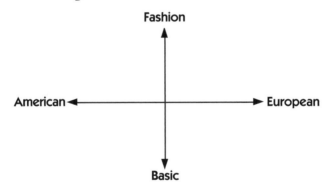

Occasionally there are windows of opportunity, or spectrums of consumer wants, that can be illustrated.

This is the place where you can use your imagination to communicate the strategy for defending this portion of the plan.

H. Tactics:

Tactics = Creative Executions.

The tactics are the creative executions themselves.

While this actual advertising should not appear in the planning document, you may include a few items that are common to all the advertising.

If the intent is to have advertising that is based on humor, it may be appropriate to make that point here and tell why humor will have a greater impact on the sales of the Brand. Or you may wish to make the point earlier in the Tone section of your Creative Strategy.

If there is something that is tactically different from what has been used before (a new look to the advertising, a new spokesperson, a new theme song) it should be communicated and defended here.

It goes here if the change is not strategic, but only tactical.

When Maytag changed from the old repairman to the younger one, this was a tactical change, not a strategic change.

For more information, please also read:

1. **The Copy Workshop Workbook**
   Bendinger, Bruce
   The Copy Workshop, Chicago, 1993. Second Edition.

   This book features additional help on developing Creative Strategy and a variety of Creative Strategy formats. Also use it for the creation of the advertising itself.

2. **Award Books: The One Show, CA Magazine**
   These are an excellent resource for looking at the best of current creative advertising.

3. **CMYK Magazine**
   1101 Clay St.
   San Francisco, CA 94108
   or call 1-800-784-0745

   This magazine features some of the best student work from around the country. It will demonstrate the level of work being done by students like you. Single issues are $7, check for current offers on subscriptions and back issues.

4. **Managing Creativity**
Kao, John J.
Prentice Hall, Englewood Cliffs, NJ, 1991.

Read the introduction for a clear understanding of creativity. Read the rest of the book to understand how to manage it.

5. **Squeeze This Whipple**
Sullivan, Luke
AdWeek Books, NY, 1998.

This entertaining book offers advice on the kind of advertising creative directors look for.

6. **The New How to Advertise**
Roman, Ken and Maas, Jane
St. Martin's Press, NY, 1992.

Chapters One and Twelve will aid with this chapter. Chapters Two, Four, and Five will aid in developing creative.

7. **The Y&R Traveling Creative Workshop**
Norins, Hanley
Prentice-Hall, Englewood Cliffs, NJ, 1990.

This book is out of print, but if you can find a copy, you'll have an invaluable resource on one of the best creative planning systems in the advertising industry.

Creative Platform

*"Thanks to copymachines
we no longer need copywriters.
What we need are ideawriters."*

—David Koch

Introduction.

A Clear Statement.

The creative platform (or copy platform) must be a clear statement that both defines the direction of what the advertising needs to accomplish and differentiates the Brand in the marketplace.

It should encompass the target audience, the factors that motivate purchase behavior, and the unique characteristics of the Brand.

The creative direction will be clearly defined through the creative platform, and it must show the strength of the Brand.

It should not be so tight that only one kind of advertising can be created. If it is too tight, the creative people will have no interest in working on the project.

If it is too loose, then there will be some probability that the advertising will not help sales. It will simply be interesting to people who see the advertising.

A Road Map.

The strategy should provide the basis for differentiation and the road map for where the Brand is going in the future.

Once it has been completed and agreed to, it should not be changed often. Advertising developed on this strategy may be developed on a regular basis.

Pepsi used essentially the same "Generation" strategy for thirty years.

Creative work should not begin without formal agreement as to what the strategy is.

Strategic Options.

In the following example, notice that the Creative Platform is not based on a cost strategy, but seems to be based on an "ease" strategy.

> *If you sew your own clothing with Simplicity Patterns, you will be able to get the clothing you want much faster and more efficiently than if you look through all the department stores and boutiques.*

Clearly, this strategy is based on research and insight into the Target Audience.

I would have guessed that the primary reason for the category was money saving, but this strategy seems to indicate that I am wrong. Be careful to not use your own opinions. Make sure your strategy and action are based on consumer wants, needs, and demands, not just what you think.

And as you pause to think about the strategy and the Target Audience, you will see there are other things going on here.

The Strategy reinforces the self-image of the Target Audience.

It doesn't say, "You can't afford to shop at stores, so you have to do it yourself." Rather, it says, "You're smart, you're capable, you can dress stylishly with Simplicity Patterns and have exactly what you want."

Furthermore, it helps differentiate the Brand by associating Simplicity with contemporary boutique fashion.

Simplicity could have also used a strategy based on quality or a strategy based on individuality. The basis for this is what the people who sew use as criteria for making selections of patterns. No other reason matters.

The format for this strategy part of the Creative Platform was developed by Wells Rich Greene.

Simplicity Patterns—Copy Platform.

Target Audience:

Women 18 to 34 with a college education.

Objective:

To establish Simplicity Patterns as the quick and easy way for the Target Audience to obtain the clothes they want.

Strategy:

To convince: Target Audience (defined above)

To buy: Simplicity Patterns

Instead of: Shopping for clothing in boutiques and stores

Because: Simplicity is the most efficient method of obtaining first-quality clothing with the right color and style.

Support: Simplicity Patterns eliminate the difficulty of searching for the right clothing because the Target Audience can select the fabric and color and because the patterns are current, durable, and active.

Considerations: 1. Easy-to-follow instructions.
2. Can be made in a few hours.
3. Sewing can avoid frustration.

Tone: Active, yet fashionable.

Ideas & Ideation

*"When you reach for the stars,
you may not quite get one. But you won't
come up with a handful of mud, either."*

—Leo Burnett

Introduction.

Did you know that Brainstorming was invented by someone in advertising? Alex Osborn, the "O" in BBDO developed techniques that are still used today. That's just one of the areas we'll cover.

The Need for Team Creativity.

As you work together, you'll also need to have ideas together. One person's idea will feed off another's. You'll have to make decisions as a group as to which is the best idea.

Together, you'll have to determine what the problem is, and then you'll have to think up the solution.

It's one of the toughest jobs in advertising and marketing. And it's one of the most enjoyable.

Three Topics.

In this section, we'll cover three things:

A. **The Ideation Process:**
   There are some surprisingly similar ways that different ideas are developed. We'll briefly summarize what we know about how people have ideas.

B. **Brainstorming:**
   There is a formalized technique, developed by Alex Osborn, that you can run in your own agency group.

C. **Team Creativity:**
Finally, we'll give you a few idea-starters on ways your agency can develop the ideas you'll need for a winning campaign.

A. The Ideation Process:

James Webb Young, a well-known copywriter who wrote *A Technique for Producing Ideas,* gave us the definition most in advertising still use: *"An idea is nothing more or less than a new combination of old elements."*

Here is the way most of us put ideas together. It has six stages:

1. **Preparation:**
This is where you and the agency team collect input and "do your homework."

During this preparation stage, you'll start by being logical, and the information will go into the left side (Verbal/Storage/ Memory) of the brain.

2. **Frustration:**
While ideas may seem logical after the fact, getting those two previously unrelated things to combine isn't always a logical process. So, unless the answer is obvious, the result is often frustration.

You and your group may be frustrated. You worked hard to get the information together—so where's the answer?

3. **Incubation:**
Now the part of your brain that associates things and makes connections goes to work. Individually, and as a group, you'll shuffle through the information—consciously or subconsciously.

And you'll associate new and old information in new combinations.

You may actually want to "sleep on it" as you mull it over. It's a natural process.

This is a time for your group to have fun. Have a pizza together as you talk it over.

4. **Illumination:**
This is the moment when you have the insight—when you make the connection you never made before.

It's the "AHA" moment. The light bulb goes on as two previously unrelated elements connect.

But don't always expect a blinding flash of light.

As Leo Burnett observed, *"The secret of all effective originality in advertising is not the creation of new and tricky words and pictures, but putting familiar words and pictures into new relationships."*

5. Evaluation:

This is difficult. And we don't know any way to make it easier.

You have to decide whether or not your idea is a good idea.

Your agency may have lots of ideas, but how do you tell the good ones from the bad ones? How indeed.

One of the ways to do this is to go back to the Critical/Analytical Left Side of your brains. While you've been having ideas, it's usually best to be nonjudgmental. Now it's time to be a bit more tough-minded. See Chapter Eleven for more detail.

It's one of the critical decisions you'll make as a team.

6. Elaboration:

Finally, you have to work on those ideas. You have to flesh them out from the initial bones of your thinking.

You may find that when you combine two of the new ideas you've created, you'll have even more new ideas.

Keep working at it. Remember that the more you know, the more things you have to combine with other things to create one of the most interesting things in our business—an idea.

B. Brainstorming:

Alex Osborn invented brainstorming in the 1930s. His book, *Applied Imagination*, was a bestseller.

It's an easy-to-understand system of ideation that you can run in your own agency group.

Brainstorming Guidlines.

There are four guidelines and six stages:

1. Suspend Judgment:

No negative comments. No critics.

Evaluation and criticism are postponed until later.

During the sessions there are "no bad ideas." (Though, of course, we know that there are.) During the session, if you don't like something, keep it to yourself. Later, there will be a time to "thin the herd."

2. "Free Wheel":

Let go of traditional inhibitions like "saying something silly." Wild ideas are encouraged.

It's easier to tone something down than think something up.

3, Quantity not Quality:

The object is to think up the most ideas possible.

Often, one idea will spark another. This is good.

4. Cross-Fertilize:

It's okay to work off of someone else's ideas. In fact, it's encouraged. Something you say may spark an idea in some-one else. And vice versa.

Don't worry about authorship. Remember, an idea doesn't care who has it.

The Six Stages of Brainstorming.

To get started, you'll need a Leader, hopefully someone who can write clearly and quickly. You'll also need lots of large sheets of paper and a room where you can tape the paper up on the wall.

Usually, you give people time to prepare, though you'll all know the topic. If you want to invite one or two clever friends, that's okay, too. Eight people is about the maximum.

Here's how it works:

1. The Problem:

The Leader states the problem. Discuss the problem.

Let people say what's on their mind related to the problem.

2. "How To…"

Next, restate the problem in a "how to" format.

This should be done in as many ways as possible.

These "How To" statements are written at the top of large sheets of paper and posted around the room, which will stimulate more thoughts and more restatements.

Everything is written down and displayed. (Now you see why you need a big room.)

3. **"How Many Ways…"**
   The group selects the first statement for the brainstorm.

   Now rewrite the statement in a "How many ways…" format.

   Everyone calls out solutions and writes them down. If the Leader starts to fall behind, write down your ideas and wait your turn. It's easy for a good group to get ahead of the person writing things down.

   As ideas dry up on the first restatement, move on to another. Ideas are numbered and built on. You can refer to a previous idea and build on it with a new idea. Do this until the group is through generating ideas. A bit of a "lull" will occur.

   As everyone takes a break, agree on which is the best "How To…" This is your Basic Restatement.

   Rewrite it clearly, and display it prominently.

4. **The Warmup—"Other Uses For…"**
   During this next stage, everyone steps away from the problem for five minutes or so.

   Participants throw out ideas related to "Other uses for…" anything… a paper clip, pizza crust, whatever. The purpose is to get everyone's mental muscles loosened up again.

5. **Brainstorm!**
   Read the Basic Restatement and call out for ideas.

   Sometimes these will relate to ideas that were already mentioned. Remention them and move on quickly.

   Write things down as quickly as possible.

   By this time, you may have drafted a second person to write things down. Or people may write down their own ideas.

   By now, everyone should be into it. Ideas are continually generated and built upon.

6. **The Wildest Idea:**
   When it seems like everyone's done, take the wildest idea generated and try to make it into something useful.

   You may want to do this with a few ideas.

   Sometimes this can stimulate one more round of ideation.

After the Brainstorm.

Now is the time for an initial evaluation by the group. With Post-Its, stickers, or colored markers, members can go around the room and indicate their favorite ideas.

Then, one or two members of the team go away and write up all the ideas, putting the favorites in the first section and all of the others in a follow-up section.

In a day or two, it's time to meet again and evaluate the best ideas from the session.

C. Team Creativity:

Over time, you will have developed working relationships as a team. There is little we can do to help you manage all the complexities of a half-dozen human beings working together.

But we can give you useful advice about how and where to do it.

"The Brain Wall."

One of the powerful aspects of brainstorming is the visual display of many different ideas. This works because it stimulates new connections. And when we make new connections, we tend to have new ideas.

So, you should find a place where you can put a lot of things up on the wall. Agencies do this all the time, that's why they have lots of rooms with corkboard and pins.

"The War Room."

Some agencies also have rooms dedicated to thinking about certain important projects. When they do, this room is usually called "The War Room." Some agencies have more than one.

If possible, your agency should try to find a War Room of your own. If it's not possible to have a room dedicated to this, try to find a room you can use regularly and get ready to put stuff up and take it down on a regular basis.

A Business of Ideas.

At an agency, ideas are everyone's job.

The better you learn to have ideas, recognize other good ideas, and work to make those ideas better, the better you'll do.

Advertising Media

In simpler times, advertising people had two concerns: what to say and how to say it. Now the issue is where, when and how can advertising reach receptive prospects. Today's toughest question is how to find your customers at the most strategic time— that's why media is the new creative frontier."

—Keith Reinhard, Chairman, DDB/Needham

Introduction.

Efficiency. Effectiveness. Target Identification.

The advertising media planning process seeks to select those media that will deliver the Target Audience or allow the advertiser to place advertising in front of the most desirable group of people using the least resources.

Quite simply, the advertiser wants the most efficient and the most effective medium to reach the identified Target Audience.

Increasing Opportunities. Increasing Complexity.

The media plan continues to grow in complexity as the media opportunities have increased.

We have evolved from three television networks that could deliver a large audience at a relatively efficient cost, to a complex world of strong local independents, "Superstations," unwired networks, cable TV, and other emerging broadcast systems like videotaped cinema advertising, in order to deliver an increasingly fragmented audience.

It is, however, still one of the key areas of advertising that relies on numbers in its decision-making process.

Clients generally feel much more comfortable with media than they do with creative, because it is quantifiable.

Increasing CPMs and a general decrease in advertising effectiveness is a concern for most marketers.

The Planning Process.

As you write the media plan, try to visualize the key buyers and users of the Brand and those who influence the buyers and users of the Brand.

A great deal of the process is to identify who these people are and how they are different from other people, where they live and work, when they buy, how often they consume what they buy, and what is the best way to reach them.

The following is set up to be similar to what you will write in the media section of your marketing planning document covering objectives, strategies, rationale, tactics, and buying.

A. Objectives:

What Will You Acomplish?

The objectives of the media plan are intended to describe what the media plan will accomplish. They should be in the same language as the marketing media strategies, which in turn are intended to describe how the marketing objectives will be fulfilled.

Refer back to the marketing strategies you wrote (Chapter Six) for the language to be used in the media objectives.

The objectives should be short and to the point. It is rare when media objectives will exceed one page.

Common objectives would include:

1. Target Audience:

The Target Audience is most often described demographically.

Gender and age are the most common demographic terms used, but additional characteristics can be added depending on the capability of the auditing service to provide ratings for a more detailed group, and the information you have to define your target audience.

If you have information that indicates you have a target audience of homemakers, it is likely that you will use daytime television.

If you know that your key consumer is a working woman, it is more likely that you will use a daypart which that woman is likely to watch—early fringe, prime access, prime, late fringe, or late night. It is unlikely that a working woman will watch daytime television (except, of course, those who tape a program).

An example of the objective might be:

> *To deliver a target audience of men 35 and older, with special attention given to those with upper income and education.*

2. Geography:

Geographically, the media objective seeks to identify where the advertising ought to appear in order to fulfill the marketing objective.

Virtually every brand sold will have a geographic skew. It is easy to understand that more snow tires are sold in Michigan than in Arizona or that more denture cleansers are sold in Florida than in Maine.

This geographic objective will identify how you give importance to those markets that will yield greater sales.

If the media plan is based on developing Brand potential, then the following example could be used:

> *To provide a base of advertising nationally, with additional advertising placed in areas with the greatest opportunity for sales as defined by a brand potential index.* (See Note A.)

If the geographic allocation of media funds will be determined by a brand development index, then the objective might be:

> *To provide a base of advertising nationally, with additional advertising placed in areas that have historically had the greatest sales.*

3. Seasonality:

The seasonal objective of the media plan will identify when sales are expected to be the greatest.

Even in Michigan, more snow tires are sold in September than in April, and more canned tomato soup is sold in October and November than during the summer.

This objective will provide the guide for what you want to do to take advantage of sales peaks throughout the year. The following might be considered for some brands:

> *To deliver advertising throughout the year in line with sales as evidenced by historical trends.*

However, if you choose to allocate funds throughout the year based on the statistical smoothing method described in Note B, then the Seasonality objective for media might look like this:

> *To deliver advertising throughout the year in line with how advertising will lead sales.*

4. Continuity, Flighting:

This objective will address whether advertising is desirable in bursts or at a lower level on a continuity basis.

An example of an objective for this section might be:
> *To deliver advertising in a continuous fashion throughout the year.*

If it is clear that sales are skewed to one season, snow tires in Michigan or ice cream novelties anywhere in the U.S., then the objective should look more like this:
> *To flight advertising delivery in line with past sales history.*

This objective might also be appropriate if you choose the advertising seasonal smoothing method.

5. Creative Constraints:

Occasionally a product will need a specific medium in order to communicate the benefit.

Generally speaking, food is better presented in a medium that will allow the visual communication of appetite appeal.

Music might be more effectively sold through a medium that offers good sound reproduction than one with good visuals—although unique album graphics and print media with a high concentration of young CD and cassette buyers may yield other advantages.

The other consideration for the media objectives based on creative constraints is when there is no quality advertising for the Brand in a given medium. (It seems the creative strategy cannot be translated into a good outdoor board for Crisco.) Then, the creative constraint might be a medium—outdoor.

An example of a media objective that addresses creative constraints for Bisquick might be:
> *To use media that allow for the visual representation of the appetite appeal of food prepared with Bisquick.*

6. Reach Versus Frequency:

Finally, the media objectives should address whether the Brand will benefit from more reach or more frequency.

An example might be:
> To maintain a four-week frequency of at least six, and to maximize reach within the budget.

B. Strategies:

Allocation.

Media strategies are statements of how media objectives will be fulfilled. Strategically, many advertisers have chosen to allocate media monies to:
1. Times of the year when sales are greatest
2. Markets that yield the greatest sales
3. Target Audiences that have proven that they buy the product

Some have become so exacting that a portion of the budget is spent in direct proportion to where and when each case is purchased.

For example, if the ABC company expects to sell 10,000 cases a year and spends $1,000,000, then they are spending $100 in advertising for each case of product that is sold. If two hundred cases will be sold in the Glendive DMA, then $20,000 will be budgeted to Glendive.

This philosophy can also work with the allocation of media impressions instead of dollars. Impression allocation is a little more accurate, but rewards each market for its sales potential (however that potential has been defined) with no regard for media cost.

This impression allocation methodology will therefore deliver the right number of GRPs to a given DMA despite its CPM being totally out of line (San Francisco for example). It would underdeliver a DMA like New York (which is very efficient) compared to a dollar allocation method.

While somewhat less common, this same system can work in the seasonal allocation of media dollars.

Continuing with the example, if 15% of sales take place in June, then it is desirable to have 15% of our media weight influence sales in June (see Note B at the end of this chapter for more detail).

Seasonal Costs.

Marketers rarely take seasonal costs into consideration when they allocate funds throughout the year because historically there just hasn't been very much difference in the cost. As delivery numbers decrease and costs for precise target groups increase, this may change.

Historically, fourth quarter has been the most expensive, and the Christmas season, along with the first weeks of a new television season, has been the most expensive within that quarter.

If we want to know if the more expensive weeks of the year are worth it, we simply develop an index to compare the difference in expected sales at that time with the premium to be paid for the advertising during the weeks under consideration.

This index could be used in conjunction with the impact of no advertising during a given period and advertising that would be greater than what the index would suggest.

Offensive Strategies.

Offensive strategies, wherein the advertiser chooses to allocate more funds to those areas where sales are poor and more funds to those months with less sales, are less common.

The idea seems great—a little more advertising in July and we can start to even out the seasonal sales curve. But there may be a strong reason why sales are poor in those particular times and places, and advertising dollars can't fix it. People just aren't going to buy more snow tires in Phoenix, and the market for hot chocolate is clearly limited in August.

On the other hand, virtually every new product must allocate its monies using an offensive strategy. Remember, you can only spend the money once.

The Media Strategy Format.

The media strategy format that follows may be shortened by combining some of the elements if the plan is not complicated. If it is very complicated, headings may be added.

1. Media Mix and Types:

The strategy statement should simply identify if there will be a mix of media or not and identify which media will be used.

If the plan will use both network and spot television, this is the same medium—not a mix.

The statement might read:

To use a media mix of television and outdoor.

Or...

To use magazines as the sole advertising medium.

2. Media Format or Classes:

This is where the plan will identify the subgroups within each medium. The strategy statement will ascertain which dayparts will be used in television and whether it will be spot or network. The statement will identify which group(s) of magazines—national, men's, news, fashion, women's service, etc.—will be used.

An example of the media format or classes strategy follows:

> *To use news-weeklies and men's action magazines.*

3. Geographic Use of Media:

The specific methodology that will be used to determine which markets will receive advertising support and which will not, should be included in this strategy statement.

Brand development indices are a good starting point for determining where marketing funds will be allocated.

Markets should likely receive a proportionately higher allocation of the available media resources based on BDI. (See Note A at the end of this Chapter.)

This would indicate a strategy like:

> *To allocate media on a market-by-market basis, using brand development as the key parameter to determine individual market advertising weights.*

It is also possible to have a strategy wherein all markets are judged to be equal. Strategically, the strategy might then be:

> *To allocate media evenly throughout the United States.*

Which markets receive advertising is of major importance in the media plan. Allocating that weight based on which markets can contribute to the greatest sales is consistent with the philosophy discussed at the beginning of this section.

4. Seasonal Use of Media:

The same is true of seasonal use of media as it is of geographic use. If the objective is to put more advertising in those months when sales have always been the best, then strategically the statement might read:

> *To advertise in key sales months with secondary emphasis given to lesser sales periods.*

For more information see Note B on Seasonality.

5. Flighting versus Continuity:

The media strategy that addresses flighting and continuity must be consistent with all other media strategies by stating how the media plan will fulfill the media objectives, which in turn are stating how (as marketing strategies) the marketing objective will be satisfied.

Specifically, the strategy might be:

To use pulsing throughout the year with two-week flights and three-week hiatus periods.

This strategy could address the objective for continuity and flighting listed in the objectives section.

C. Rationale:

This is where the plan is to be defended. (Some media planners prefer to give the rationale for each segment after each strategy. That method is also sound for structure and understanding, but we will illustrate the rationale as a separate segment.)

The defense or substantiation for the plan should convince the reader that the media plan will contribute to the fulfillment of the marketing objective.

Comparison to Alternate Plans.

Very often, this requires a comparison of the recommended plan to another strong plan, particularly if the Brand has been using a significantly different plan than the one you are recommending.

For Example.

If the media plan is one which uses a foundation of magazines with a little spot television for reinforcement to the low reading quintiles and to give additional geographic support to DMAs with strong brand potential indices, then an alternate plan might consider all television.

Network would replace magazines for the national segment of the plan, with spot being unchanged. This alternate plan can be used to show the strength of the recommended plan.

Under no circumstances should this alternate plan be a "straw man" used solely to show substantiation for the recommended plan. It should be a real and substantive alternate.

This rationale, or defense, should be broken into two key parts:

1. Support of Strategy:

This is the substantiation for how the media strategies of the plan will satisfy both the media objectives and the marketing objectives. If the media objectives are clear, then substantiation of those media objectives will be easier to communicate.

2. Support of Delivery and Efficiency:

This part of the Rationale should seek to cite quantitative support for why the plan will fulfill both the media objectives and the marketing objectives.

A very clean defense is to simply show that Plan A delivers +21% more GRPs than Plan B, or that Plan A delivers more GRPs to the low-reading quintiles; thereby, not underdelivering a major segment of the target audience.

D. Tactics:

The tactics segment of the media plan includes the specifics of how the plan will work, and what it will look like.

The following list is intended as a starting point to describe the media plan. Usually each of the following points are charts or tables of numbers with little or no explanation.

Each should be on a separate page.

1. Media Vehicles:

This chart should be a simple list of the vehicles recommended by the plan, separated by medium.

2. Reach, Frequency, and GRP Summary:

These numbers should be shown by quarter and total year. The following is a good setup for the chart that will be completed for this tactic. Fill in the numbers for the plan you are working on to see how it looks.

Exhibit "A"

ABC Brand
Reach, Frequency, and Gross Rating Point Summary

	1st Q		2nd Q		3rd Q		4th Q		FY '00	
	R/F	GRP	R/F	GRP	R/F	GRP	R/F	GRP	R/F	GRP
National:										
— Magazines	__	__	__	__	__	__	__	__	__	__
— Network TV	__	__	__	__	__	__	__	__	__	__
— Total National	__	__	__	__	__	__	__	__	__	__
"A" Markets:										
— Spot TV										
—Total "A" Mkts	__	__	__	__	__	__	__	__	__	__
"B" Markets:										
— Spot TV										
—Total "B" Mkts	__	__	__	__	__	__	__	__	__	__

Please take note that the reach, frequency, and gross rating points are not additive between "A" and "B" markets, because "A" market viewers will not see television that is aired in "B" markets.

3. Cost Summary:

The Plan should also be shown by quarter and by total year. Some corporations will require that a specific split in the dollars be maintained from quarter to quarter or from first half to second half (i.e., no more than 60% of dollars may be spent in the first half, or no more than 40% of dollars in any one quarter).

This chart will allow the reader to ascertain compliance with corporate financial philosophy. (Columns, lst half, and 2nd half, may be required additions.)

The following is a good setup for the chart that will be completed for this tactic. Fill in the numbers for the plan you are working on to see if the numbers are consistent with your intent.

ABC Brand
Cost Summary ($M)*

	1st Q		2nd Q		3rd Q		4th Q		FY '00	
	$	%	$	%	$	%	$	%	$	%
National:										
— Magazines	—	—	—	—	—	—	—	—	—	—
— Network TV	—	—	—	—	—	—	—	—	—	—
— Total National	—	—	—	—	—	—	—	—	—	—
"A" Markets:										
— Spot TV	—	—	—	—	—	—	—	—	—	—
—Total "A" Mkts	—	—	—	—	—	—	—	—	—	—
"B" Markets:										
— Spot TV	—	—	—	—	—	—	—	—	—	—
—Total "B" Mkts	—	—	—	—	—	—	—	—	—	—

* Percent of total budget by medium

The chart should show the percentage for each medium by time (i.e., 26% of magazine dollars are spent in the first quarter).

The percentage column under FY '00 should show the percent that each medium represents of the total budget.

Again, please take notice that the dollars are not additive between "A" and "B" markets, because "A" market viewers will not see television that is aired in "B" markets.

4. Flow Chart:

The flow chart is a visual representation of everything that will be in the media plan for a full year.

A separate flow chart should be completed for every market that has a different media plan. If there are two groups of markets that will receive extra weight, then there will be three flow charts—one for the national plan, one for "A" markets, which will receive the highest level of local support, and one for "B" markets, which will also receive additional weight, but at a level below the "A" markets.

The flow chart should contain the following elements:

a. Media:

Show what media will be used, at what level, and when the advertising will appear (or be heard) via that medium.

Be sure to include specific vehicles and the size of the advertisement for newspapers and magazines (unless the list is long, then include it in a separate chart—see Tactic 1), day-parts and GRP levels for television, GRP levels, or showing for outdoor, and number of spots per week for radio.

If possible use a different pattern to designate each distinct element of the plan.

b. Seasonality:

A Seasonality index should be included at the top of the chart to indicate sales indices for each month of the year.

This allows the reader to quickly see when advertising will appear in relationship to the key sales months.

c. Budget:

The dollar budget for each medium should be included on the far right side of the chart.

This allows the reader to compare costs of the various elements of the plan easily.

d. Reach & Frequency:

These numbers should be calculated on a Target Audience basis and filled in at the bottom of the flow chart. This allows the reader to see instantly how well the plan delivers the Target Audience, without thumbing back through the charts to find the total numbers.

Finally, the flow chart should contain the Brand name, a designation for the year, as well as the date when the plan was completed, and the planner's initials at the bottom of the page.

See the Flow Chart on page 209 for more detail.

5. Sales to Advertising Comparison:

The advertising to sales numbers should be shown in two ways:

1. over history, and

2. for this year's plan in comparison to sales in each DMA.

a. History:

This chart is used for substantiation of the budget.

It shows how advertising dollars, brand sales, and the resulting case rate have changed over time.

Exhibit "C"

ABC Brand
Advertising , Sales, Case Rate—Comparison
(Index versus year ago)

	Fiscal Year 1999		Fiscal Year 1998		Fiscal Year 1996	
	Dollars	(Index)	Dollars	(Index)	Dollars	(Index)
Advertising Bdgt	$9150.0M	(109)	$8425.2M	(112)	$7551.3M	(106)
Cases Sold	4596.1M	(109)	42166.6M	(112)	3764.8M	(106)
Case Rate	$ 1.99	(100)	$ 2.00	(100)	$ 2.01	(100)

Please notice that the budget needs no substantiation once the reader agrees to the marketing objective, because the case rate has been consistent over a three-year period.

Detailed substantiation would be necessary if the marketing plan author chose to change the case rate or methodology for the allocation of funds for some reason. But·since the plan recommends continuity within the realm of what has been done in the past, the reader must agree after seeing the numbers.

b. DMA by BPI:

This chart is used for substantiation of the geographic allocation of the media funds and should show the quantity of dollars in comparison to the brand potential index.

Exhibit "D"

ABC Brand
Advertising to Sales Potential Comparison

	Media Allocation		BPI	Ratio
	Dollars	Index		
Abilene-Sweetwater	___	___	___	___
Albany, GA	___	___	___	___
Albany-Schenectady-Troy	___	___	___	___
Albuquerque	___	___	___	___
Alexandria, LA	___	___	___	___
Alexandria, MN	___	___	___	___
Alpena	___	___	___	___
Amarillo	___	___	___	___
Anniston	___	___	___	___
Ardmore-Ada	___	___	___	___

The ratio column is a mathematical comparison of the media allocation index to the Brand potential index. It can be subtraction or division. It doesn't matter—the purpose is to allow the reader quick access to the information by showing the markets that are in line with one another and which markets are inconsistent.

The chart should be completed through all 213 DMAs.

6. Competitive Media & Sales Review:

This review will act as substantiation for both the media and the marketing of the plan. Remember, some of this information was developed for the Situation Analysis.

a. Category Sales History:

This chart may be used to defend the marketing objectives by showing history as support for future projections. It should show the brands to which growth is accruing over time.

Exhibit "E"

ABC Brand
Category Sales History
(Index & Change versus year ago)

| | Fiscal Year 1999 | | | | Fiscal Year 1998 | | | |
	Sales	Index	Share	Chg	Sales	(Index)	Share	Chg
ABC Brand	___	__	___	__	___	__	___	__
Brand D	___	__	___	__	___	__	___	__
Brand E	___	__	___	__	___	__	___	__
Brand F	___	__	___	__	___	__	___	__
Brand G	___	__	___	__	___	__	___	__
Brand H	___	__	___	__	___	__	___	__
All others	___	__	___	__	___	__	___	__
Total	___				___			

This chart will make it easy for the reader to see which brands are growing, which are declining, and the vitality of the category.

b. Competitive Case Rates:

A case rate is the number of dollars an advertiser allocates to the advertising budget for each case sold.

The competitive media spending chart (see the Situation Analysis) can be combined with the sales chart (Exhibit "E") to make a category case rate chart in order to see how the Brand's spending rates compare with the category.

203

ABC Brand
Competitive Case Rates ($M)
(Index & Change versus year ago)

	Fiscal Year 1999			Fiscal Year 1998		
	Sales	Media	Cs Rate	Sales	Media	Cs Rate
ABC Brand						
Brand D						
Brand E						
Brand F						
Brand G						
Brand H						
All others						
Total						

The Case Rate.

The case rate is a type of budget preparation similar to the percentage of sales methodology. A simple percent of sales methodology can be substituted for those brands and categories that do not use the case rate method.

7. Target Group/User Analysis:

This segment will support the Target Audience selection made in the People part of the marketing strategy. This same Target Audience is used in the media objectives.

The Target Audience should, at a minimum, be substantiated using the standard demographic parameters of gender, age, income, education, and professional status. When it is important, include other parameters provided by MRI or SMRB, or from primary or other secondary research that has been gleaned on behalf of the client.

The chart that substantiates the demographics of the Target Audience of Viva Paper Towels might look like this:

Viva Target Audience Demographics
Paper Towels Category
(Incidence of Usage, Index to Average)

	All Users		Heavy		Light		Viva		Bounty	
	Incd	Indx	Incd	Indx	Incd	Indx	Incd	Indx	Incd	Indx
Age:										
— 25–34	84.7	100	34.0	95	12.6	98	13.7	93	38.9	95
— 35–44	85.0	100	40.5	112	10.0	77	15.8	107	42.1	102
— 45–54	87.6	104	38.8	108	10.4	81	15.1	103	42.4	103
— 55–64	85.5	101	38.9	108	10.9	84	18.5	126	44.8	109
— 65+	84.4	100	32.4	90	20.2	157	14.9	101	43.8	107
Income:										
— $60M +	89.5	106	44.0	122	8.3	64	20.3	138	49.0	119
— $50–60M	86.6	102	43.1	120	8.7	67	17.6	119	46.9	114
— $40–50M	86.6	102	41.2	114	8.8	68	16.8	114	44.0	107

Source: SMRB

Notice that in the portion of the chart that addresses age, enough age breaks are included to substantiate our Target Audience age of 35 to 64. It is easy to see that usage of Viva is significantly lower under age 35 and over age 64. This chart will make it easy for the reader to see this difference quickly. Additionally, this age target will put Viva in a good position to attract heavy users, not light users.

The income portion of the chart need not continue past the $40,000 break because it is a straight line continuum. It may be sufficient to simply target Viva to "upper income."

The same type of information should be continued in this chart for education and professional status. Simmons does not break out gender for the paper towel category, so it is not included here.

Be sure to read the county size information because it can help identify if the Target Audience is located in center city areas or in rural areas. This would impact the geography allocation part of the media plan.

It is likely that psychographic parameters should also be included. Most often actual research will be unaffordable to determine which psychographic groups will be interested in the Brand.

After studying the characteristics of the groups, it is likely that some conclusions can be drawn based on other information you have available for users of the Brand.

8. Detail on Planned Medium:

A decision grid should be developed for the primary medium that is planned.

Note A in Chapter 8 gives some detail on decision grids and how this discipline can be used to make a decision concerning which markets (DMAs) are appropriate for the Brand to buy extra advertising.

That same decision grid discipline can be used to determine which vehicles to include in the plan within an already established medium.

If magazines have already been established as the primary medium for Treetop Apple Juice, vehicles in rank order of value could be established by using parameters like CPM, cost, and reach against the Target Audience (W 25-34), against category (apple juice) users, and against orange juice users.

Other parameters that could be considered might be editorial content, number of days reading time, or number of children in the household. The list of other information to consider is virtually endless.

The chart used to determine the values of the parameters might look like this:

Exhibit "H"

Treetop Apple Juice
Vehicle Selection Parameters
(Raw Numbers)

	CPM	Cost	Reach W 25-34	Reach Cat use	Reach O.J.	Circ
Magazines:						
Better H & G	$ 12.09	$ 119.0 M	17.7	20.6	20.0	8,143.0 M
Cosmopolitan	14.33	53.2	13.2	8.2	8.0	2,760.0
Country Living	17.42	43.7	5.6	6.6	5.1	1,833.8
Family Circle	10.80	76.1	16.7	19.0	18.6	5,922.5
Gourmet	19.34	24.6	2.2	2.0	2.0	806.3
McCall's	11.77	69.2	17.0	15.5	14.5	5,142.5
Redbook	12.61	65.9	17.8	11.6	26.2	3,950.5
Seventeen	13.85	35.2	2.5	3.5	3.1	1,752.3
Woman's Day	10.96	73.1	14.3	16.9	16.4	5,571.6
Working Mother	24.52	30.5	3.0	2.7	2.5	905.4

Source: SMRB, SRDS

206

The magazines considered in the decision grid should meet some basic constraints—over 800,000 circulation, minimum brand reach, etc. The reasons must be able to be substantiated.

Turning Numbers Into Values.

The next chart will turn these numbers into values.

The first step is to determine which of these parameters is the most important and to give them values which add to one hundred.

The decision grid chart would then look like this:

Exhibit "I"

Treetop Apple Juice
Vehicle Selection Decision Grid
(Calculated Values)

| | CPM | Cost | Reach | | | Circ | Total |
			W 25-34	Cat use	O.J.		
Values	35.0	5.0	20.0	15.0	10.0	5.0	100.0
Better H & G	31.3	1.0	19.9	15.0	7.6	5.0	79.8
Cosmopolitan	26.4	2.3	14.8	6.0	3.1	1.7	54.3
Country Living	21.7	2.8	6.3	4.8	1.9	1.3	38.8
Family Circle	35.0	1.6	18.8	13.8	7.1	3.6	79.9
Gourmet	19.5	5.0	2.5	1.5	7.6	0.5	36.6
McCall's	32.1	1.8	19.1	11.3	5.3	3.2	72.8
Redbook	30.0	1.9	20.0	8.4	10.0	2.4	72.7
Seventeen	27.3	3.5	2.8	2.5	1.2	1.1	38.4
Woman's Day	34.5	1.7	16.1	12.3	6.3	3.4	74.3
Working Mother	15.4	4.0	3.4	2.0	1.0	0.6	26.4

Source: SMRB, SRDS

The magazines that are the best choices for Treetop, based on the decision-making criteria established, are *Family Circle* and *Better Homes & Gardens,* with *Woman's Day* a little farther down the list. *McCall's* and *Redbook* would also be good choices.

Every chart in the marketing plan should have the initials of the person who prepared the chart, the date of the preparation, and the source of the material.

Additional Charts.

It is likely that additional charts may be required to fully describe the media plan.

For example, it may be that a chart comparing plan "A" to plan "B" on a quarterly GRP basis will make the the convincing argument for the second part of the Rationale. That chart should be developed and included in this Tactics segment.

This is the fun part of the project—finding new ways to present the information and new ways to substantiate the plan.

Too many people use the time allotted to simply complete the project and have no time to have fun with it. That's sad. A lot of work has been done—now take some time and play with some of your ideas.

E. Buying:

The last segment of the media plan contains the instructions for the buying group. These instructions should contain two parts.

1. Constraints:

List those items that are to be restricted from the media buying. An example here might be that the client prefers to avoid television programming that is controversial in nature.

2. Rationale:

This is where the defense or reasoning for the buying direction is provided.

The part of the plan allocated to buying may be extensive, but it also may be as short as a paragraph in length.

For more information, please also read:

1. **Advertising Media Planning**
   Sissors, Jack Z. and Bumba, Lincoln
   NTC Business Books, Chicago, 1992. Fourth Edition.

   While most of this book will be useful to you when you are writing this segment of the plan, look specifically at Chapters Eight through Fifteen.

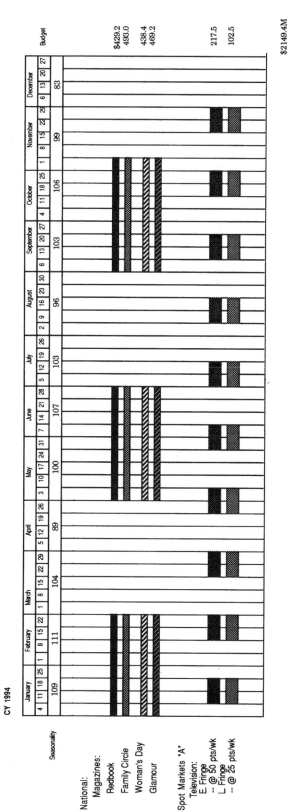

Media Flow Chart

Flow Chart
ABC Brand

Geographic Allocation of Media Dollars

"Fish where the fish are biting."

—Unknown

Introduction.

Allocate Based on Sales Potential.

The geographic allocation of media dollars should be based on sales potential. The purpose of this section is to illustrate how to determine sales potential by DMA.

The Geography part of the Situation Analysis was used to determine those areas that have had the greatest history of sales as evidenced by BDI. This Note A will show how to transform the BDI (Brand Development Index) into a BPI (Brand Potential Index).

We will seek to project the Brand's sales potential in every district, region, state, or DMA in the country.

If a BDI is not available as the base, then this process will be more difficult, but a projection of sales by DMA can still be made.

If a BDI is available, it is the first step because it is a measure of the history of the Brand's success, adjusted for population.

It is likely that this history will be repeated if nothing new has been implemented. Most often, however, the next step is to adjust the BDI by factors other than sales that may impact on those sales in the coming year.

Selecting Parameters.

There is no specific number of parameters that should be used to adjust the BDI, but I usually recommend that students seek seven or more parameters. The selection of these parameters should be based on what will contribute to the sales of the Brand. *Your goal is to think of what influences the Brand's sales.*

It may be the incidence of the target group by DMA, but it could also be some outside characteristic.

Examples.

Ivory Bar Soap, for example, works better in soft water than it does in hard water. A measure of the water hardness by DMA would help to understand Ivory's sales potential. Mufflers wear out faster in states that use salt to control ice and snow. Highway department information that tells where and how much salt is used might be used to project future sales for Midas Mufflers.

If the usage of the Brand is tied to some other product or category (butterscotch topping is probably tied to the sale of ice cream) then the sales of that category could be used to project sales of the Brand. If you look, you will be surprised at the number of outside influences there are—hamburger & ketchup, syrup & pancake mix, bar soap & water softener, fish & lemons, etc.

You will soon begin to see that the writing of a marketing plan contains many of the same elements found in sleuthing.

Incidence of Current Users.

Another parameter to consider is the incidence of current users (or target audience) on a DMA basis.

The U.S. Census can provide the information, or check *Sales and Marketing's Survey of Buying Power.*

MRI or SMRB can provide some information, on a regional basis only. While that is better than no information at all, it is not very sensitive.

Work to find the information on a DMA basis. It is possible to gain this information on the incidence of age and gender, income, education, etc., on a DMA basis.

If you are certain of the Target Audience, then where these people exist should produce better geographical sales.

If, for example, you know that people who earn more than $40,000 a year have a higher propensity to buy your Brand, then you might factor that information into the decision-making process.

Do not, however, use the absolute number of people in an DMA who earn $40,000 a year or more. Use instead the percent of people in the DMA who earn this amount.

The absolute number will give too much importance to the physical size of the DMA. While that may be important, make sure you can control the importance of all parameters by making them comparative to all others, and by having a reason for doing so.

Calculating the BPI.

Let's assume we are seeking to increase awareness of Midas Muffler and Brake Shops among young professional women.

The first step is to calculate BDI by DMA.

Next, information needs to be found that we judge will impact the sales in each DMA during the period of time for which the plan is written.

All this information can then be put on one chart or table.

The BPI is calculated by simple mathematical weighting to determine the BPI. The chart itself could look like the one that follows.

Exhibit "A"

Midas Muffler and Brake Shops
Brand Potential Index FY '00

	BDI	Hwy Salt	% U.S. Pop.	Incidence of the Target Group W 18-34	$40 M+	Coll Ed	BPI
Abilene-Sweet	___	___	___	___	___	___	___
Albany, GA	___	___	___	___	___	___	___
Alb-Schen-Troy	___	___	___	___	___	___	___
Albuquerque	___	___	___	___	___	___	___
Alexandria, LA	___	___	___	___	___	___	___
Alexandria, MN	___	___	___	___	___	___	___
Alpena	___	___	___	___	___	___	___
Amarillo	___	___	___	___	___	___	___
Anniston	___	___	___	___	___	___	___
Ardmore-Ada	___	___	___	___	___	___	___
Total							

Sales Potential Rationale.

The Media segment of the planning document should contain an overview of the markets with the greatest sales potential. This would be found under geography, and the substantiation for why those markets have the greatest sales potential under the rationale heading.

That substantiation is a defense of the parameters shown on the chart chosen to adjust BDI in the decision grid.

It is a simple task to point out why a greater incidence of women 25 to 34 in a given DMA will impact on sales (if that is the target audience).

Take care to avoid just defining the parameter; justify why that parameter will impact on future sales.

After all, if the reader agrees with your choice of parameters and the weighting, they must agree with your conclusions.

Offense or Defense.

The decision to develop a defensive or offensive strategy will be saved for the strategy segment of your document, but you will find this a difficult decision.

Most packaged goods manufacturers choose the defensive strategy because there is history of success and they are seeking to reduce risk. Areas where business is strong represent genuine potential. It is likely that there are historic and geographic reasons why the brand is preferred in this area.

Business has inertia. Remember, inertia means things at rest will tend to stay at rest and things in motion will tend to keep moving.

Tide will probably sell more detergent next year in Denver simply because Tide has sold more detergent in Denver every year for the past twenty years.

On the other hand, the low BDI areas have an appeal.

Sometimes it is easy to see that all they need is a little more advertising pressure to make these markets into real opportunity areas. Clearly, they yield less than their fair share of the marketplace, and it may be that a small adjustment in the plan will put a low BDI market more in line with what it should yield.

But remember: every dollar you allocate to a low BDI area is a dollar you may not spend in a proven high BDI area.

This is the reason for a Brand Potential Index.

Search for New Ways to Look at Things.

Part of the fun of the media portion of the plan is finding new ways to accomplish what you want and new ways of defending that plan.

Sometimes it is appropriate to make up new formulas.

For example, a BDI or BPI (Brand Potential Index) is commonly referred to geographically, but an index that is similar to BDI or BPI could be developed to show history or sales potential by demographics or Seasonality.

These are useful, but less common, so you will need to find a new name for them, like Demographic Development Index or Seasonality Development Index.

Seasonal Allocation of Media Dollars

"Fish when the fish are biting."
—Unknown

Introduction.

When?

Media planning is often described as the determination of the who, what, when, and where of advertising.

Discussion of the "when" of media planning, however, is often reduced to a discussion of scheduling.

The purpose for this discussion is to make the case for a more exacting methodology for the allocation of media dollars (or impressions) on a monthly or seasonal basis.

Advertising Should Lead Sales.

Marketing (including media) monies have historically been placed in those months when the greatest return is expected.

Most often this has translated to the allocating of media funds in direct proportion to the months when the greatest percent of sales has historically taken place.

Clearly, the goal is to build Brand awareness during the period when the potential consumer is most likely to be influenced.

Most often this requires advertising to lead sales.

To simply allocate advertising dollars by using percent of sales to directly determine percent of media budget is insufficient because this method does not allow advertising to lead sales. It assumes that advertising works instantly.

Advertising can be adjusted for the period of time necessary for the potential consumer to understand the advertising message.

A stronger impact could be made by allocating money just prior to the period when sales are anticipated.

A. Smoothing:

The intent of this explanation is to show how statistical smoothing can be used to allow advertising to lead into the key selling periods.

To do this, it is necessary to know the speed at which the advertising works—or how fast the consumer learns. There are very few brands that advertise that have this knowledge.

A likely assumption is that the learning time would show one-third of our advertising to be motivating in the month in which it appears, one-third would take a month for the consumer to digest, and the last third would need two months to make an impact.

This lead-in to specific months of delivery is called *two-month smoothing.*

It is likely that a brand employing high frequency during a four-week period would require a shorter smoothing period because awareness levels would likely be higher.

Low frequency would require a longer smoothing period.

A creative product with higher recall would shorten the smoothing period.

B. Method:

The budget that will be spent in each month can be determined by allocating the budget in percentage terms directly in line with monthly sales percentages.

In Exhibit "A" (page 219) the monthly sales figures are used directly for the original monthly budget percentages. In May, 8.9% of sales (index 107 to the average month) translates to 8.9% of the budget. The example calls for an annual budget of $7,500M.

The next step is to smooth the monthly budget. Based on the assumption of learning time, simply divide the budget by three and allocate that one-third of the budget to the month when the sales are expected, one-third to the prior month, and the last third to the month before that. In July, for example, we expect 9.4% of the Brand's sales.

This equates to a monthly budget of $705.M.

One-third of that money ($235.M) will be spent in July, one-third in June, and one-third in May. The June and May monies will be leading into the July sales period. In August, the monthly budget is $772.5M. One-third will be allocated to August ($257.5M), one-third to July (again, because July advertising will help to make sales in August), and one-third in June. And so on. When the thirds are added again, the new allocation will show $662.5M in July. This is $42.5M less than the monthly allocation would call for and represents 8.8% of the budget (index 94 versus the original monthly budget or sales percentage).

C. Rationale:

This two-month smoothing methodology for the allocation of seasonal media (or marketing) dollars is important for three reasons:

1. Statistically accounting for the time it takes for the advertising to educate current and potential consumers both in Brand awareness and conversion to the Brand will aid the advertiser to be more precise with the use of media or marketing funds.

2. Recognition of learning time could provide the Brand with information that could impact calculation of effective frequency. This in turn could allow the Brand to determine an optimum spending level.

3. In the absence of learning time information, a two-month lead time may not be precise, but the result will likely lead to a better understanding of how consumers are influenced, and the time it takes to make that influence felt. This in turn will allow the Brand to have a clear understanding of the seasonal budget impact on sales.

D. Conclusion:

Smoothing can allow advertising to lead into sales instead of assuming that advertising works instantly.

The lead-in period is a function of the learning time required by the advertising and can likely be dictated by product life cycle and the impact of the creative product.

Understanding this learning period can contribute to the knowledge necessary for the amount of frequency needed to build Brand awareness and conversion to the Brand.

Smoothing will ultimately aid in market share growth for the Brand, since it provides message weight delivery proportionate to when consumers will buy and in line with how those consumers learn.

Chapter Eight
Note B

Exhibit "A"

Seasonal Allocation of Media Dollars
Two Month Smoothing

	Percent Sales	Seasonal Index	Percent Budget	Budget	Third	Third	Third	Budget	Smoothed Percent Budget	Index
						Smoothing				
January	6.9	83	6.9	$ 517.5	$172.5	$162.5	$205.0	$540.0	7.20	104
February	6.5	78	6.5	487.5	162.5	205.0	187.5	555.0	7.40	114
March	8.2	98	8.2	615.0	205.0	187.5	222.5	615.0	8.20	100
April	7.5	90	7.5	562.5	187.5	222.5	222.5	632.5	8.43	112
May	8.9	107	8.9	667.5	222.5	222.5	235.0	680.0	9.07	102
June	8.9	107	8.9	667.5	222.5	235.0	257.5	715.0	9.53	107
July	9.4	113	9.4	705.0	235.0	257.5	170.0	662.5	8.83	94
August	10.3	124	10.3	772.5	257.5	170.0	220.0	647.5	8.63	83
September	6.8	82	6.8	510.0	170.0	220.0	190.0	580.0	7.73	114
October	8.8	106	8.8	660.0	220.0	190.0	255.0	665.0	8.87	101
November	7.6	91	7.6	570.0	190.0	255.0	172.5	617.5	8.23	108
December	10.2	122	10.2	765.0	255.0	172.5	162.5	590.0	7.87	77
Total	100.0	100	100.0	$7500.0	$2500.0	$2500.0	$2500.0	$7500.0	100.00	100

Sales Promotion

*"The manufacturer who finds himself up the creek
is the short-sighted opportunist
who siphons off all his advertising dollars
for short-term profits."*

—David Ogilvy

Introduction.

Promotion and Advertising Should Work Together.

The purpose of this part of the marketing document is to outline the events that will work in concert with the advertising.

Sales Promotion is differentiated from advertising since it is a tangible motivation to do something—a bribe, or more politely, an incentive.

A twenty-five cent coupon good on the purchase of McDonald's French fries is 25¢ worth of good motivation to buy french fries at McDonald's.

The marketing plan is quite often evaluated on its adherence to Integrated Marketing Communication principles. That simply means everything works together for a common goal.

Synergism is the old name for it, and it is still defined by Webster. The bottom line is that the promotion plan and the execution of that plan should work in concert with the advertising.

The discipline is the same in the marketing plan as it has been for every section. The objectives of the promotion plan are intended to describe what the promotion plan will accomplish. As we have discussed before, they are marketing strategies.

Two Parts: Consumer and Trade.

The promotion plan is divided into two major parts: Consumer Promotion and Trade Promotion. Quite often, the same objective(s) can be used for both the consumer and the trade promotion, and quite often the two work together.

Example: Nestle.

When the plan was written for Nestle to gain new distribution in video stores, the promotion plan used to support that called for a case allowance to the video store, and consumer advertising stated that Nestle could now be enjoyed with a movie.

A cents-off coupon was added for motivation.

The two sales promotion events worked in concert. Synergy.

Example: Polident.

Occasionally, one promotion can serve both consumer and trade.

When Polident Denture Cleanser introduced Polident II, that plan recommended including two tablets in one package.

These "two-packs" were then given to the trade (retailers) when they purchased a predetermined amount of regularly packaged Polident II.

The trade sold the two-packs in end-aisle displays for a nickel.

The consumer was delighted to try something new for such a small price.

The result was that one promotion was directed to both the trade and the consumer.

At a minimum, the same objectives should work for all consumer promotion, and the same objectives should work for all trade promotion.

A. Consumer Promotion:

Consumer promotion is directed at the end user, the consumer.

Examples of consumer promotion events include: coupons, rebates, contests, sweepstakes, bonus packs, samples, temporary price reductions, and premiums—on-pack, near-pack and self-liquidating.

Here is how to structure this Section:

1. Current Situation:

The written market planning document should give a little history of what has worked in the past and what has not. Cite results in comparison to previous years and to those areas that have received special promotion events and those that have not.

For example, if you are writing a marketing plan for Bisquick. You had an on-pack shrink-wrapped cookbook sales promotion event in test market, and sales were up by +7% in the test areas. A comparison chart might look like this:

	Test Period	Year Ago
Promotion	+ 7%	+ 2%
No-Promotion	− 1%	+ 1%

You might make the argument that the recipe book promotion increased business in the test area by 8% because the control area was down 1% in the test period.

Even if there is no event in test market, use this space to indicate what promotion events have been used, what the competition is using, or what the current thinking is on the brand as it relates to promotion events.

2. Objectives:

The objectives are lifted directly from the marketing strategies. An example of solid sales promotion objectives might be:

> To establish KCNR radio as one of the five radio stations pre-selected for use in the cars of the target audience.

It is likely that this would have a strong tie-in to the creative objective.

3. Strategies:

The strategies provide detail on how the objectives will be accomplished. While the objectives outline what is intended, the strategies tell how it will be done. The following strategy example might have been used by KCNR:

> To convince local automobile resellers to preset the middle radio button to KCNR.

This strategy might also work well with the creative objective and strategy that outlines that KCNR (for center) wants to be the center of everything with which it comes in contact.

4. Rationale:

The objectives and strategies are defended here.

The first preference is to defend the key elements of the promotion plan quantitatively. But however you decide to defend the plan, it should be done so that management is convinced that this will contribute to the volume or other number objective for the Marketing Plan in its entirety.

There is increasing pressure being brought to bear against promotion events—they must not only provide short-term incentives to purchase, but they must also contribute to the long-term Brand image.

5. Tactics:

This is the place to describe the specific sales promotion events and how they will work in detail. Quite often there is more than one event. If this is the case, they should be named or numbered to differentiate between the events.

A tactic from our KCNR example might be:

> *To provide an incentive to the automobile resellers in the form of on-air KCNR mentions of the automobile reseller name and campaign line.*

This tactic also provides the automobile reseller an opportunity to use IMC in the execution of his or her marketing plan.

6. Payout:

Each promotion event should contain a rationale in the form of justification of the budget.

In our KCNR example, this section of the plan would show the cost of the on-air mentions for the reseller (or in this case, the lost opportunity cost), and compare this cost to the benefit of having radios turned to KCNR.

More commonly with a packaged goods brand, the payout would show the volume needed to pay for this promotion.

A chart similar to the one shown under "Current Situation" on the previous page might be used here.

B. Trade Promotion:

The Rise of the Retailer.

Trade promotion is directed at the middle man.

If the Brand on which we are working is a packaged good product sold in grocery stores, drug stores, or mass merchandisers, then the retailer is the trade.

Probably the most common trade promotion events are advertising allowances and display allowances. Some manufacturers treat stocking allowances as trade promotion events.

One of the most important changes in marketing has been the increased strength of the trade.

The advent of Universal Product Code (UPC) information that can provide daily information on sales has shown the retailers exactly what is moving and what is not.

"Slotting Allowances."

Retailers have become aware of their power in the marketplace and have required such things as Slotting Allowances for new products to gain distribution. These slotting allowances can be quite significant in some cases—particularly for new products.

As a result, marketers have spent a great deal of time, energy, and money fostering trade relations.

The Trade May Have Different Motivation.

For franchise operations such as automobile dealers and fast food restaurants, the trade is the franchisee.

What motivates the trade to do something is not necessarily what motivates the parent company or manufacturer. The trade objectives and strategy must address this motivation.

The trade objectives for Promotion will be lifted directly from the Marketing Strategies.

The trade portion of the sales promotion segment of the marketing document will have the same subpoints as the consumer promotion side. Be sure to include: the current situation, objectives, strategies, rationale, and an outline of the specific events that will be used.

For more information, please also read:

1. **Strategic Advertising Campaigns**
   Schultz, Don E., and Barnes, Beth E.
    NTC Business Books, Chicago, 1994. Fourth Edition.

   Chapter Thirteen pertains to sales promotion.

2. **Your Advertising's Great...How's Business?**
   Frankel, Bud and Phillips, H.W.
   Dow Jones-Irwin, Homewood, IL, 1986.

   This is a practitioners' guide to sales promotion.

3. **Advertising and The Business of Brands**
   Bendinger, Avery, Altman, et al.
   The Copy Workshop, Chicago, 1999

   See Chapters Seven and Nine of this introductory text for more information on sales promotion.

4. **Sales Promotion Essentials**
   Schultz, Don E., and Robinson, William
   NTC Business Books, Chicago, 1992

   This book is a good introduction to basic techniques.

MarCom

" The future ain't what it used to be."
—Yogi Berra

Introduction.

Advertising campaigns have grown. They now include public relations, direct marketing, event marketing, and more.

Sometimes elements are included that address personal selling, packaging, or promotional products.

These are all referred to as marketing communications, or MarCom for short. This chapter will address these segments of the marketing document.

Not every plan will contain all, or even any, of these elements. But if they are in the plan, they need to be in the marketing strategy (see Chapter Six), and they need to be here in this segment as well.

A Little History.

Many of these MarCom disciplines emerged from tactics.

Event promoters helped to develop event marketing.

Catalogue marketers developed the techniques of direct marketing as they searched for better ways to sell what was in their catalogues.

Printers, who printed the cardboard for promotional displays became better at sales promotion in order to sell more printed cardboard.

Even today, a terrific movie placement opportunity or a CEO's love for golf or car racing can impact decision making in a very undisciplined fashion.

Public Relations.

Public relations involves influencing a group of people, called a public, in the interest of promoting the Brand.

This segment will address how the public relations part of the plan can contribute to fulfilling the marketing objective. After all, that is what the strategy is all about. In most cases, the public relations part of an advertising campaign will be Marketing Public Relations (MPR), not Corporate Public Relations (CPR).

Your MPR must work with the advertising and the sales promotion, to maximize effectiveness. This is called synergy.

1. Current Situation:

The first step is to outline what is currently happening in the area of public relations. Some of the questions that need to be answered are:

- What has been the history?

- What has worked in the past?

- Do we anticipate any news in the coming year or period covered by the plan?

2. Objectives:

The second part is the objective. The Public Relations Strategy, outlined in this section, will be identical to the marketing strategy for public relations outlined in Chapter Six.

An example of a public relations objective is:

To enhance Nuprin positioning as the preferred analgesic for relief from sports-inflicted pain.

While this objective is a marketing public relations objective relating to publicity, there could also be objectives relating to a whole host of other elements including corporate public relations.

3. Publics:

Public relations address publics instead of target audiences. The two terms mean the same thing, but in public relations they are expressed as a public instead of a target. A public for a broad-based public relations plan within an advertising based marketing plan might be stakeholders.

Stakeholders, of course, are employees, vendors, customers, stockholders, and anyone else that has anything else to do with the Brand.

Schultz and Barnes note that to be truly integrated, marketing communications need to address internal as well as external audiences.

They observe that in many large companies with well-paid executives and well-funded programs, it is often the lowest-paid employees that deliver the messages to consumers.

4. Strategies:

Strategies are how you intend to fulfill the objective. While the public relations objective is the same generation as the marketing strategy, the public relations strategy is one lower generation.

An example of a public relations strategy is:

> *To influence stakeholders to support Charles Schwab online stockbrokerage due to its variety of research sources.*

5. Rationale:

In this segment, a case must be built for why the strategy is correct. Be sure to include why this particular strategy will fulfill the marketing objective better than any other strategic direction.

Public relations is a way to influence public opinion by providing newsworthy information to the media. It can be a supplement to advertising, but differs from advertising because you do not have control over the final product.

Direct Marketing.

Direct marketing is selling the Brand directly to the consumer.

This segment of the marketing plan will address how direct marketing can help to fulfill the marketing objective.

1. Current Situation:

The segment on direct marketing is similar to other introductory segments of the advertising based marketing plan. The first step is to record what has worked in the past, what is currently working, and any other circumstances that would impact the planning.

There may be aspects of this current situation that may be of benefit to the overall situation analysis.

2. Objectives:

The Direct Marketing objective is next. It will be identical to the marketing strategy for direct marketing outlined in Chapter Six. There could be objectives that relate to both inbound and outboard telemarketing, direct mail, direct response, direct television, etc.

An example of a direct marketing objective for direct mail is:

To establish the Land's End catalogue as a resource for casual clothing and accessories.

3. Target Audience:

Who is the intended audience? The intended target of the direct marketing should be recorded here.

To deliver messages to a target of working women with children at home.

4. Strategies:

The direct marketing strategy designed to fulfill the direct marketing objective goes here. The direct marketing objective is designed to fulfill the marketing objective. An example might be:

To convince current and potential Land's End customers to request a Land's End catalogue.

5. Rationale:

Defend why this will work. It is insufficient to just state that you believe the plan will work.

It is important to provide strong support for why this plan will help to deliver the marketing objective.

Direct marketing requires a clear understanding of where to find members of your target group. This probably means database management.

Don't forget that about 20% of America moves every year. That means if your information is two years old, a third or more of your information is probably incorrect.

Event Marketing.

Event marketing is marketing to consumers in a special environment called an event.

This is the part of the advertising campaign plan that outlines how the Brand will communicate directly with current and potential customers through a specific event.

There is great variety of events that are available to the Brand.

For a brand like Mobil Oil, the arts may provide a fertile field for potential events.

On the other hand, a consumer product like Bank of America may want to be involved with sporting events; Apple Computers may be more comfortable with an environmental event.

1. Current Situation:

Again, it is important to outline key information on what has been done in the past. This segment can be detailed and include past history, current users, geography where event marketing has been used in the past, seasonality of events, and competitive information.

This could include what events competing brands have used and what success they have had.

This detailed information could also be used in pubic relations or direct marketing.

The Brand could also use an abbreviated version that only states what has been used in the past period immediately before the writing of the plan.

2. Objective:

The objective will be identical to the marketing strategy for event marketing. This in turn will fulfill the marketing objective:

> *To establish Mobil Oil as a community-minded business through arts involvement.*

3. Strategies:

The event marketing strategies will help to fulfill the objective. An example might be:

> *To involve women 35+ with the NutCracker to relay the civic and arts attitude at Mobil Oil.*

David Ogilvy said "strategy is about choice" more than a quarter of a century ago. It is still true.

A brand like McDonald's may have the resources to be active in virtually every marketing communications category.

It can be surprising in how many MarCom categories even small brands are participating.

The choices made in those categories is what strategy is all about.

4. Target Audience:

This is a clear and distinct identification of the people likely to be involved in the event and those who will likely be interested in the Brand:

To deliver the event to women 35+.

This Mobil Oil event may be against a marketing objective designed to give support to stock prices on Wall Street.

5. Rationale:

Again, the reason why this will help to increase stock prices must be clearly stated in this section. The support may be linked to any variety of reasons, but it must be clear and it must be substantiatable.

Virtually every advertiser will be a presenter at a trade show at some time or another. This is also an event. The target group changes from consumer to trade, but the principles are the same.

Event marketing is different from public relations because it tends to work with consumers; public relations tends to work with the media and internal company audiences.

Miscellaneous.

Any other element of the advertising campaign can be included here. For example, online activities.

You should at this point understand that the current situation should be outlined, and that the objective for this additional element to the plan should match the marketing strategy.

A tactics section can also be added to any element of the advertising-based marketing plan.

Warning.

If you are in a class at a university, or a small business, be careful to not to try to do too much. If you do, it can eat you.

Your best strategy will be to identify those marketing communications disciplines that best reinforce your marketing strategy in terms of impact and efficiency and to then limit yourself to those ideas and disciplines.

If you choose to develop work in every possible discipline, you will be developing a more balanced, more thorough plan than if you did not.

The key to this thinking is to remember that everything is a trade-off.

The first step is to develop a long list of options, calculate their cost and benefit, then choose.

For more information, please also read:

1. **Strategic Brand Communication Campaigns**
   Schultz, Don E., and Barnes, Beth E.
   NTC Business Books, Chicago, 1999. First Edition.

   This new book features their new approach to Integrated Brand Communications (IBC) and is more MarCom focused. It is much different than *Strategic Advertising Campaigns*.

2. **MaxiMarketing**
   Rapp, Stan, and Collins, Tom
   McGraw-Hill, NY, 1987

   A Direct-Marketer's approach to MarCom

3. **Under The Radar**
   Kirshenbaum, Richard
   AdWeek Books, NY, 1999

   A bright young ad agency's look at new ways to make MarCom work.

4. **Introduction to Marketing Communications:**
   An Integrated Approach
   Burnett, John, and Moriarty, Sandra
   Prentice-Hall, Upper Saddle River, NJ, 1998

   A solid introductory textbook with an IMC focus.

Evaluation

*"A man who carries a cat by the tail
learns something he can learn in no other way."*
—Mark Twain

Introduction.

The Need for Evaluation.

The success or failure of the marketing plan is determined ultimately by its ability to deliver the objective. Unfortunately, often this is not quite a particularly sensitive measurement.

Occasionally, the marketing objective will be fulfilled despite the marketing plan. Or the marketing plan may be brilliant, but some unforeseen change in the competitive environment will prevent the fulfillment of the objective.

When these situations arise, a good evaluative method will help to determine the quality of the individual elements of the plan.

The intent of the Evaluation section of the marketing planning document is to outline how this evaluation will take place.

It may be evaluated totally on how well the objective is delivered, but more than likely there will be other measures that provide information on the success or failure of the individual elements within the plan.

Interim Evaluation Measures.

Interim measures on the quality of the creative product that compare attitudes of consumers on a variety of parameters toward the brand (this year versus last) may aid the advertiser. A midyear evaluation can make the plan stronger before the end of the year.

This helps to eliminate the all-or-nothing nature of fulfilling marketing objectives. The idea is simple: try to get a midyear progress report instead of waiting for the end of the year.

Most large packaged goods manufacturers track sales on a monthly basis in order to evaluate progress.

It is common to track sales two ways: this year versus last year and versus projection (also known as "against plan" or "against budget").

With the advent of scanning machines, it is possible for manufacturers to have sales information, virtually daily, by grocery store. This information probably has limited usefulness, because it provides too much detail for the manager to absorb.

The key evaluative tools that will track the Brand's progress toward the marketing objective are obviously sales and share.

However, some of the interim tools that will help determine what is impacting sales and share might be:

1. **Copy testing**
2. **Attitude measurement for the Brand**
3. **Awareness measurement for the Brand**
4. **Advertising awareness measurement**
5. **Usage measurement**
6. **Purchase motivation assessment**

Evaluating Media.

A media analysis might provide information on the quantity of GRPs delivered into a specific geographic area during the past six months. This in turn could let us know if the media pressure is up or down versus the previous period.

The same information might be available for sales promotion or publicity or merchandising. This information would be developed through a detailed business analysis.

This section is not intended to provide this information. It is intended to provide a plan to measure consumer reaction to these elements of the marketing plan.

Example: Good Seasons.

For example, if you are the Brand Manager on Good Seasons Salad Dressing, and you knew that Little Rock had been receiving +150 GRPs a week (total is 600) in each of the advertised weeks for the past six months when compared to the control market of Birmingham (450 GRPs), then we could compare the impact of that extra 150 GRPs.

We could compare that impact by looking at sales or market share, but if we had a tracking study in place we could compare the results of such attitudinal measures as:

- Good Seasons tastes fresher than other salad dressings.
- Good Seasons is one of the best tasting salad dressings.
- Good Seasons is easy to prepare.
- Good Seasons is one of my favorite salad dressings.

If the tracking study has been set up so respondents can evaluate these measures on a five point Likert scale, then we can start to get a measure of progress by comparing the evaluations over time.

A. Current Situation:

How We Are Evaluating the Marketing Plan.
The section should outline what is currently being used to evaluate the marketing plan.

It may include tracking studies or any of the information-gathering techniques.

The current situation might outline the objectives, strategy (including methodology), and the expected learning or benefit of any evaluation technique that is currently in place.

B. Objective:

Marketing Strategy for Evaluation.
The objective of the evaluation section of the marketing planning document is the same as the marketing strategy for evaluation. It will specify what will be evaluated and what we want to learn.

For example:

> To determine attitudes of the target audience toward both Texaco and its advertising.

This objective sets the stage for what information is needed in order to track progress in the coming year. It is possible that there will be multiple evaluation objectives in a given year.

C. Strategy:

There May Be More Than One Strategy.

The strategy, as always, is written to describe how you intend to accomplish that objective. There may be several strategies for each objective.

For example in the case of Texaco, the strategy might be:

1. *To gain qualitative insight for how consumers think about Texaco, how they use gasoline in general, and what they think of Texaco specifically.*

2. *To conduct a quantitative attitude, usage, and awareness study during the second quarter to verify or refute information gleaned in the qualitative study.*

Multiple Objectives, Multiple Challenges.

If there are multiple objectives, there will be strategies written to support each of them.

Remember, objectives are what you want to do, and strategies are how you intend to do it.

D. Tactics:

Tactics/Methodology.

The tactics of the evaluation segment of the plan are sometimes called the methodology.

Here you will list the methods for gaining the information.

With the Texaco example, the strategy was to acquire qualitative information.

An example of the tactics might be:

To conduct two focused group sessions in the first quarter in order to gain consumer insight to the marketing elements of Texaco.

These group sessions will be conducted in a medium BDI area and with a medium to high CDI.

The groups will seek to determine consumer attitudes toward gasoline consumption in general and about Texaco specifically.

Question Areas.

If a listing of question areas has been developed it might be included here, but more often this will be left for a specific recommendation following the approval of the marketing document.

Summary.

What You Plan to Learn.

This same process will be followed for each individual measure you hope to have for the marketing plan.

The Evaluation section of the marketing planning document outlines what is to be done in the coming year—or the period under consideration for the marketing plan.

It differs from Chapter Two, Research, since the research segment is intended to summarize what you have learned in the past that will contribute to this marketing planning document, and, in turn, for the marketing of the Brand itself.

For more information, please also read:

1. **Successful Advertising Research Methods**
   Haskins, Jack, and Kendrick, Alice
   NTC Business Books, Chicago, 1993.

Test Marketing

"...testing is the name of the game."
—David Ogilvy

Introduction.

At Least One Test Market.

All good marketing plans contain at least one test market.

Exceptions to this rule should be rare.

Test Marketing, or simply testing, is altering the marketing plan in one market to find the effect of that alteration.

Testing is a way to learn the power of new marketing possibilities without risking all the geography in your franchise.

Example: New Creative Strategy.

We may have interest in a new creative strategy.

The old one has been working for many years, and sales have been solid. This was the case on Bob Evans Sausage business.

The business was good, but we believed sales could be increased by convincing current customers to use sausage more often—at lunch or dinner instead of just breakfast.

We had evidence to believe that current users would have interest in using more of the product if we showed them how.

We developed a test market to determine the impact on sales of an increased usage strategy.

The actual test was to run recipe advertising in women's service magazines in Cincinnati in order to leverage usage.

We chose Cleveland as a control market. Cincinnati was the only market to receive magazine advertising.

We reduced the quantity of television advertising going into the Cincinnati area to avoid also testing an increase in the dollar allocation to advertising.

This is a good example of test market design.

Objective, Strategy, Tactics.
It is the purpose of this segment of the marketing document to outline the test market(s) and the expected outcome(s).

The test market will be described by outlining objectives, strategies, and tactics in executional detail.

Poor Arguments Against Test Markets.
Some may maintain that if business is poor it probably needs "fixing." They state that attention should be paid to solving the problems at hand and attention should not be diverted into setting up a somewhat risky test market.

These critics of testing always point out the lack of resources for a good solid test market.

Both of these arguments miss the point.

If test markets had been in place, there is a strong probability that the business would not be in trouble, because the manager would have been learning new ways to market the Brand.

There would be at least one more piece of learning available.

Additionally, test markets do not have to be expensive and the learning can make the difference between a profitable brand and one that is not quite making it.

Recommendations.
Many marketing planning documents recommend at least one test. Some recommend many tests in order to increase learning for future years. These tests might be in many different elements of the plan.

Almost anything can be tested. David Ogilvy, in his book *Ogilvy on Advertising*, cites that Procter & Gamble is such a formidable competitor because they are disciplined. *"Their guiding philosophy is to plan thoroughly, minimize risk, and stick to their proven principles."* They reduce risk through testing.

Take care to select two or three markets for testing. The markets should not be contaminated by competitors' testing or unusual behavior as it relates to the category.

Selecting a Test Market.

It is unlikely that a refried bean manufacturer would test market in Buffalo. Refried beans are not consumed in Buffalo at the same levels that they are in Arizona or Texas.

The markets should be representative of the remainder of the United States (and Buffalo is a chronically depressed area, not exactly the best place to to test a new product).

Pick control markets to go with the test markets so that the effect of the test can be measured against specific markets, and not just compared to the remainder of the United States. The selection of the markets for testing takes some care.

Peoria is a good example. It is a Midwestern market with a good mix of working, middle-class consumers. It is a relatively small DMA, which makes it more affordable than testing in Chicago or Indianapolis.

Selecting a Control Market.

Marketers may choose a test market in Peoria and compare the sales results to those in Ft. Wayne. Ft. Wayne might be chosen as the control market for the test because it is about the same size as Peoria, has about the same seasonality of sales, and has about the same percentage of the market as represented by the target audience in both markets.

If the history of sales is about the same in both markets, and they have about the same brand and category development indices, then they are a good match.

Other Determining Factors.

Some marketers choose more than one test market to determine how the test will work in high development areas and in low development areas or in markets with some other skew.

Others have a requirement that a test market must represent a given percentage of the United States—one or two percent—to avoid having too small of a testing environment. Others will test in a very small environment like Alpena, Bend, or Presque Isle to avoid the high cost of larger markets, then test again in the more expensive, but more substantive markets after success has been proven in these mini-markets.

Ten Factors.

Here are ten factors from which you may want to gain actual market information in a test market environment:

    1. The power of an alternative copy strategy.

2. The effect of an increase in advertising weight.

3. The impact of an increase in price.

4. The result of increasing the value of the standard cents-off coupon used on the Brand.

5. The acceptance of a product change.

6. The result of an alternate distribution system.

7. The consequence of implementing an ongoing publicity campaign for the first time.

8. The outcome of targeting a new audience.

9. The acceptance of moving the Brand into new geography.

10. The effect of moving marketing funds to a new season of the year.

Here is the structure for presenting Testing recommendations in your Planning Document.

A. Objective:

The objectives in the testing part of the marketing document are the same as the marketing strategies in Chapter Six.

An example of a testing objective might be:

To determine the sales impact of a +50% increase in advertising impressions.

An explanation of how this objective will help fulfill the marketing objective will increase the chances of acceptance.

B. Strategies:

How Learning Will Take Place.

The strategies, as always, will outline how the objective will be met, or in the case of testing, how the learning will take place.

If the test is a complicated one, several strategy statements may be necessary (as it was in media), but if the marketing test is not complex, one strategy statement may be all that is necessary.

It might be as simple as:

> To use the television medium to carry the increased weight in a medium-development test market.

This strategy gives sufficient information about how the objective will be fulfilled, but needs more information in the tactics section to let the reader know exactly what is going to happen.

C. Tactics:

Also Known as "Method."

This section is sometimes called the method section and is used to outline precisely how the test market will be implemented.

> To increase television weight in Cincinnati by +165 GRPs to a total of 495 GRPs (index 150) per flight for a one-year period.

> The weight will maintain the current proportions between the daytime, early fringe, and late fringe dayparts.

A flow chart should also be attached so the reader can clearly see when the test plan will go into effect.

D. Rationale:

Management Is Entitled to a Convincing Argument.

This is the defense for why the test market will likely contribute to the marketing objective.

It is the reason to believe that the premise behind the test will provide better results than whatever is currently the standard.

There are limited opportunities for test markets, and management is entitled to a convincing argument on behalf of the value of each and every test market recommendation.

Support your point of view.

Quantitative and qualitative research and sales results will be presented here as substantiation for the test market.

E. Evaluation:

Also Known as "Payout."

This is the place to outline what the definition of success will be. Some call this section "Payout."

For example, if it will take an increase of +13% in sales in order to pay out the +50% increase in advertising, then that should be established here.

For more information, please also read:

1. **Successful Advertising Research Methods**
   Haskins, Jack and Kendrick, Alice
   NTC Business Books, Chicago, 1993

2. **Strategic Advertising Campaigns**
   Schultz, Don E., and Barnes, Beth E.
   NTC Business Books, Chicago, 1994. Fourth Edition.

   Chapter Four relates to this chapter on research.

   Chapter Five (Research) and Chapter Fifteen (Evaluation) are valuable for understanding testing.

3. **Advertising Media Planning**
   Sissors, Jack Z. and Bumba, Lincoln
   NTC Business Books, Chicago, 1993. Fourth Edition.

   Chapter Seventeen has a good review of testing and test markets.

4. **Confessions of an Advertising Man**
   Ogilvy, David
   Atheneum, NY, 1980.

5. **Ogilvy on Advertising**
   Ogilvy, David
   Crown Publishers, NY, 1983.

Appendix

The Presentation:

Speech and Visual Support

"In the ad game, the days are tough, the nights are long, and the work is emotionally demanding. But it's all worth it because the rewards are shallow, transparent and meaningless."

—Anonymous

Introduction.

Congratulations.

You have just finished a grueling experience—you have written your first Marketing Planning document. This is no easy task.

Most students will have invested about a hundred and fifty hours or more to get to this point. If this is a semester-long project, you will have spent about fifteen to twenty hours a week getting the marketing planning document written.

You have now completed about two-thirds of the work needed to finish the marketing planning process.

The next segment is the presentation of your work. It is easily the last one-third of the work.

At the university level, the presentation is usually a twenty- to thirty-minute slide show of your work.

At the professional level, the presentation can last up to two hours.

Now for the bad news.

It is more difficult to write and give a twenty-minute presentation than a two-hour presentation.

You must present everything that is in a two-hour presentation, but condense it into a twenty-minute period.

Here is what you must do.

A. Objective:

Sell Your Ideas.

A presentation is an opportunity to sell your ideas.

Therefore, the objective of this segment of the process is to convince your target audience, probably your client, that your ideas are the best ideas available.

One of the easiest methods to convince the group that your work is the best is to have the most finished work, the best-looking presentation.

Early in my advertising agency career, someone told me that the ideas that get sold to clients may not always be the best ideas or concepts, but they are always the best executed. He meant that they were always the ideas that had the best finishing touches, the best art work, the best slides, the most professional presentation.

Whether you're in a class or a contest, your objective is to win.

And that means the best presentation.

B. Elements:

There are two key elements of the presentation—the Planning Document and the Creative Presentation.

1. The Planning Document:

First you need to provide a review of the written planning document. Usually this is given in the same order as the marketing document—Situation Analysis, Research, Problems and Opportunities, Objectives, Budget, Strategies, Creative, Media, Promotion, and Evaluation.

Testing will be inserted into that segment of the plan for which the testing is taking place. For example, a 50% increase in media impressions test would be inserted into the Media segment of the presentation.

Research with yogurt users might appear in any number of places—Marketing Strategy, Creative Platform, or Media Plan.

2. The Creative Presentation:

The second part of the presentation is the presenting of the creative product itself, the ads.

This is usually done during the Creative segment of the plan, but can be done throughout the presentation.

It is not unusual for a presentation to begin by telling the audience what you are going to show them—including some of the creative work. Then demonstrate it in the Creative segment by showing how the strategy and the creative work together. Show it again. Then at the end tell them again what you have shown them earlier.

You have now had a frequency of three and have broken the threshold necessary for learning.

C. Start Early:

Some Good Advice You Will Probably Ignore.

Everyone will give you advice to start work on the creative product and the presentation as early as possible. You, however, will ignore them because you are smarter than they are.

You are a Senior—the top of the college pecking order. You can pull it out at the last possible minute. Maybe.

A Bad Example.

One year I was coaching a team, and we were going to present at the AAF/NSAC the next morning.

After meeting with the District Coordinator, I came back to the hotel to discover that we did not have Spanish language radio yet. This was ten o'clock the night before presentation.

One of the team members recorded the commercial in the bathroom of the hotel room at two in the morning. We won the District competition, so maybe you seniors can pull it together at any late date—but you're pushing your luck.

Do Yourself a Favor.

If you start early you'll have more opportunity to revise your presentation and make it better.

More important, if you just finish on time you'll also limit your learning. And, while winning is nice, the real value is learning skills that will help you in the business world.

One of the key learning experiences in preparing a marketing (including advertising) campaign of this nature is being able to go back and look at what you did when you are finished.

And since you now know more than you did when you started, you can probably find some ways to make your work better. This will reinforce your learning, and enable you to have a stronger plan and develop better skills.

D. Write the Presentation:

Written Language vs. Spoken Language.

Writing the presentation will require slightly different language than that in the written portion of your document, because we all speak differently than we write.

To verify this, after you write something, read it out loud.

And you might want to note the amount of time it takes to speak it.

More Good Advice.

Each member of your team should write the speech for the segment of the plan that they wrote for the planning document.

When you start to write your segment of the presentation, you might want to start by setting the margins on your computer to leave at least forty percent of the page blank. This will allow you to draw in the first rough illustrations and ideas for slides—so that you can see what the presentation will look like to the audience as you are giving the verbal portion of the presentation.

PowerPoint also has formats for notes and handouts that you might find helpful.

Identification—Dates and Initials.

You will quickly find there is a lot to keep track of in this process.

It's a good idea to put the initials of the person who authored that particular page and the date at the bottom of each page so you will know what revision you are using.

It is likely that you'll rewrite the presentation several times before you finally get it the way you want it.

E. Create Slides:

Slides or Charts?

You can use a variety of methods to visually support your presentation.

Overhead transparencies or acetates are common in the business world. These work well to illustrate charts or tables of numbers, and it is easy to walk up to the screen and touch the number you are talking about in order to make a point.

You could also use charts. These could be large pieces of paper (24" x 36" or larger) mounted on cardboard or foam core. Or you could use a smaller format (14" x 17") in a flip-chart format. Flip charts work well when presenting to a small number of people.

The problem with these methods is that they are not very exciting.

And your team is in a contest that you want to win.

In a competitive environment, use PowerPoint.

While there are better and more sophisticated ways to present your work, PowerPoint is the standard. Use it.

The slides are used to reinforce what you are communicating verbally at the time the slide is being shown. In your PowerPoint presentation, there are three types you will use in your presentation:

1. *Computer Generated Slides:*

The two major categories of computer generated slides are:

- Type slides
- Graphic slides

Both are used to reinforce what you are saying.

Type Slides.

If you are talking about the objectives in the Media section, you will probably have the media objectives on a slide.

These are type slides.

"Build" With Progressive Slides.

You might even make it a set of progressive slides, where the first slide shows the first Target Audience objective in bright yellow Helvetica type. Like this:

Media Objectives:

- **Objective 1**

The second slide might show the first Target Audience objective in tan Helvetica, and the second (geographic) objective in bright yellow Helvetica type.

Media Objectives:

- Objective 1
- **Objective 2**

The third slide would show the first two objectives in tan and the third (seasonality) objective in bright yellow.

Media Objectives:

- Objective 1
- Objective 2
- **Objective 3**

And so on.

This progressive sequence is called a "Build." Whatever colors, type faces, or graphic devices you use, the key is that you make it easy for the audience to follow your sequence.

Support Important Points.

You may also use type slides to support a point you're trying to make.

For example, if you're giving a presentation for Dannon Yogurt you may have a slide in the Situation Analysis segment that states the following:

24.1% are over 55

This would indicate that 24.1% of all female homemakers are 55 years of age or older. You would cite in the speech that this information comes from the Spring 1996 report from Mediamark Research, Inc. You might also consider putting the Source material in small type at the bottom of the slide.

This is a good slide because, like a billboard, it does not contain too much information.

There is a danger of having too much type on the slide so that your audience spends time reading the slide and not listening to you.

It can also be difficult to present a slide that is simple.

If you have a complicated graphic slide like a media flow chart, you have to immediately explain it in your speech.

A type slide can just be put on the screen with little explanation, because it is already part of the speech—it's there to reinforce what you are saying.

Graphic Slides.

The graphic slide needs explanation; the speech is there to explain the graphic.

The computer can be used to generate unusual graphics that help to explain the strategic positioning of the Brand.

The mnemonic device (memory graphic) shown in Chapter Seven could be made on the computer and used throughout the presentation to support the strategic direction.

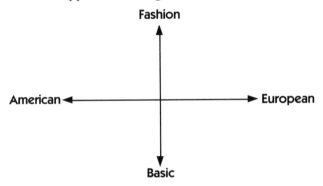

These slides can be generated on your computer in a number of ways. PowerPoint also has chart and graphic capabilities.

2. *Creative Slides:*

You should also use slides to present your Creative work. You may also want to use layouts, which will also be in your plans book— but it is best that you also integrate the Creative work into your presentation.

Print Advertising.

The print advertisements you have written and designed should be put into your PowerPoint presentation.

If you wrote and designed the ads on the computer, then you can generate the slides of those ads the same way.

Television in PowerPoint.

When it comes to television, you can show the individual frames of your commercial on screen in PowerPoint and read or play a prerecorded sound track of the copy.

New video techniques are becoming available, and you may be tempted to make a video commercial.

But be cautious in switching from one format to another. It is one more thing that can go wrong.

Another reason for caution—the potential of a commercial that is only in storyboard form may be greater than the reality of a commercial produced by inexperienced people with inadequate skills and equipment. This is not a home-video competition.

This discipline can be used for creative in other media as well.

3. *Miscellaneous:*

There will be a variety of slides you may have to take with a camera for your presentation. Digital cameras make this easier than ever.

For example, if you want a slide to show the selection of magazines you are recommending, you will have to buy the magazines, spread them out on a table, and take a slide. The digital image can be integrated into your PowerPoint slide fairly easily.

If you are recommending transit advertising and you want to show a bus with your work on the side, then you will have to convince someone at the local transit authority to let you put your art work on the side of the bus so you can take a slide for your presentation.

Convincing this person to let you put it on an active bus so that you can get a picture of the bus in traffic will be a test of your salesmanship. (Taking a shot of the bus and fitting your art work to the desired space is not quite as good, but if someone is skilled in Photoshop, it's suprising what can be done.)

F. The Creative Product:

Staging Your Creative.

The presentation is primarily an opportunity to show the creative work, because the creative product should not be included in the marketing planning document.

There is a natural buildup that takes place, a curiosity that needs to be developed before you show the creative advertising product and after management or the judges have had an opportunity to read the Marketing Planning Document. Once curiosity has been built up, then it's the right time to show them the creative product.

It will be easier to convince them that the executions you are recommending will contribute to fulfilling the Marketing Objective.

Seven Good Guidelines.

This book is not a forum for what the creative product should and should not contain, but here are seven observations you should be aware of when entering student contests like the one sponsored by the American Advertising Federation.

1. **If there's a creative judge from the client, don't point out too many flaws with the current campaign.**

   Remember: one of the judges may have created it.
   This is a good rule for all advertising professionals.
   Be careful how you tell anyone that their work stinks.

2. **The best work has a good idea behind it.**

   The premise can be any variety of things, but it has to go beyond just saying the Brand name in a clever fashion. There must be a real reason for the creative idea.

3. **The better your work looks, the higher the probability of winning any competition.**

   Find an artist to do the finish work on your advertising. If it looks like a student project, it will be judged to be inferior to more professional-looking work.

4. **Make sure the advertising is fresh; it shouldn't look like any other advertising around anywhere.**

   Go beyond what other people have done. Be "creative."

5. **The advertising should be on strategy.**

   This shouldn't be a problem since you wrote the Strategy as well as the advertising. But be sure to evaluate your advertising against the Strategy. Ask hard questions. The judges will.

6. **Use the campaign line on *everything*.**

   Use it at the end of all the advertising—on the television, newspaper, magazine, radio, outdoor, transit, and ball caps.

   If you're recommending sky writing, it should be what is written in smoke. Put it on the cover of the "leave-behind."

7. **Do something you don't think anyone else will do.**

> Write original music, create a campaign in Spanish, use testimonials of famous people and get their voices on tape. Find a way to differentiate your campaign from all others.

Use Your Good Ideas.

Occasionally you will have a great idea for a magazine advertisement, but you're not recommending magazines in the media plan. Do not ignore the idea. Find a way to use it.

That may mean you have to go back and rewrite the media plan or add a test market, and find a reason to substantiate the decision to recommend magazines.

But it could also mean that you just show the work in the presentation and tell the truth. You have a great idea, but you don't know if it can be used or not.

That way, you get credit for the idea, but don't have to defend its use.

"Learn" Your Audience.

No matter what the presentation, "learn" your audience.

If you are working for an advertising agency, then your audience is your client.

If you're working for a small startup company, your audience is the entrepreneur who started the business. But if you're a team member in the AAF/NSAC, your audience is comprised of the judges. Learn as much about these people as you can.

Presenting "safe" advertising can be good in some cases when the audience is conservative, but it can be deadly when working professional creative people are your audience.

G. Rehearse:

And Rehearse Some More.

The next step is to rehearse what you have created. Practice makes perfect. Rehearse, rehearse, rehearse.

If there is someone in your group who has taken a theater class or two, so much the better. If you have an opportunity to take a theater class before the presentation, do it.

Dramatic techniques can get the attention you need.

There are many professionals who believe that they can rehearse too much. There should be, they reckon, a certain amount of spontaneity to the presentation of the campaign. That is correct—for professionals who have two hours to present their work. Students do not, so their presentations must be rehearsed.

Present Before You Present.

Present the work as often as you can before the District competition, if you are competing in the AAF contest.

When I was at the University of Kansas, we had a five-hour drive to St. Louis for the presentation. The team rehearsed the presentation ten times in the van on the way to the District competition. That year, the team won the District against some very good competition.

Sometimes when you rehearse a presentation it begins to sound memorized. You have to go beyond that point. You have to make it a theatrical presentation; it is memorized, but it doesn't sound like it.

For more information, please also read:

1. **How to Create and Deliver Award Winning Advertising Presentations**
   Moriarty, Sandra, and Duncan, Tom
   NTC Books, Lincolnwood, IL, 1989

2. **A current book on PowerPoint.**
   There are a number of books that are quite adequate, your team will need a useful reference to help make the most of this program.

Presentation Example

University of Oregon
Nestle Presentation

Misty: We _are_ the team you have been waiting for. We are the University of Oregon, and

our objective is to win.

Our strategy is to convince you to select the University of Oregon over all other campaigns

because it is superior in quality based on a strong creative product, tested promotions, and an extensive media plan.

Now for a sample of our strong creative product.

Tape: Nestle. That's not nessel, neeslay, or nest-el-ay. Nestle makes chocolate. The very best chocolate, which is a language we all understand. Nestle creates this confection to satisfy any tongue that craves creamy delicious chocolate. There's no better way to say it. Now you can go anywhere and speak Nestle. Nestle. When all you want is Chocolate.

Final Notes:

Next Steps:

"Never give up.
Never give up.
Never give up."
—Winston Churchill

Introduction.

If you read at the rate that most people do, you have read this book in a few hours. Hopefully, I've given you a few tools to craft a marketing planning document.

This is a skill that will last you a lifetime.

The Next Step.

Do it.

The next step is simple. "Just do it."

The first time you write a marketing planning document, you'll think it is an incredible task. When you are halfway through the Situation Analysis—when you have to find competitive spending information—you'll begin to believe it is not possible to gain enough information to complete this document.

You are right, and you are wrong.

One of Parkinson's minor laws is that the Marketing Plan will expand to fill the time allotted.

The more time you spend on it, the better it will be, but also the longer it will take. Get into it early on so that you can enjoy the process.

If you're an entrepreneur, the first time through the process may take six months or longer. The second time will only take a few weeks.

If you're a student finishing this document for a contest or for an Advertising Campaigns class, it clearly will take you the entire term to complete the document and give a presentation.

Don't Give Up.

Many times you will work around the clock.

Don't give up, it will be worth it.

Next time, when you are working for JWT in Chicago or Y&R in New York, or P&G in Cincinnati, you will finish it in a month or so.

Best of all, next time, you will get paid for it.

The AAF Contest.

Whether You Win or Lose...

If you are competing in the AAF NSAC competition, you may find that this is one of the most involving activities in your college career.

And, like any contest, you'll play to win.

And, like many contests, there will be only one winner (plus Regional winners—an honor in itself) and many who do not win.

Well, Here's a Little More Good News.

Whether you win or not, you'll find that the skills you developed preparing for this contest will serve you well.

One of the reasons the AAF and the participating sponsors support this competition is that it is one of the best "real world" training grounds for students. It is worth all the effort you can put into it.

Be Prepared.

The AAF contest prepares you for the deadlines, pressures, and high standards that are part of the competitive world of marketing—where you are not just competing for a grade or a prize, but for the very survival of your company in the marketplace.

If you work hard, you'll be preparing yourself to succeed in the real world. And that's a prize everyone can win.

The Finished Product.

The First Time is the Hardest.

I know how hard it is. Every year, I watch a new group of students wrestle with one of the most demanding tasks in business. And every year, I hear from a few former students.

So here is my last bit of good news. It gets easier.

There are Two Reasons.

So, a couple of years from now, when you're at Lintas or Wells or with some brand-new company that needs your help, when you're asked to write a marketing planning document, you'll know how to do it.

And it will be easier for at least two reasons:

First, you'll know what the finished product should look like.
Second, you'll have better resources and better backup.

But even with the resources available at a large advertising agency, you wouldn't be as prepared to write the document if you hadn't been through the process first while you were still at the university.

Life on the Learning Curve.

Knowledge and information are the driving forces of our economy. Learn to use them and learn how to learn.

Work hard, learn the process, and learn the Brand.

Learn to excel and learn to lead.

If you're going to work for an ad agency, a marketer, or run your own business, you'll need everything in this book.

And a lot more that isn't.

So...good luck! I hope you reap the enjoyment and satisfaction that comes from learning to do a job well.

Schedule:

Notes:

Resources: